university for the creative arts

Maidstone, Oakwood Park, Maidstone, Kent, ME16 8AG
Return on or before the last date stamped below. Fines will be charged on overdue books.

Frontispiece: Winchester Discovery Centre, Hampshire, library night view

Published by
Ashgate Publishing Limited
Wey Court East
Union Road
Farnham
Surrey, GU9 7PT
England

Ashgate Publishing Company
Suite 420
101 Cherry Street
Burlington
VT 05401-4405
USA

www.ashgate.com

British Library Cataloguing in Publication Data
Renewing our libraries : case studies in re-planning and
   refurbishment
   1. Library buildings - Great Britain - Design and
   construction - Case studies 2. Library architecture - Great
   Britain 3. Library planning - Great Britain
   I. Dewe, Michael
   022.3'0941

Library of Congress Cataloging-in-Publication Data
Dewe, Michael.
   Renewing our libraries : case studies in re-planning and refurbishment / by Michael
Dewe.
      p. cm.
   Includes bibliographical references and index.
   ISBN 978-0-7546-7339-2 (alk. paper)
   1. Library buildings--Great Britain--Design and construction--Case studies. 2. Library
buildings--Ireland--Design and construction--Case studies. 3. Library architecture--Great
Britain. 4. Library architecture--Ireland. 5. Library planning--Great Britain. 6. Library
planning--Ireland. I. Title.

   Z679.2.G7D495 2008
   022'.30941--dc22
                                                                                          2008019107
   ISBN 978-0-7546-7339-2

Mixed Sources
Product group from well-managed
forests and other controlled sources
www.fsc.org Cert no. SGS-COC-2482
© 1996 Forest Stewardship Council

Printed and bound in Great Britain by
TJ International Ltd, Padstow, Cornwall

Contents

List of Figures   *ix*
List of Tables   *xi*
List of Contributors   *xiii*
Preface   *xv*
Acknowledgements   *xvii*

Introduction   1

1   Renewing our Libraries – Forces for Change   3
     Michael Dewe

PART 1: HERITAGE LIBRARY BUILDINGS – ENHANCING THE PAST FOR THE PRESENT

2   Leek Library, Staffordshire: Listed, Linked and Limited –
     Opening up Service and Perception in a Victorian Building   21
     Hilary Jackson and Alan Medway

3   Long Eaton Library, Derbyshire: An Art Nouveau Gem Reborn   31
     Robert Gent and Don Gibbs

4   Torquay Library, Torbay: Refurbishing an Art Deco Style Building   41
     Katie Lusty

PART 2: NEW STYLES OF PROVISION – WIDENING THE LIBRARY ROLE

5   Winchester Discovery Centre, Hampshire: Discovery Centre and More   57
     Richard Ward

6   National Library of Wales: The Visitor Experience Project   67
     Mark Mainwaring

PART 3: REMAKING UNIVERSITY LIBRARIES – CREATING MODERN LEARNING AND RESEARCH ENVIRONMENTS

7   Kenrick Library, Birmingham City University: From Dismal to a
     Dynamic Refurbishment   79
     Judith Andrews

8   Glasgow University Library: From Book Warehouse to Lighthouse
     for Study   89
     Helen Durndell

9   Hartley Library, University of Southampton:
     From Accretion to Integration, 2002–2007   101
     Mark Brown and Richard Wake

PART 4: EXTENDING THE LIBRARY – MODERNIZING AND ADDING SPACE

10   Dublin City Library and Archive: From Concept to Reality   113
     Deirdre Ellis-King

11   The London Library: Changing to Stay the Same but Expansion
     and Renewal   123
     Inez T.P.A. Lynn

12   Malmö City Library, Sweden: Beauty vs. Efficiency –
     Planning for User and Staff Needs   133
     Gunilla Petterson

13   Waterford Central Library: A Space For All   145
     Jane Cantwell

PART 5: LIBRARY REFURBISHMENT PROGRAMMES – FORGING TEMPLATES FOR BUILDING RENEWAL

14   Barnsley Central Library: There and Back – Remaking Libraries   159
     Kathryn Green, Jane Lee and Wendy Mann

15   Coalville, Birstall and Enderby Libraries, Leicestershire:
     Case Studies in Renewal   173
     Margaret Bellamy

16 North Yorkshire Libraries: Creating a New Library Brand 183
Julie Blaisdale

17 Lowestoft, Stowmarket, Lakenheath and Felixstowe Libraries, Suffolk:
Refurbishments that are Prize-winners 195
Mike Ellwood

**PART 6: (1) SNAPSHOTS: SOME REFURBISHMENT CASE STUDIES
IN BRIEF (2) CASE STUDIES REVIEWED**

18 Snapshots: Some Refurbishment Case Studies in Brief 221
Michael Dewe and Alan Clark

19 Case Studies Reviewed 243
Michael Dewe

Bibliography *267*
Index *271*

List of Figures

Frontispiece: Winchester Discovery Centre, Hampshire, library night view   ii

2.1   Leek Library, Staffordshire, exterior   23
2.2   Leek Library, Staffordshire, interior   26
2.3   Leek Library, Staffordshire, children's library   28

3.1   Long Eaton Library, Derbyshire, exterior   32
3.2   Long Eaton Library, Derbyshire, children's library   34
3.3   Lending library with stained-glass window to the rear,
Long Eaton Library   35

4.1   Torquay Library Service, Torquay Library, interior   42
4.2   Torbay Library Service, Torquay Library, first floor   45
4.3   Torbay Library Service, Torquay Library, balcony   48
4.4   Torbay Library Service, Torquay Library, ground floor plan   52

5.1   Plan of Winchester Discovery Centre, Hampshire   62
5.2   Winchester Discover Centre, Hampshire, library central space
(CAD view)   63
5.3   Winchester Discovery Centre, Hampshire, express library
(CAD view)   65

6.1   National Library of Wales, Aberystwyth, the Drwm, rooftop view   68
6.2   National Library of Wales, Aberystwyth, the Drwm, the courtyard view   72
6.3   National Library of Wales, Aberystwyth, aerial view   73

7.1   Kenrick Library, Birmingham City University, group study rooms   83
7.2   Kenrick Library, Birmingham City University, Level 4
before refurbishment   85
7.3   Kenrick Library, Birmingham City University, Level 4
after refurbishment   85

8.1   Glasgow University Library, exterior   89
8.2   Glasgow University Library, library levels   93
8.3   Glasgow University Library, study area   97

9.1   Hartley Library, University of Southampton, exterior   102
9.2   Hartley Library, University of Southampton, reception desk   107

9.3   Hartley Library, University of Southampton, open area   109

10.1   Dublin City Library and Archive, exterior (original building)   114
10.2   Dublin City Library and Archive, reading room   118
10.3   Dublin City Library and Archive, library extension   119

11.1   The London Library, model showing old and new elements   128

12.1   Malmö City Library, perspective of three library buildings   134
12.2   Malmö City Library, The Calendar of Light   137
12.3   Malmö City Library, The Castle   138

13.1   Waterford Central Library, exterior   146
13.2   Waterford Central Library, information desk   149
13.3   Waterford Central Library, children's library   153

14.1   Barnsley Central Library, ground floor   161
14.2   Barnsley Central Library, coffee bar   163
14.3   Barnsley Central Library, children's seating area   167

15.1   Leicestershire County Library Service, Coalville Library   177
15.2   Leicestershire County Library Service, Birstall Library,
       children's area   180
15.3   Leicestershire County Library Service, Enderby Library   181

16.1   North Yorkshire County Libraries, Knaresborough Library, exterior   186
16.2   North Yorkshire County Libraries, Knaresborough Library, interior   188
16.3   North Yorkshire County Libraries, Eastfield Library, interior   189

17.1   Suffolk County Libraries, Lowestoft Library, exterior   198
17.2   Suffolk County Libraries, Lowestoft Library, interior   199
17.3   Suffolk County Libraries, Stowmarket Library, children's area   205
17.4   Suffolk County Libraries, Felixstowe Library, interior   214

18.1   Plymouth Campus Library, University of Plymouth, atrium   227
18.2   British Museum, Great Court and Round Reading Room   231
18.3   Walsall Central Library, exterior   235

List of Contributors

Judith Andrews
Director of Library and IT Services, Birmingham City University

Margaret Bellamy
Head of Library Services, Leicestershire

Julie Blaisdale
Assistant Director (Library and Community Services), North Yorkshire

Mark Brown
University Librarian, University of Southampton

Jane Cantwell
City Librarian, Waterford City Libraries

Alan J. Clark
Coordinator, Designing Libraries Project, University of Aberystwyth

Michael Dewe
Library Buildings Consultant

Helen Durndell
University Librarian, University of Glasgow

Deirdre Ellis-King
City Librarian, Dublin City Library and Archive

Mike Ellwood
Project Manager, Libraries, Archives and Information, Suffolk

Robert Gent
Assistant Director, Cultural and Community Services, Derbyshire

Don Gibbs
Assistant Director, Libraries, Archives and Information, Derbyshire

Kathryn Green
Chief Libraries Officer, Barnsley Metropolitan Borough Council

Hilary Jackson
Principal Librarian, Library and Information Services, Staffordshire

Jane Lee
Information and Resources Officer, Barnsley Metropolitan Borough Council

Katie Lusty
Professional Services Librarian, Torbay

Inez T.P.A. Lynn
Librarian, London Library

Mark Mainwaring
Director, Department of Corporate Services, National Library of Wales

Wendy Mann
Operations Officer, Barnsley Metropolitan Borough Council

Alan Medway
Group Manager, Library and Information Services, Staffordshire

Gunilla Petterson
Malmö City Library

Richard Wake
Deputy Librarian, University of Southampton

Richard Ward
Head of Library and Information Service, Hampshire

Preface

Neighbouring the modern British Library on the Euston Road is the Victorian gothic St Pancras Station and Hotel, whose height and colouring came, incidentally, to influence the design of British Library building. St Pancras Station was neglected for many years, became a likely victim of demolition but, with advocates like John Betjeman and the Victorian Society, it was thankfully listed Grade I in 1967.

Now, after a further period of decline, this heritage station building has finally been renovated and refurbished, reopening in late 2007. In doing so the neglect has been made good, the new elements have had to blend with the old features, unused parts of the station complex have been brought into use, and shops, a champagne bar and public art have given life to its new role as the London station for Eurostar. One commentator has said that 'The station's rebirth is a slap in the face for the old-is-useless mob and all their claptrap about outdated structures'.[1]

As the case studies in this book demonstrate, the background to the renewal of St Pancras Station reflects many of the concerns and issues surrounding the renewal of the UK's library buildings, such as the need to make good a period of neglect and lack of investment, the challenge of blending old parts of a building with new, contemporary elements, and the opportunity to bring life to old but now modernized premises. And, in doing so, perhaps overcoming the view of those who might prefer new build to refurbishment and remodelling.

Some of the UK libraries instanced in this book have a similar national architectural standing to St Pancras Station: listed building such as the British Museum Round Reading Room (1837), the John Rylands Library, Manchester (1905) and Swiss Cottage Library, Camden (1964) by Sir Basil Spence. Of the many other libraries (some of which are also listed buildings), described and mentioned in the following pages, their worth, especially in their renewed form, is in the continuing value placed on them locally by the communities they serve.

And so with the wish to heighten their profile, provide a better service, modernize their environment and increase use, many libraries of all types in the UK have refurbished, remodelled and, where necessary and possible, extended their existing buildings. Much has been achieved in this regard across the UK in recent years; more continues to be done and needs to be accomplished to renew our libraries.

This book is to some extent a record of what has been achieved by way of renewing our libraries in the late 1990s and the early 21st century: both in the UK and, to a much smaller degree elsewhere in the world. The main aim of this set of case studies, however, is to provide librarians, architects and others with examples of what has been undertaken in order to highlight the aims, processes, design issues – and the problems that have been overcome – that lead to successful

Acknowledgements

I would like to thank Dymphna Evans at Ashgate for suggesting the theme of this book, that I should compile it and for supporting its progress. Thanks also to the proofreader, Helen Parry, and to Gemma Lowle and Claire Jarvis, of Ashgate, for seeing this book through to publication. My thanks are also due to my good friend and former research assistant, Paul Drew, for all his administrative and other help, such as dealing with the illustrations, in the preparation of this book. My illness has delayed publication a little, but thanks to a friend and colleague, Alan Clark, Coordinator for the Designing Libraries Project, University of Aberystwyth, who offered timely assistance with a chapter, matters have gone more smoothly than expected. The contributors also have my thanks for responding so promptly to my invitation to participate and for their timeliness in meeting deadlines, as do those who have been responsible for the illustrations. I also add my customary thanks for the use of the library and information facilities of the Hugh Owen and Thomas Parry libraries of the University of Aberystwyth and the National Library of Wales. Without their resources and study facilities it would have been impossible to contribute to and edit this book.

Introduction

The major part of this book consists of 16 case studies of building renewal, mainly in the UK, and covering a range of libraries serving a wide variety of readers and communities. The buildings concerned date from the late Victorian period to the latter half of the twentieth century, notably libraries of the 1970s. The buildings include:

- a national library
- three university libraries
- libraries of 11 public library services, of which two are from the Republic of Ireland and one from Sweden
- an independent library.

Each case study, as will be seen, has its own distinctive project characteristics: it may involve more than one building in the case of some public library services. Contributors, however, will usually cover a number of common themes. These include:

- reasons for the refurbishment
- the planning, design and refurbishment process
- the design solution that was eventually proposed and adopted
- an account of the library service and design outcomes that were finally achieved
- any problems, delays and difficulties that occurred during refurbishment
- an evaluation of the refurbishment and its impact on the library community.

The case studies in this book, discussed in Chapters 2 to 17, are arranged in five categories (Parts 1 to 5). In devising these categories, it was taken as read that every library wanted to improve its services, make the best use of available space and create a modern library environment, and so other aspects of library renewal have been highlighted in creating the following categories:

- heritage library buildings – enhancing the past for the present
- new styles of provision – widening the library role
- remaking university libraries – creating modern learning and research environments
- extending the library – modernizing and adding space
- library refurbishment programmes – forging templates for building renewal.

Using these headings, however, means that case study libraries sometimes fall into more than one category and so what seemed important to the editor (and gave more evenly balanced groupings) has guided the arrangement of which chapters were placed in which parts. While not wanting to take a library sector approach with these categories, the nature and aims of academic library refurbishment suggested that those case studies were best kept together as a single group.

Following the case studies, Chapter 18 provides brief details of a number of other UK and non-UK library refurbishments that have come to the attention of the chapter's joint authors.

As well as chapter notes, where appropriate, a short bibliography listing further references is provided for those who wish for additional information on the various aspects of library planning and design.

Preceding the case studies, a preliminary chapter (Chapter 1) looks at the need for library building renewal and provides a brief survey of the current library scene. It identifies drivers and influences for the refurbishing and re-planning of libraries, with particular attention given to government policies, influential reports, library campaigns and the funds made available to renew the library 'estate'. A final chapter (Chapter 19) reviews the contributed case studies, bringing out the common features, concerns, achievements and outcomes stemming from this upsurge in library building renewal projects.

A concluding remark needs to be made about the terms used in this book to describe what happens when library buildings are renewed. The terms include 'makeover', 'upgrading', 'refurbishment', 'transformation', 'improvement', 'remodelling', 'rebuilding', 'renovation', 'modernizing', 'remaking', 'revamping' and the word 'renewal' itself. Of all these 'refurbishment' is commonly used as shorthand to signify a variety of material changes to the library, for example, its layout, décor, furniture and equipment, accessibility, interior organization and physical structure. What exactly a library has experienced by way of 'refurbishment' will be made clear in the full description of the case study concerned.

Chapter 1

Renewing our Libraries – Forces for Change

Michael Dewe

Introduction

Libraries of all kinds are in a state of transition, as they seek to offer new services, embrace changed social attitudes, adapt to new ways of working and respond to the demand for more agreeable surroundings. They have to be ready to take up the challenges of providing new formats, using new technologies, welcoming new management ideas and seeing the incorporation of developments in architecture, construction and interior design in their buildings.

A new library building provides the perfect opportunity to face the challenges and opportunities of a particular time – in this case the early years of the 21st century. And in recent times a number of high-profile new library buildings in all library sectors have resulted, such as Brighton Jubilee Library and Bournemouth University Octagon Library, attracting media attention, prizes and awards.[1]

In addition to these new building, however, there is a host from earlier periods which make up the library estate, and scores dating from the first decades of the period after the Second World War. Many of these libraries may be short of space and lack modern amenities – and public libraries in particular have received constant criticism about the quality of their physical environment – which make it difficult for them to meet today's challenges. The response has been a substantial increase in the number of public library refurbishments – such as Saffron Walden Library, Essex, and Barry Library, Vale of Glamorgan – sometimes involving the extensive remodelling and extension of the existing premises.[2] The academic sector too has responded to its particular circumstances and requirements by upgrading and extending existing libraries, including those at Glasgow, Birmingham and York universities, as well as constructing new ones, such as those at the Open University and the Saltire Centre, Glasgow Caledonian University.[3]

This chapter will note some of the drivers for change and in particular examine the role of national and home governments in promoting and assisting the development and improvement of library buildings through policy-making, funding and the work of various agencies. Lessons from the past, however, seem to suggest that whatever the motivation and forces for change there is a cyclical pattern to renewal of individual library buildings.

Public libraries – a little bit of history

Take, for example, Hendon Library, a neo-classical building, originally opened in 1929 to considerable acclaim. As Hendon Central Library it was extended, remodelled and refurbished in 1973, providing an increase of around 50 per cent of its floor space, enabling improved lending and reference services. It was refurbished once again in 2004 and reorganized over three floors plus an upper first floor.[4]

The cycle of refurbishment during Hendon Library's 75 years of existence seems to suggest that public library buildings receive a significant 'makeover' only after a number of years have elapsed. This is not exceptional as the 'little bit of history' below will show. Even library buildings pre-dating the 1920s Hendon Library – and often still in use today – have been refurbished, remodelled and extended, with various periods of time elapsing between each such renewal.

In the early 1980s the author completed a study of the late Victorian/Edwardian architect, Henry Thomas Hare, who was well regarded, both by architects and librarians of the time, as an expert in the design of public library buildings.[5] While there were early unsuccessful project proposals, Hare was responsible for the executed design of nine public libraries which were opened between 1897 and 1909, projects either commissioned or won in architectural competitions; some were funded by Carnegie. A century later a number of them, such as those at Hammersmith, Fulham and Harrogate, still continue in use.

Chronicling the changes that occurred to each building, from the time of its opening to the time of the study, some 70 or 80 years later, was quite instructive. It showed that public library buildings were only substantially altered (sometimes including an extension) and refurbished every 20 or 30 years. Such changes were usually brought about by:

- new library methods – such as a change from closed to open access
- the closing-down of particular department such as a newsroom or museum
- a change in service emphasis from reading on the premises to lending
- the introduction of new services such as a music library
- the need for more space for staff.

In undertaking these changes in the past there is no doubt that librarians felt that they were modernizing their library service and the physical environment in which it was offered. And while the nature of these changes is of interest to the library buildings historian, equally worthy of note is the significant time lapse that often occurred between major library changes leading to refurbishment, space reorganization and extension. The Hendon Library cycle of building renewal thus appears to be a common feature of public library history and one that needs to be less infrequent if such acts are to be seen as carefully planned rather than acts of almost desperation.

Building renewal

Building renewal is very much up to the initiative of individual local authorities and their library services responding to opportunities for changes to library provision, operations and premises. The success of renewal, as an alternative to erecting a new library building, shows that in the right circumstances, the conservation and re-use of existing library premises are worthwhile. The danger, however, of relying on local initiatives, with their probable lengthy intervals between building upgrades, means that the physical condition and appearance of public libraries (both inside and out) may deteriorate in ways that are not necessarily helpful for their public library image or quality of service.

It would be a mistake, however, to imagine that this problem relates only to the UK's public libraries of a somewhat elderly vintage, as many of the libraries in use today, especially branch libraries, date from the library building boom years of the 1960s and 1970s and many do not seem to have experienced that expected cycle of renewal.

However, the quality of a public library service is not just a simple question of building renewal, important (if irregular) though that may be, but relates to its modern role and the role of staff. And here there may be conflict between the traditionalists, who focus on a book-orientated service, and those modernizers discarding the 'library' description for new titles like Idea Store or Discovery Centre.[6]

Drab and dismal

By the 1990s this neglect of the public library estate, whether built prior to or after the Second World War, and the cost of bringing premises up-to-date, were being recognized. A number of publications and reports, such as *Overdue, Better Public Libraries* and *Who's in Charge?*,[7] had highlighted the situation, characterizing some public libraries as of outmoded design, drab and dismal and poorly located. It was suggested that without change (and not just to buildings) public libraries would have a limited future. As will be seen, measures would be put in place to help remedy the situation of inadequate public library buildings through the central influence of the Museums, Libraries and Archives Commission (MLA) and to heighten people's awareness of the value and availability of their public library service.

Formal government recognition of the poor condition of public library buildings, and the probable cost of making them good, is to be found in a House of Commons report on public libraries.[8] However, a number of library building initiatives, stemming from the *Framework for the Future*[9] action plan, were already under way, although these were concerned with new builds as well as the refurbishment of public libraries. This concern for library buildings has to be seen as part of New Labour's belief that public buildings – aligned to a central government vision – enable the improved provision of public services – witness its *Buildings for the Future* secondary schools building programme and the Prime Minister's Better Public Building Award.

For public libraries, a government plan, influential publications, the work of government-funded agencies and the funding mechanisms themselves – while still depending on local initiative, library service and building developments, including refurbishment – reflect a centralized view of the modern library service and its preferred outcomes. These include the broader requirements of libraries contributing to community regeneration and social inclusion.

Framework for the Future

The ten-year plan for public libraries, *Framework for the Future*, was published by the Department of Culture Media and Sport in 2003. Following the report, the department commissioned the MLA to prepare an action plan of projects and programmes to support the report's three main aims. The report recognized the need for modern library premises and the promotion of best practice in the planning and design of library buildings and three projects were subsequently put in place to ensure their achievement.

Designing Libraries website

Following a pilot in 2004, a library buildings database was launched in 2005, led by the Chartered Institute of Library and Information Professionals (CILIP) through a steering group. Seen initially as being for public libraries, 'Designing Libraries: the gateway to better library buildings', is now more than just a database of descriptions and images of library buildings and is also actively working to include other types of library, both from at home and abroad. The website, managed by a team at Information Services, University of Aberystwyth, now includes news items on recent library building projects, a photo gallery, statistics, RSS feeds, an e-mail list and a toolkit – references to print material and links to relevant organizations, for example library suppliers. The website is now seen as an essential planning resource for all those involved in the design (and renewal) of library buildings, as it shares experience and best practice, raises standards and helps raise the profile of libraries and their buildings.

Of 256 libraries listed on the Designing Libraries database, which covers the year 1995 to date, 92 (32.6 per cent) are examples of the refurbishment of both small and larger libraries. By comparison, new buildings account for 40.8 per cent (115 libraries), conversions 19.1 per cent (54 libraries) and extensions 7.4 per cent (21 libraries). Putting refurbishment and extensions together means that their total runs a close second to new build.[10] In answer to a parliamentary question, however, it was said that 'almost 200 "significant" refurbishments' of public libraries had taken place in 2006–2007, set against 40 closed branches.[11]

Given the ongoing success of the Designing Libraries website project, it was funded for a further two years to March 2008 and work is being actively carried out to ensure its continuation after that date.

Workshops in library design

A series of one-day workshops were arranged by the CILIP to assist library staff to develop effective space planning and design skills and show participants how they could make improvements to their library. A small number of reports were produced about these workshops and these are now available online.[12]

Related events organized by the MLA included a seminar in early 2007 called 'The better management of library buildings' and, with Society of Chief Librarians, a 'Landmark libraries atelier'. The atelier, held at Swiss Cottage Central Library, Camden, focused on the librarian's role in the library building project process, the roles of other partners and tools for monitoring the building process.

Audit of public library buildings

The MLA commissioned an audit of English public library buildings aimed to investigate their present physical condition and to provide an estimate of what it would cost to repair and refurbish them to an acceptable standard. The audit collected the following details about library buildings:

- condition of the building infrastructure
- quality of design and currency
- compliance with legislation
- heritage or listed status
- external condition
- quality of furniture and fittings
- cleanliness
- signage
- suitability for the installation and development of ICT services.

The report, published in July 2006, does not provide a mass of detail nor does it draw conclusions but offers a high level analysis of survey responses together with a summary of the complete survey. The authors of the report recognize certain weaknesses:

- 'the survey [responses] have been collated and analysed without any independent assurance and are based entirely upon authorities' responses to the questions posed'.
- From the survey, 'only half of all library authorities have an asset management strategy'.

Results of the survey

Of 149 English library authorities, 136 (91 per cent) responded, so providing a representative and helpful picture of the present condition of library buildings. Major report findings are:

- The total value of library buildings owned by the 136 library authorities is £1.5 billion (£1.6 billion if all authorities are included).
- 3629 library buildings were identified in the survey (3,988 if all authorities are included).
- Gross library space, including internal and external space (both public and non-public) is 9 million square metres (9.9 million square metres, if all authorities are included).
- Using a simple definition of 'satisfactory' as fit for purpose, 70 per cent of library buildings were considered fit for purpose. Of the 30 per cent not so considered, 24 per cent did not meet health and safety standards. However, if the Disability Discrimination Act (DDA) compliance was taken into consideration, then 70 per cent of the survey buildings were not fit for purpose.
- The estimated cost of making all library buildings fit for purpose is around £692 million (£760 million if all authorities are included). This includes money to make good a routine maintenance backlog of £119 million (£130.8 million if all authorities are included), plus an estimated £66 million (£73 million if all authorities included) to meet health and safety, DDA compliance and other building regulations.

As will be seen, the results of the survey, which only apply to England, found 70 per cent of libraries satisfactory and fit for purpose , the major issue for all libraries, those considered satisfactory and unsatisfactory, being DDA compliance. However, the audit helped in putting a case 'to government and others for funding a programme of building/refurbishment and to help develop library authorities' estate strategies'.

While the buildings audit and its implications are very much central to the quest to create better new library buildings and to improve existing accommodation, the impact of the other two projects – the Designing Libraries website and workshops in library design – should not be overlooked.[13]

Funding

In the countries of the UK various central funding streams have been made available to improve public library buildings in whole or in part. As will be seen, this funding is sometimes associated with particular library campaigns, such as those under the umbrella of the Reading Agency and Love Libraries campaign.

Big Lottery

In October 2006, it was announced that the Big Lottery Fund was putting £80 million into 'strengthening the place of libraries in community life'. Developed with the MLA, the scheme provides capital funding to improve library buildings and create space for such community activities as reading groups, advice services, local history workshops, mother and toddler groups, community meetings, exhibitions and performances, healthy living workshops, language courses and family learning.

Library authorities England have bid for funds of between £250,000 and £2 millions for projects lasting up to three years. Bids had to 'clearly demonstrate that local communities are actively engaged in the development, delivery and management of the projects'. Fifty-eight successful bids for the English regions were announced in 2007 out of the 125 or so applications. They included such projects as that of Lancashire County Council, awarded nearly £1.5 million to extend and refurbish Colne, Haslington and Lancaster libraries to create flexible spaces for learning, arts, performance, talks, virtual space, families, heritage and well-being and to act as a sanctuary for all. At Bradford, a £1.5 million grant has been allocated to transform the Edwardian Manningham Library into a family and community facility offering a range of activities. The transformation will improve energy efficiency, and externally a recycling and community garden area will be provided.[14]

One ambition for the scheme is that it will provide models which other library services can endeavour to imitate. As such lottery money cannot be spent on core items; however, it has led to the criticism 'that libraries are wasting their money on unnecessary extras'.[15]

Wales

CyMAL (Museums Archives and Libraries Wales), was established in Wales, in 2004 as a new division of the Welsh Assembly government. It oversees a variety of projects including 'Libraries for Life', Strand One of which is the sharing of nearly £1.5 million amongst 15 Welsh libraries in 2007-08 to refurbish and upgrade their buildings.[16] The refurbished Oystermouth Library by Swansea City Council in 2005 had demonstrated what such a makeover could achieve by way of increased visits (31 per cent in the first year), increased requests, and increased adult and children's book issues – for children under five book issues rose by 102 per cent.

The project funding is not for a complete library refurbishment but for particular schemes, costing around £90,000 to £100,000, such as a community room, ICT training room, attractive children's area and better facilities for disabled people.

Scotland and Northern Ireland

In Scotland, eight projects aimed at improving public library services across the country, and amounting to £440,000, have been awarded from the Public Library Quality Improvement Fund, administered by the Scottish Library and Information Council (SLIC). While the awards are not specifically for the improvement of library premises, the provision of better ICT facilities, self-issue technology and collections of reading materials in languages other than English are bound to have space implications and benefits for libraries.

In addition to funding new library buildings the Northern Ireland's Department of Culture, Arts and Leisure (DCAL) has funded around 20 minor schemes and work to make libraries DDA compliant. DCAL has also supported a major refurbishment at Armagh Library, and at Bangor Library a refurbishment and extension, due for completion in 2008, during which year a major refurbishment of Newtownstewart Library will begin.[17] DCAL's 2003 important report, *Tomorrow's Library*, includes costed plans for library building improvements.[18]

Library awards and campaigns

The promotion of better library buildings is clearly helped by central guidance, publications and funding, although in England and Wales, for example, such funding is limited to particular purposes and to successful bidders. Further promotional benefits are derived, however, from the publicity from library building awards and campaigns that aim to improve the physical appearance and content of the public library.

Public Library Building Awards

Established in 1995 and organized by the CILIP's Public Libraries Group, the Public Library Building Awards are awarded every two years. The competition is open to new and refurbished public libraries across the UK and the Republic of Ireland. Early competitions (from 1999 to 2003) had a converted/refurbishment category, and there was an award for both a large and a small library in this group. Winners in the refurbished category included Burnley Central (1995), Putney (1999) and Lowestoft (2003) libraries.

Since 2005, the categories have been focused on areas considered of key importance in building design, practice, management and use, such as interior design and accessibility, and awards may be made for parts of a building. Winners in that year included the refurbishment of Swiss Cottage Library, London Borough of Camden and Hamilton Town House Library, South Lanarkshire. The latter won in two of the six award categories.[19]

In 2007 the competition received 33 entries of which 16 were longlisted and eight shortlisted. Winners included the refurbished Carnegie Library at Prestonpans, East Lothian, and the modernization of Handsworth Library, Birmingham. The delegates choice of those attending the Public Library Authorities Conference in Glasgow from the 16 longlisted libraries was Felixstowe Library (see Chapter 17).[20]

Love Libraries campaign

As part of its campaign for England's public libraries, 'Love Libraries' helped with the 2006 transformation of three libraries in 12 weeks.

- Coldharbour Library – a bland and dowdy 1960s box redecorated inside and out.
- Newquay Library – when opened in 1962 by John Betjeman, the library was an example of good design but it needed bringing up to date. The refurbishment is briefly described in Chapter 18.
- Richmond Library – an 1880 Grade 2 listed building.[21]

The Reading Agency

A charity formed in 2002, the Reading Agency sets out to improve the reading experience by inspiring, challenging and supporting libraries, mainly public libraries. Following a Big Lottery award of £575,000, the agency is working with library services across England to set up 20 Book Bars 'where young people will be able to enjoy and share reading with friends and peers'.

The Book Bars – now known as 'Headspaces' – are places in libraries where young people can relax, read favourite books and magazines. 'Book waiters' will serve them coffee and their chosen book. Twenty locations have been selected as Book Bar development sites in the next three years and will provide 'a discrete space for young people within a planned new library or youth café or as part of a refurbishment programme'. Examples of those to be set up in refurbished libraries from 2007 to 2010 include those at Buxton (Derbyshire), High Street Library (Bolton), High Wycombe Library (Buckinghamshire) and Padstow Library (Cornwall).[22]

Academic libraries

Another little bit of history

One of the world's most famous library interiors is the Long Room, the old library of Trinity College Dublin. Finished in 1732, it consists of two rows of shelving divided by a central gangway above which was a gallery. By the mid-nineteenth century, and now receiving books under copyright legislation, the library found itself with space problems as well as a dangerous roof. Not without some controversy, the agreed solution (completed in 1861), was to raise the roof slightly, replacing the original flat ceiling with barrel-shaped one, and to shelve the gallery, repeating the layout on the floor below it.

What the visitor sees and so admires today is not, therefore, the library interior as it was in the early eighteenth century but a nineteenth-century renewal, a response to library and structural needs. And although still a working library, alongside other modern libraries on the site, the Long Room has become a major tourist attraction, as well as a book museum and exhibition space with other facilities close by.

As with public libraries there may be long intervals between physical changes to an academic library, which can alter its appearance, and also its internal geography, as when, for example, a new entrance is created at a different location to the original or a library extension is erected. The challenge here, as with all heritage buildings such as the Long Room, Trinity College Dublin and others like the John Rylands Library, Manchester, and the Wilkins Library, University College London, is the successful blending of the old and contemporary elements of the building to make a successful new whole.

Forces for change

Like librarians in public libraries, there have been external pressures as well institutional ones for academic librarians to re-evaluate existing premises, as well as provide new buildings. In the 1990s, and through to the present time, higher education institutions have found that:

- Student numbers have grown.
- Institutions have grown through expansion and mergers.
- There has been a convergence of library and computing services.
- Changes have taken place in research, teaching and learning, facilitated by information and communications technology (ICT).

In a number of institutions the use of the 'learning centre' description for the library has helped to signal the response to these developments.

Follett Report

Part of the answer to these developments was a need for improved physical and information technology facilities, as demonstrated by the findings of the 1993 Follett Report.[23] This declared that libraries were under pressure, that there were serious shortfalls in space and that funding had not kept pace with IT developments and the opportunities it presented. The situation could be remedied by significant capital expenditure on new and refurbished buildings as well as ICT.

As a result of Follett over 100 new academic library building projects were embarked on in the 1990s and into the 21st century. These projects, to improve the library as a place of resort for all, included new build, the rationalization of the number of service points in some instances, refurbishments, extensions and accessibility. The emphasis of these building projects was on flexibility and the future-proofing of space.[24]

Funding

With two thirds of the money coming from institutional funding and one third earmarked capital grants from the funding councils, a range of building projects was made possible, including refurbishment of a number of library and information services. More library building improvements were still needed, however, and funds were made available in England through the Funding Councils' Poor Estates Initiative 1998–2003.[25] Institutions, particularly the older universities, are able to benefit from fundraising from alumni and others for library building projects. Libraries in the higher education sector may also benefit from funding from, for example, the Wolfson Foundation.

The Scottish Funding Council has published *Spaces for Learning*, which includes a number of case study libraries of which Glasgow Caledonia University is one, a refurbishment project.[26] In Wales the Higher Education Funding Council (HEFCW), through its widening access programme, has made disability capital funding available to higher education institutions to help them comply with disability legislation. The money is to be used for adapting buildings and other estates work.[27]

Providing guidance and assistance to those undertaking library projects, whether new build or refurbishment, are the Society of College, National and University Libraries (SCONUL) and the Joint Information Systems Committee (JISC).

Society of College, National and University Libraries

SCONUL has a strong commitment to providing information and guidance on library building provision. Its Working Group on Space Planning has amongst its terms of reference the wish to 'Raise awareness of good space as a key institutional strategic resource'.[28]

Associated with the working group's activities are the SCONUL Library Design Awards originally made every five years (now changed to every three years), which have been awarded to both new buildings and refurbishments.[29] SCONUL also arranges building visits to libraries from time to time: the visits in 2006 were to Glasgow Caledonian and University of Glasgow libraries, the latter a major refurbishment and expansion (see Chapter 8).

The SCONUL Library Buildings Database includes details of new as well as refurbished libraries, such as the University of Lincoln Library, the J.B. Morrell Library, at the University of York and the Hartley Library, University of Southampton (see Chapter 9). In 2008 the SCONUL database was incorporated in the buildings database of the Designing Libraries website.

Joint Information Systems Committee (JISC)

JISC describes itself as supporting 'education and research by promoting innovation in new technologies'. Amongst its interests is a concern for 'new environments for learning, teaching and research', with advice offered on planning and designing technology-rich learning spaces.[30]

Designing Spaces for Effective Learning (2006) is a JISC publication whose aim is to provide the post-16 sector with succinct and essential information to do just that. It highlights the impact of learning technologies on various physical spaces and provides ten examples of new and refurbished UK projects in the further and higher education sectors. It includes floor plans and a prototype floor plan for a learning centre.

Further education

Sponsored by Cymal, the publication *Services Supporting Learning in Wales* provides the means for evaluating Welsh further education learning resource services.[31] Drawing heavily on Scotland's *Resources and Services Supporting Learning*,[32] it asks a variety of key questions. The first being 'Does the learning resource service provide an effective learning environment?'. Sub-questions include:

- Does the environment encourage study? – noise, differentiated space, etc.
- Do the LRCs have effective internal and external signage?

Funding, published guidance, best practice examples and an innovative response to educational challenges have resulted in a substantial number of new and refurbished structures in the UK higher and further education sectors as the case studies demonstrate.

National libraries

Following the opening of the new British Library building close to St Pancras Station in 1996, it is the National Library of Wales in Aberystwyth – out of the UK's three national libraries – that has perhaps undergone the greatest reorganization and refurbishment of its premises. This is reflected in the inclusion of a case study on the project (see Chapter 6), showing its more inclusive approach to users; its educational services development; better reader, exhibition and ICT facilities, as well as public facilities such as a shop and restaurant. Making national library reading rooms more inclusive and accessible at, for example, the British Library, as not always meet with approval by more longstanding readers.

Special libraries

The need for change and refurbishment has also been on the special libraries agenda. For example, the Kennel Club Library was established in 1985 and is the largest canine library in Europe. The need for greater space as well as other requirements led to a major refurbishment of the library in 2006. Changes in technology and staff interaction with users, and the need for DDA compliance, have resulted in changes to the furnishing of other special libraries, such as those of the Law Society and Lincoln's Inn.[33] The Wellcome Library reopened in its old home that includes a state-of-the-art conservation studio; exhibition facilities, conference centre, café and bookshop are part of the nine-storey building next door to the library.[34]

Renewal and rebirth

Library buildings, but particularly public library buildings, have sometimes been given a bad press in recent years. The poor condition of the library 'estate' has been seen as contributing to declining library use – bad buildings put people off – while new and refurbished premises, with longer opening hours, modern facilities, different layout and stock, social space and a more welcoming staff, are viewed as a means of drawing people, especially the socially excluded, into libraries. And, as the following case studies reveal, the immediate impact of new or renewed premises on library use and visits would seem to justify this attention to library premises, refurbishments in particular. Interestingly the situation in the US, as revealed the *Library Journal*'s six-year summary in 2006, shows that the total of additions, remodellings and renovations regularly slightly exceeds the number of new buildings[35] – indicating, perhaps that the push to renew our library buildings is not just a UK concern.

This opening chapter has surveyed the current library scene, identifying drivers and influences for the refurbishing and re-planning of libraries. Particular attention has been paid to the influence of government initiatives, campaigns and funds to renew the library public library 'estate'. Other kinds of library too have shared in this process of modernization and development, as the case studies described in the following chapters demonstrate, although the emphasis is on public libraries as the most numerous group. This imbalance is remedied to some extent by the 'Snapshots' chapter (Chapter 18) with its greater emphasis on academic and other types of library.

All this activity might be seen as an unprecedented concern for the provision of high-quality library buildings to meet the needs of a modern society. However, while this present upsurge of activity and interest in library buildings, with its obvious results, is to be welcomed, there has always been a continuing improvement to the publicly funded library estate. For example, in 1990–4 there were 165 new academic and public library buildings and 73 refurbishments, as well as 33 extensions and 110 conversions across the two library sectors.[36] Prior to this period, that is from 1984–9, however, the emphasis was on new buildings, the conversion of buildings for library use, and extensions.[37]

The question is whether this current concern for the refurbishment of library buildings is an example of cyclical renewal (as discussed at the outset of this chapter), but now on a wider front and for a more sustained period of time than hitherto – and therefore likely to soon come to end – or whether this momentum for change and improvement of the library estate can be maintained into the future. This is a topic that will be returned to in the concluding chapter of this book, as part of the lessons learned from the case studes that follow.

Notes

1   Dove, A. (2006), 'The pleasure principle: Brighton Jubilee', *Library + Information Update* **5** (7–8), 48–51.

2   On the transformation of Saffron Walden Library, Essex, *see* Salisbury J. (2007), 'Building for the future', *Public Library Journal* **22** (4), 26–8. On the renovation of Barry Library, *see* Jones, S. (2007), 'New library – new opportunities', *Y Ddolen* spring, 18–19.

3   Hyams, E. and Hunt, M. (2006), 'The partnership approach to building new', *Library + Information Update*, **5** (7–8), 40–2; Howden, J. (2007), 'The Saltire Centre: a new space for learning', *Library + Information Update* **6** (6), 28–31.

4   For details of its current arrangement, *see Barnet London Borough, Barnet Libraries, Hendon Library*, available at: www.barnet.gov.uk/library-hendon. 20 February 2008.

5   Dewe, M. (1981), 'Henry Thomas Hare (1860–1921): an Edwardian public library architect and his work', thesis, Department of Librarianship, University of Strathclyde.

6   For a discussion, *see* Ward, R. (2007), 'Public libraries' in *British Librarianship and Information Work 2001–2005*, edited by J.H. Bowman (Aldershot: Ashgate), 14–28: 22–6.

7 Leadbeater, C. (2003), *Overdue: how to create a modern public library service* (London: Demos); *Better public libraries* (2003), (London: CABE and Resource); Coates, T. (2004), *Who's in Charge? Responsibility for the public library service* (London: Libri Trust and Laser Foundation); for comment, *see* Goulding, A. (2004) 'Who's afraid of *Who's in Charge'*, *Journal of Librarianship and Information Science* **36** (4), 147–50.

8 House of Commons, Culture, Media and Sport Committee (2005), *Public libraries: third report of session 2004–05* (London: HMSO).

9 Department for Culture, Media and Sport (2003) *Framework for the Future* (London: DCMS).

10 *Designing Libraries: the gateway to better library buildings, statistics* available at: www.designinglibraries.org.uk/stats/data/?=catproj. 20 February, 2008. Libraries listed in the database may be counted more than once, if for example a refurbishment includes an extension.

11 'England loses 4 branches, gains 200 refurbished buildings' (2007), *Library + Information Update* **6** (12), 17.

12 *MLA programmes, library design workshops*, available at: www.mla.gov.uk/programmes/framework/framework_programmes/Library_design_workshops. 20 February 2008.

13 *MLA programmes, audit of library buildings*, available at: www.mla.gov.uk/resources/assets//L/librarybuildings_10218.pdf. 20 February 2008.

14 A full list of awards is given in Wilkie, S. and Nichol, J. (2007), 'Winning the lottery: the successful community libraries', *Library + Information Update*, **6** (12), 34–7: 36.

15 'Big Lottery wins' (2007), *Library + Information Update*, **6** (12), 3.

16 *Welsh Assembly, Cymal,* available at: http/new.wales.gov.uk/topics/cultureandsport/museumsarchiveslibraries/cymal_4/libraries/WLPSI/?lang=en. 20 February 2008.

17 *Northern Ireland, Department of Culture, Arts and Leisure, library buildings,* available at: www.dcalni.gov.uk/index/libraries/library_buildings.htm. 20 February 2008.

18 Department of Culture, Arts and Leisure (2003) *Tomorrow's Library: views of the public library sector* (Belfast: Department of Culture, Arts and Leisure).

19 Harper, P. (2006), 'Library design has arrived', *Library + Information Update* **5** (7–8), 35–9. This article reviews the PLBA scheme and identifies design trends and the use of interior design professionals: Gosport Discovery Centre is a case study.

20 McDermott, N. (2007), 'Inspiring public spaces', *Public Library Journal* **22** (4), 5–9; *CILIP, Public Libraries Group, Public Library Building Awards*, available at: www.cilip.org.uk/specialinterestgroups/bysubject/public. 20 February 2008.

21 Rushton, K. (2006), 'Library makeover campaign launched', *Bookseller* (5222) 24 March, 3.

22 *Reading Agency*, available at: www.readingagency.org.uk/youngpeople/headspace. 25 February 2008.

23 The Follett Report: Joint Funding Councils' Libraries Review Group (1993), *Report* (Bristol: HEFCE).

24 Atkinson, J. and Morgan, S. (2007), 'University libraries' in *British Librarianship and Information Work 2001–2005*, edited by J.H. Bowman (Aldershot: Ashgate), 57–81: 65–6.

25 Higher Education Funding Council for England (1997), *Improving Poor Estates: invitation to bid* (Bristol: HEFCE); for a list of refurbished academic libraries for 2001–2005, *see* Dewe, M. and A.J. Clark (2007) 'Library buildings' in *British Librarianship and Information Work 2001–2005*, edited by J.H. Bowman (Aldershot: Ashgate), 372–89: 385–6.

26 Scottish Funding Council (2006), *Spaces for Learning* (London: AMA Alexi Marmot Associates).

27 *Higher Education Funding Council Wales, widening access*, available at: www.hecfw.ac.uk. 25 February 2008.

28 *SCONUL, space planning*, available at: www.sconul.ac.uk/hottopics/spaceplanning. 25 February 2008.

29 McDonald, A. (2002), 'Celebrating outstanding new library buildings', *SCONUL Newsletter* 27, winter, 82–5.

30 *See*, for example *JISC, infokits*, available at: www.jiscinfonet.ac.uk/infokits/learning-space-design. 25 February 2008.

31 *Services Supporting Learning in Wales: a quality toolkit for evaluating learning resource services in further education colleges* (2005) (Cardiff: fforum).

32 Scottish Further Education Funding Council (2003), *Resources and Services Supporting Learning: a service development quality toolkit* (Glasgow: Scottish Library and Information Council).

33 Serota, M. (2007?), *Principles of Library Design*. Also available: at www.serota.co.uk.

34 'A Wellcome return' (2007), *Library + Information Update* **6** (5), 10.

35 Fox, B-L. (2000), 'Betwixt and between', *Library Journal* **131** (20), 42–54: 54.

36 Harrison, D. (ed.) (1995), *Library Buildings in the United Kingdom 1990–1994* (London: Library Services Ltd), 11.

37 Harrison, K.C. (ed.) (1990), *Library Buildings 1984–1989* (London: Library Services Ltd), 12.

PART 1

Heritage Library Buildings – Enhancing the Past for the Present

Fabulous renovation – absolutely stunning, well done! The building is much improved, more space, lighter, brighter but still retains the stain glass!
– Comment on Long Eaton Library, Derbyshire

Chapter 2

Leek Library, Staffordshire: Listed, Linked and Limited – Opening up Service and Perception in a Victorian Building

Hilary Jackson and Alan Medway

Factors which secured and informed the project

Background

In 2001 Staffordshire embarked on a programme of refurbishing its libraries. The County Council invested the sum of £3 million in the programme to improve library buildings. For Staffordshire Libraries this represented a huge investment and followed years of little or no money spent on or in libraries. In the previous 20 years Staffordshire had built two new libraries and refurbished five, two of which are now in the unitary authority of Stoke-on-Trent. Expenditure had been limited to the very bare essential maintenance items and the main thrust of the asset management policy was to keep buildings warm and dry. The libraries were dull and dingy, and brown seemed to be very much the primary colour.

Drivers for change

The driver for change was the Best Value (BV) review of libraries in 2000, which showed that the library service in Staffordshire was only 'fair'. The review resulted in a five-year plan to improve the library service which had widespread political support and brought with it funding to initiate fundamental improvements to the service. This process became known as the 'Library Vision'. As with all best value reviews there was a wide-ranging public consultation exercise, which included the setting up of a number of focus groups throughout the county. These followed on from the household survey commissioned by the county council to gather information from residents on their perception of all county council services. MORI conducted the survey and recruited the members of the focus groups. These groups represented a cross-section of each of the various communities selected and included a broad age range and both library users and non-users. There were four key messages that came out of the focus groups: the public wanted better access to libraries, improved marketing, better stock and lighter, brighter environments.

What can you see through the shop window?

Among the many things the public wanted to see in their library environment were bright colours, comfortable seating areas and the provision of refreshments. They also wanted libraries to meet a number of different needs with different zones for different users: areas for quiet study and local history were important. It was also clear that customers wanted a fast-track area with multiple copies of the latest bestsellers so that, short of time, they could access the latest books quickly with self-issue and return. They also wanted to see more IT, more information and access to other services and all provided by happy smiling staff. There was a resounding 'no' to connecting libraries to supermarkets as people considered shopping to be a chore and the library to be a pleasurable experience to be savoured and enjoyed.

One of the other key features of the BV exercise was to look at opportunities for partnership working and explore the benefits of shared facilities. These would provide economies of scale in terms of costs and staffing and each would benefit in terms of users accessing each others' services. The development of one-stop shops, the drive towards e-government and increased work with district councils provided the impetus for many of the library service projects.

Style

All these requirements had to be accommodated in a variety of buildings of various ages and styles and it was decided that while there should be a certain 'look' to our libraries, with bright colours and light wood tones, each library should be refurbished in a style appropriate to the building. The branding of the service has been achieved through signage and a house style for publicity, livery for the mobile libraries and a publicity campaign that was designed to change the traditional view of libraries. This ties all the libraries together and creates a brand that is 'Staffordshire Libraries'.

At the same time the library service worked with consultants to apply retail principles to libraries with the aim of improving the users' experience of the library environment. The aim was to remove clutter, improve stock presentation and identify the natural flow of people through a building. A series of quality standards were introduced, setting benchmarks for stock presentation and display and ensuring that libraries are tidy, clean and fragrant. At the same time we took a robust approach to posters and notices, adopting a principle of 'less is more' and with an emphasis on the positive rather than the negative. All the library staff have been trained and engaged in this process and embraced the 'House Doctor' approach with great enthusiasm.

Planning and design process

A unique building

Figure 2.1 Leek Library, Staffordshire, exterior

The Staffordshire library to be discussed in this chapter is the Leek Library housed in the Nicholson Institute. Opened in 1884 this provided a lending library, reference library, reading room, newsroom, and museum and art gallery. Since 1888, the Nicholson Institute has been held in trust by a number of public bodies. Latterly, the overriding responsibility has fallen to the county council, a situation which makes for an interesting working relationship with the two other main stakeholders.

The building has a number of rooms and balconied galleries and much of this space had not been open to the public for some time due to access and health and safety issues.

The building is a source of civic pride in Leek and is a Grade 2 star listed building. Consequently, many of the more ambitious aspirations for the development were quashed by English Heritage; a passenger lift attached to the exterior being one such suggestion. Staffordshire had employed a firm of architects – Bryant, Priest, Newman – to develop innovative design for the some of the county's library refurbishment programme. The challenge was to provide a modern library environment that at the same time was sympathetic to the historic building.

Public consultation

Expectations of a library refurbishment at Leek had been high for a long time before Staffordshire's Library Vision. The library in Leek is housed in the Nicholson Institute, which is also home to other services and providers, including an art gallery and museum. There was an expectation that all these services would be improved. The range of views for a mutually beneficial development of public facilities in Leek were influenced by those from the other two main stakeholders – Staffordshire Moorlands District Council and Leek College of Further Education – whose premises stand at either side of the Nicholson Institute. The agreement was that consultation would take the form of a user group, which would consist of councillors and interested parties. This group started meeting in 2001, and met intermittently until the final plans were developed and agreed in the summer of 2005.

Desire for integration

The integration of services between Staffordshire County Council and Staffordshire Moorlands District Council was a key aim of the project, and the first stage was the development of a one-stop shop in the district council offices.

This facility was to allow immediate access to some library services from the district council's customer service desk where customers can now return items, select books from a quick-pick area and have them issued, access the People's Network, pay fees and charges and make general enquiries. The design of this particular area to some extent fell outside the remit for the refurbishment, but informed the ideals of the provision from within the library, as well as being dependent on the progress of developing a bridge link. The library itself would integrate some community museum provision within its design.

The spine

Each refurbishment in Staffordshire had at least one element that made it different from the others. Leek Library boasts 'the spine', which was designed in response to one of the concerns about developing the listed building. This was the amount of service trunking and fixtures that would need to be attached to the walls of the library. Previous developments had not given due consideration to the original fabric of the building with the result that they were cluttered and damaged.

The spine incorporates book shelves, display cases, computer workstations, cabling, electrical supply and integrated lighting. Entrance archways are attached to book shelves, which are in turn attached to the service counter. Bays of shelving are punctuated with display cases and each right-angled turn opens up a new section of stock to explore. The linked 'vertebrae' are covered with a coloured pelmet arrangement, the colours progressing through the spectrum of the rainbow. The effect is to make exploring the library an intriguing experience, whilst simultaneously drawing difficult space into a holistic concept without diminishing the prominence of individual genres of stock.

Restoration

Bringing a contemporary concept of style and service into a listed building was never going to be achieved without compromise. The need for a bright, modern and attractive environment does not sit easily with Victorian grandeur and austerity. The pre-eminent achievement of this refurbishment project was to bring a visual appeal to the service with a trail that leads users to the children's library, the adult lending library or the one-stop shop without any feeling of incongruent changes in space. Meanwhile, the walls and panels that were features of the original building are restored and painted in an attractive and complementary dove grey, freed of hanging cables and fixtures and forming an elegant backdrop to the modern 'spine'.

Customers accessing IT and reference services ascend the stone staircase to the upper floor, where a colour scheme that reflects the original has been employed to give a distinctive ambience to the room. The room has its own 'mini-spine', housing computers, refreshments and library stock.

Figure 2.2 Leek Library, Staffordshire, interior

Problems, delays, difficulties

Listed building consent

The listed building status of Leek Library has been a challenge in achieving a refurbishment that is both modern and complimentary to the building. However, the end result does bring a pleasing mixture of the new and old, and the population of Leek can once again be rightly proud of this facility. There was early consultation with English Heritage, as it was clear that little progress would be made without their input. The Grade 2 star listing required that both building and furnishings were considered.

One of the key requirements for listed building consent for this project was to commission a paint scrape to establish the original colour scheme. The result was a detailed analysis of the original paints and colours used which revealed a rather drab scheme of maroon and brown; clearly the Victorians did not expect users of the building to be distracted by bright colours. There followed some delicate negotiations with the local conservation officer about colour and it was agreed that this scheme would be preserved on one wall of the building.

The lighting also proved to be contentious. The original had been gas lighting, so could not be replicated, but suitable shades and fittings had to be sourced to fit in with conservation expectations. Windows could not be replaced unless they replicated those already in use. Such work inevitably lengthened the construction process, as well as increasing costs. Plans then needed to be modified to ensure that as much of the scheme as possible was still achieved.

The steps

Both library clients and architects believed that the concept of integrated services, described previously, could best be delivered by establishing a common entrance through the district offices. The main entrance previously was a broad set of stone steps leading to an entrance hall and up again to the ground floor and then to the upper floor of the library. The proposal to restrict this entrance to a fire exit met with nothing short of an outcry from members of the user group. Press reports soon escalated this to wider public consternation, which at times became disproportionately vitriolic.

Eventually plans were adjusted to allow for a continuation of use of these steps, although this was no longer the main entrance. The condition and gradient of the steps and the cobbled approach to them had been an issue in the past. However, public will to preserve this part of the building's heritage won through.

Design of the bridge link

The bridge link was a major construction project within the refurbishment project. This development brought more than its share of difficulties as two buildings of different age and floor levels were to be linked together, whilst access to a car park behind both buildings was maintained.

Once achieved, the bridge link allowed members of the public access to a range of District Council and County Council facilities and services all under one roof, albeit in two separate and neighbouring buildings.

The link is a modern glass structure with simple clean lines joining the two buildings. It is close both to the service desk in the district council office and the library counter on the ground floor of the library. The bridge has a width of 1.7m, and so some book stock can be displayed on it using paperback spinners, without restricting the access. There is book stock on display in the one-stop shop area near to the link, so a visual connection to the library is made with content as well as guiding.

Evaluation

Design outcomes and improvements to service

The transformation of the library has been spectacular. As well as the visual impact of the spine, the relocation of areas of service has had great effect. A children's library was created in the room that had formerly housed a reference library.

Figure 2.3 Leek Library, Staffordshire, children's library

The space here is both interesting and adaptable. Group activities and school class visits are now more easily achieved and the scope to be creative with the space has been greatly increased. The rest of the lending stock follows the maze of the spine for particular genres and sections. The audiovisual stock is close to the service counter, and so cumbersome and ugly security cases are not used. The teenage zone has a cosy niche and the provision of PCs in the lending and children's areas is unobtrusive but effective. The siting of display cases in a busy section of the library raises customers' awareness of aspects of Leek's history that are regularly exhibited.

The area that has been developed as a reference and IT section opens up some original architectural features that many citizens will not have seen previously. Yet the room effectively incorporates the service provision, allowing for private study and computer use, as well as learndirect courses facilitated by a private provider, Exchange.

A small room adjoining this has been developed as a local studies space.

Increased use

While the library refurbishment was taking place, the service was maintained in the district council one-stop shop. Although use of the service dipped on average the monthly reductions were only 30 per cent on visits and 42 per cent on issues. This was considerably less than in other locations, where temporary facilities had been set up.

Following this there has been a steady recovery in performance, especially since March 2007. People have, it seems, regained the habit of using their town library. Monthly issues are back to between 15,000 and 16,000 and monthly visitors again stand at about 23,000.

In August 2007 issues rose to 18,015 and visits rose to 24,751. This will have been due in no small part to efforts to promote the Summer Reading Challenge, although a general increase in use of the library has been noted by staff.

Impact on community

Early reactions were mixed as one might expect in such a prominent and historic building. Some of this will have been a result of the wrangling over the main entrance, which although resolved continued to highlight negativity over modernization. Many found the new arrangement of the building hard to grasp, and resistance to change, even in the detail of where things where now kept or sited, was clearly vocalized.

However, many appreciated the bright new interior, extensive new children's library and increased investment in book stock, although they were less vocal in their enthusiasm.

Change is never welcomed wholesale and this refurbishment has taken some time to gain acceptance. Increased use is starting to show, which gives some cause for optimism for the future.

The library and one-stop shop services are better positioned for a positive impact on the community. The library service has undergone a county-wide staffing restructure, which has resulted in a full team system being established at Leek Library. The opportunities for this team to work with community partners to promote the library have never been better.

Leek Library continues to function within the confines of a listed building, but the refurbishment and the links to other services helps it to stretch out beyond its limits to deliver 21st-century services.

Chapter 3

Long Eaton Library, Derbyshire: An Art Nouveau Gem Reborn

Robert Gent and Don Gibbs

This brief chapter can do no more than give a flavour of the transformation that has been effected in a run-down library in the centre of a small industrial town in Derbyshire. A building which appeared to have reached the end of its useful life, and which was experiencing declining levels of use, has been reborn as a modern, thriving resource at the heart of the local community. That community has supported the 'new' library enthusiastically and their enthusiasm is shared by the staff, who have a new pride in their library and their service. The feeling is best summed up in the reaction of the first young person to walk through the door of the vibrant new children's library; he stopped in his tracks, his eyes wide, and breathed the one word, 'Wow!'

Long Eaton is a small industrial town of around 20,000 people in the valley of the River Trent, within the Nottingham/Derby conurbation. Its former prosperity rested principally on the textile industry and the nearby ironworks at Stanton-by-Dale. In the latter years of the twentieth century it suffered from the decline of those traditional industries, and from increasing unemployment, poor housing and limited infrastructure. Despite its difficulties, however, and its location within the larger conurbation, it retains a clear identity of its own and a genuine sense of community.

An unappealing and defective building

The origins of the town's library epitomize that sense of local identity and the optimism which characterized the period of economic growth in the early years of the century. Long Eaton Library was opened in 1906 following a local appeal for subscriptions but the bulk of the funding for the building itself came from the Carnegie United Kingdom Trust. Local businesses, organizations and individuals provided funding for furniture, fittings and book stock.

The library, a Grade II listed building, stands in a small park on the edge of the main shopping street, and is a fine example of Art Nouveau design. Its features include a remarkable stained glass window and some notable tiling, including an impressive mosaic above the main doors.

Figure 3.1 Long Eaton Library, Derbyshire, exterior
Source: Richard Belton

By the late twentieth century, however, the library was presenting a shabby face. Over many years, the interior had been remodelled to accommodate changing patterns of service, and new resources had been shoehorned into limited space. While the range of resources, including books, local studies resources and IT were excellent, their presentation was unappealing. The children's library, in particular, was housed in a 'temporary' wooden extension that had long outlived its anticipated life span. The original design features had long since lost their appeal: the stained-glass window, imprisoned behind a mesh screen, had become almost indecipherable.

The building fabric, too, was a cause of concern. Heavy rain brought regular flooding of staff and public areas, resulting in the growth of mould on exterior walls. The costs of continuing maintenance were high, owing to the constant procession of running repairs.

All in all, the library and its appearance belied the reputation for excellent service which Derbyshire County Council had gained: so much so, that Best Value inspectors judged the building 'disgusting' and expressed particular concern over the uneven floor, which resembled 'a small boat at sea'.

Nor was the building easy or convenient as a workspace. Multiple enquiry points, cramped workrooms, makeshift storage for audiovisual items, all made for poor efficiency and growing risks to health and safety.

Planning the renewal

With the introduction of the Single Capital Pot approach to local authority capital funding, Derbyshire County Council conducted a review of its property with a view to identifying those premises most in need of attention. As a result of this exercise, Long Eaton Library was earmarked for renovation, with the Cultural and Community Services Department making a contribution from its own budget for security, furnishing and shelving.

As a first step, library staff were asked to consider an ideal scenario, and all contributed their own ideas of how they would like the building to develop. A corporate project team was recruited and a design brief created which would form the basis of a tender. Mansells was selected as the approved contractor and an early meeting was held with all interested parties – the contractor, staff in the library, corporate and departmental ICT experts, the county council's architect, heating and electrical engineers.

Early agreement was reached on those services which would be retained and enhanced – accessible cloakroom and baby-changing facilities, extensive ICT provision – and those which would be added or altered – a loan service for console games, rationalization of enquiry points.

English Heritage's involvement

From a very early stage enormous emphasis was placed on securing the support of English Heritage and the local civic society. This was not a straightforward process. For example, the design envisaged moving an original glazed screen which acted as a barrier to people entering the building. Before approval could be obtained, library staff had to prove, using early photographs of the building, that the screen was not in its original position. English Heritage insisted that the screen be used in the building and it was employed to create an effective wall for the library office, providing a good level of natural light. The approval process for this simple operation took over six months to accomplish.

For the project as a whole it was necessary to obtain listed building planning consent, and the inspector's report was positive:

> The building is a grade 2 listed building and its importance as a rare example of the Art Nouveau style in this country is recognized. I consider the scheme, as amended, offers an acceptable balance of available resources and design response to its context. The main concerns about the external appearance of the proposal related to the screened

and non-public location of the proposed extension at the rear of the listed building. I consider that the character and appearance of the original building is not adversely affected by this proposal at the rear, replacing a 1960s timber extension. The design has attempted to resolve the opposing styles and massing of the original building and the 1960s extension. The link between the old and new, utilizing glass bricks for the external wall would provide a clear visual contrast between the original building and the extension.

Restoration and enhancement

Many other original features have been lovingly restored and enhanced. The stained-glass window and skylights benefited greatly from cleaning and it was notable how many library users became aware of them for the first time, after ninety-nine years. A courtyard area was created at the rear of the library to provide a source of natural light to illuminate the stained glass. Mosaic and tiling features were restored, the damaged tiles being replaced with new tiles carefully sourced to match. Long-standing ventilation problems were resolved with the reinstatement of the original ventilation system, using vents in the roof and the floor to allow a natural flow of air. Old and ineffective electric fans in the roof area were removed.

Figure 3.2 Long Eaton Library, Derbyshire, children's library
Source: Richard Belton

Partition walls, which had been added over the years, were taken down, to open up the area and encourage users to explore. Glazed panels were used to restore the original design concept, with light being allowed to flow in and good views over the small park from many parts of the library.

Modern radiators were chosen to be sympathetic with the original style of the building.

In many other ways the building has been enhanced. The demolition of the 1950s wooden extension which housed the children's library and its replacement with a brick-built extension enabled the creation of a bright, modern children's area with easy access and good supervision by staff and parents or carers alike. The adjoining teenage area, like the children's library, has ample face-on display, comfortable seating and dedicated ICT provision.

Throughout the building shelving and furniture was selected to maximize the flexible use of the space, with an emphasis on low level, accessible island shelving. As the library lacks a meeting room, this means that the body of the library can be simply converted to create space for events.

With the support of Derbyshire County Council's Arts Service, a striking display case was designed to showcase exhibits from the county's Ballantyne collection of ceramics. The case houses regularly changing displays of artefacts and high-quality crafts, from the Ballantyne collection and elsewhere, and is the focus for a thriving programme of craft workshops.

Public ICT provision is now a cornerstone of libraries, museums and archives services in Derbyshire, with over 700,000 half-hour sessions booked in 2006–2007. There is a firm commitment to retaining the principle of free access to the Internet, in line with the council's wider objectives around access and equality. ICT was therefore a key feature of the new design, with a suite of PCs in the library, separate provision for children and younger adults, and dedicated 'storybook' PCs, carrying a range of animated stories, for younger children. The PC suite is configured so that it can be used independently by individuals during the day, or as a setting for group learning out of hours.

Access and security were improved, with CCTV coverage, automatic doors and greatly improved sight lines. There was already a ramp at the entrance to the library, which was more than adequate.

**Figure 3.3 Lending library with stained-glass window to the rear,
        Long Eaton Library**

Source: Richard Belton

Compromise and problems

Inevitably, there were some compromises. The library still has no dedicated meeting room or separate learning centre. Storage and office space are at a premium. A section of the library had been used for occasional local art exhibitions, and the space available for this was reduced in order to make way for more accessible shelving. A small but vociferous minority made it clear that, in their view, this was a step too far.

The implementation was far from trouble free. The condition of the roof and floor proved worse than expected – the inspectors' judgement that the floor resembled a small boat at sea was no exaggeration. The complete replacement of corroded sections was necessary and this not only added several months to the proposed six months' closure, but added several hundred thousand pounds to the construction costs, taking the total to well over £1 million.

Service, refurbishment and closure

The original proposal had been to close half the library, while work was carried out on the other half, but this proved to be impossible, and the library was closed to the public for almost one year. There were no alternative premises in the town centre and a mobile library service was identified as the most economical means of retaining a library service presence. Sadly, a large supermarket chain proved unwilling to make space available in its large, town centre car park, and the mobile library was eventually sited adjacent to a leisure centre some way from the main shopping area. This undoubtedly damaged service take-up to a greater extent than had been anticipated. The service was, however, appreciated by people with mobility problems and those living near the parking site. Fortunately, storage space was identified in another library for existing and newly purchased stock.

Access to the site was not easy for library staff who were planning service provision concurrently with the construction work. This meant that where the location of switches, heating pipes and other fittings differed from that shown on the plan, last-minute alterations were necessary to the configuration of shelving and display.

Although communications with suppliers were generally good, there were some problems with the plans for shelving. Where adjustments were requested they were not always reflected in subsequent iterations of the plan, and the supplier made some alterations without consultation. Library staff were obliged to liaise on site with fitters to amend the plans in situ. These issues highlighted the need to liaise closely with design teams at the supplier level, and not merely with those whose job is to sell products.

During the extended closure, staff from Long Eaton Library were employed at a range of locations around the county – in other branch libraries and assisting with acquisitions and local studies provision. It was important to maintain a team approach and a sense of identity with the new library through regular communications.

PLUS and consultation

The short timescale between obtaining capital funding and the commencement of the work, and the complicated negotiations necessitated by the library's listed building status, meant that there was no time for extensive public consultation. However, the Public Library User Survey (PLUS) comments had for a considerable time focussed on the inadequacies of the library with comments such as:

> The library has looked for a long time in urgent need of a cash injection.
> More PCs for internet information.
> Move PC into Stevenson room.
> Wheelchair access insufficient.
> Unable to reach the top shelves.
> Building needs modernization. Heat in summer excessive.
> Location of video phone poor – light from window behind reflects.

All of these comments were addressed in the work undertaken and the responses are described elsewhere in this chapter.

Consultation was held with local children to discuss options and types of furniture; colourful bright and flexible furniture was chosen to ensure their needs were met. There was also consultation with both the proprietors and users of the neighbouring playgroup.

An extension of provision for black and minority ethnic groups was made to reflect the changing nature of the communities served and the growing needs of these communities e.g. in relation to a specific requests for a broader range of stock books, magazines and newspapers in Urdu, Punjabi and Hindi were acquired. Bollywood films on DVD and music from Bollywood films on CD also became part of the core stock of the library.

The building was opened by David Lammy MP, the Minister for Culture, in October 2005, to considerable acclaim and interest from local people. Many commented in writing about the light, bright and airy appearance of the library. Ironically, given that the book stock was 6000 volumes larger, a number of users expressed regrets that we had disposed of so many books. This was undoubtedly a result of improved circulation and the provision of more easily accessible shelving, dispensing with the high and low shelves which had made life so difficult for many users.

The small child discovering the children's library on that first morning was not the only person to experience the 'Wow!' factor.

Disabled users and their representative bodies have been highly complimentary about the improved access and circulation, the clear guiding, the range of resources for those with visual impairment, and the extensive provision of adaptive technology. For example, on such user working with the deafblind commented:

> I work for Deafblind UK as the Regional Development Officer for Derbyshire and Nottinghamshire. My role is to raise Deafblind awareness in these two specific areas. After visiting the refurbished Library last week with one of our members who has a dual sensory loss we were both extremely impressed with many aspects of the design and layout of the library. In particular the height of the shelving, the lighting, the walkways, the large print selection, the clear signage, the friendly staff...

The refurbishment received extensive coverage in the local media and the wider East Midlands media. An interview with the deputy director was broadcast on BBC East Midlands on the day of the official re-opening.

The refurbishment has met with overwhelming support from the local community. Usage has increased dramatically and comparative figures are shown for July 2004 (the last complete month of business before the library closed) and August 2005 (the library re-opened on 2nd August).

Table 3.1 Long Eaton Library: Comparative membership and use statistics, 2004 and 2005

	July 2004	**August 2005**	**Percentage change**
New members	129	698	+440%
Visits	8 474	13 780	+63%
Issues	16 256	23 600	+45%
People's Network sessions	1 500	2 275	+52%

Since reopening, the library has welcomed an average of more than 20 new members every day; 44 per cent of these have been children and young people.

The following comments serve to sum up the reaction of local people:

> Fabulous renovation – absolutely stunning, well done! The building is much improved, more space, lighter, brighter but still retains the stained glass! Also love the shiny new stock, and all the new pc's, well worth the wait!

> The new lighter, brighter library is fantastic. It makes my two children aged three and two want to sit down and look at the books rather than just pick up and go! It is a very important place for children and now they enjoy coming for longer.

Learning lessons: post-project review

Overseeing the refurbishment of a library can be a challenging task, particularly if you only have a few opportunities to direct such projects. The challenge is great but … you should also learn from the experience! Many issues arose during the refurbishment of Long Eaton Library. Learning from the positives and avoiding some of the mistakes made in future projects helps save time and money, as well as a few sleepless nights and many headaches. Following the completion of the refurbishment a post-project review meeting was arranged by Derbyshire County Council's Property Services section. This was seen as powerful learning opportunity that would leads to continual improvement in the service provided by Property Services but also provide valuable lessons for the public library service in developing future capital projects. It was an opportunity to capture knowledge, to learn and improve and to focus on the facts and not a time to cover mistakes and pass blame

The following list of headings covered at the post-project review is intended as a prompt for areas that need to be considered but it is not meant to be comprehensive:

- brief/design
- timescales
- cost/budget
- planning
- communication/meetings both internal processes and with contractors etc.
- staffing
- partners e.g. Property Services, contractors, corporate IT etc.
- monitoring
- satisfaction – client/customer
- marketing.

The work completed on Long Eaton Library was also the subject of a dissertation by a student at the University of Derby who looked at the refurbishment critically and brought together their design, regulatory, structural and technological learning to assess the project.

The Local Authority Building Control (LABC) National Built in Quality Awards, which recognize and reward the most forward-looking people and organizations and the most innovative construction projects completed within the East Midlands region, named it winner in the Best Access/Disability innovation section

The contractor, Mansells, was also awarded a Green Apple Award, presented by environmental campaigner Dr David Bellamy, in recognition of the environmentally friendly nature of the work.

Chapter 4

Torquay Library, Torbay:
Refurbishing an Art Deco Style Building

Katie Lusty

Background

For a number of years there has been a gradual downward trend in the use of public libraries throughout the country. The reasons put forward for this decline are many and varied, and include such factors as changes in lifestyle, competing leisure activities and the failure of public libraries to present and market their services effectively. However, the decline in usage has coincided with a prolonged period of under-investment and budget cuts experienced by the great majority of library authorities.

Torbay Library Services became a unitary library authority in 1998, following three years of severe budget reductions experienced by the former Devon Library Services. This meant that the new Torbay Library Services started life as a low-spending authority, and this was exacerbated by further reductions in its resources fund, the net result being a deterioration in the quality of stock available for loan and information, which in turn resulted in a steep decline in visitor numbers and stock issue figures.

Whilst many authorities have experienced similar decline, the drop in Torbay's performance was above average. Clearly there was an urgent need to halt this decline and then enter a period of growth.

Following the publication of *Framework for the Future*, a working party was convened, consisting of senior management representatives of the library service and councillors, whose aim was to produce a blueprint for the next ten years. The inadequacies of Torquay Library, in terms of size and facilities, were recognized.

During 2003 an opportunity arose for Torbay Library Services to submit a target under the Local Public Service Agreement (LPSA) between Torbay Council and the government. Inevitably the target had to be 'stretching' in nature. One of the agreed targets for the library services was to 'Increase the usage of Torbay's libraries'. To achieve the target we had to increase:

- the number of visitors to our libraries by 15 per cent (from 625,421 in 2003–2004 to 719,950 in 2006–2007);

- the number of active borrowers by 12.5 per cent (from 14,340 in 2003–2004 to 16,132 in 2006–2007) with an 'active borrower' defined as someone who borrows something on at least four different occasions during a year;
- the percentage of library users who judge the quality of books and other materials to be good or very good (from 72 per cent in 2003–2004 to 80 per cent in 2006–2007).

Figure 4.1 Torquay Library Service, Torquay Library, interior

Source: Remploy

The targets certainly were stretching, and not for the faint-hearted, but with a determination to halt the decline in the use of our libraries, and the added incentive of £75,000 pump-priming money to help us meet them, we knew that this was an opportunity we had to take.

An early decision was that our best chance of success of meeting our targets was to radically improve Torquay Library. Our strategy for meeting the targets goes beyond the scope of this chapter and I will therefore focus on the main elements that led us to the refurbishment of Torquay Library, how we went about it and what we experienced along the way.

Planning and design process

To help us meet our targets Torbay Library Services enlisted the help of the consultants John Stanley Associates. Part of the recommendations included changes to the way we marketed our services, displayed our products and set out our buildings. Some of the recommendations were used to help us formulate our plans for the refurbishment at Torquay.

This decision coincided with the award of funding for a capital project, on health and safety grounds, to completely re-wire Torquay Library. The project also included renewed lighting for the building. Clearly it made sense to combine the two projects.

Our first task was to appoint a project manager for the library service to oversee the two projects, and a member of the management team was appointed.

The second task was to convene a group of library staff who would develop the ideas for the refurbishment.

With regard to the refurbishment we had two main aims in mind, the first being to obtain maximum value for money and benefit for our customers, and the second was to realize a refurbishment that would sympathize with, rather than ignore the magnificent 1930s Art Deco style building.

The Torquay Group arrived at a number of broad considerations:

- There should be an emphasis on zones.
- The Art Deco features in the building should be retained/enhanced.
- New furniture/fittings should be light rather than dark.
- A clockwise customer flow should be achieved.
- We may need to refurbish/reshape existing counters rather than replace them as funding is limited.
- Re-carpet and paint as much of the public area as possible.
- There should be more seating/relaxing areas.

We also recognized that we had to prioritize those areas that we wished to refurbish. The initial wish was to focus our efforts on three areas, the priority order for which was as follows:

- the hub (main area of the library) – approximately 205.61m^2
- the Interactive Zone – approximately 51.45m^2
- reading area – approximately 78.44m^2.

The above considerations formed the broad outline of our original specification, which was then put out to tender to five suppliers.

Three suppliers responded to our tender with realistic proposals.

After much consideration and consultation, the final supplier, Remploy was selected. Reasons for the selection included value for money: even at the early stages we realized that we were going to be able to achieve far more than we had originally thought possible. We were also impressed with the way the design ideas fitted with our vision to bring the library into the 21st century, but also be sympathetic to the surroundings.

We quickly came to a number of conclusions:

- If we refurbished our existing counters we could extend the refurbishment to include the children's library and reference library.
- Improvements to the outside of the building would take far too much of the relatively limited budget (e.g. cleaning the stonework would cost in excess of £10,000).

Design solutions

Colour

Some of the most difficult decisions were around the choice of colours used. A specific colour group was convened (consisting of creative individuals, including a local set designer/artist, who had volunteered their help). We were also assisted by a particularly knowledgeable colleague from Environment Services.

Research was conducted into possible Art Deco colour palettes as the palette suggested by Remploy was quickly rejected.

The group decided on a scheme of green and cream (to be warm and rich, more 'butter' than 'buttermilk' the group noted) with touches of bronze (or tulip red). Ultimately a colour 'art deco cream' was identified. This was to be the main paint colour, with 'features' picked out in a 'bronze'. The carpet colour in the main areas was to be green, and the chosen (Futura) shelving cream.

The notable exception to the above scheme was the children's library where young people opted for red shelving and blue carpet. After some debate it was decided that the Inter@ct room would also have blue carpet to highlight it being a different area (and we did not want to replace the existing blue blinds!).

Our existing chairs were recovered in a claret red.

Furniture

Remploy worked with us to come up with complementary furniture and colours, from black leather sofas and cream shelving with green guiding to comfortable seating and desking. They even designed beautiful bespoke 'Art Deco' wooden end panels as a special feature for our fiction shelving.

Figure 4.2 Torbay Library Service, Torquay Library, first floor

Source: Remploy

The main changes

With a complete repaint and carpet throughout (with the exception of the local studies area which has subsequently been refurbished), the other main overall change was to the lighting.

It is incredible the impact that correct levels of lighting can make, changing a dark and gloomy place to a bright, light, inviting building! We were exceedingly fortunate to be able to have input as to the light fittings, resulting in 'portal' lighting to reflect our Art Deco theme and coastal location, and striking fittings on our upper floors.

The key changes to the different areas of the library were as follows:

- Balcony
    - bar height computer desking added with adjustable stools
    - strong branding.
- Relax
    - dedicated library catalogue and PC
    - new seating and working areas
    - magazines with face on display (previously in the reference library).
- Information
    - open flow from the main library
    - comfortable seating area
    - improved study area
    - improved public access computer layout
    - removal of steel shelving and replaced by refurbished wooden shelving
    - new community information board
    - refurbished and relocated counter.
- Hub
    - drinks vending machine
    - more seating
    - relocation of fiction into central area with bespoke 'Art Deco' end shelving
    - increased shelving.
- Inter@ct
    - PCs retained
    - Xbox 360 added
    - flat screen TV added (set to music channel)
    - sofa and stools added
    - new audio units added.
- Children's library
    - new shelving
    - study/PC areas incorporated.

Branding

We worked with our corporate communication team to ensure a strong branding identity for the service.

Project team

As well as the Torquay Group, the main project team consisted of the project manager (Torbay Council) for the re-wiring work, a representative of the electrical contractor, library supplier, industrial services and the library project manager.

We owe a huge debt of thanks to all the Torbay Council staff based at Aspen Way, the electrical contractor, IT services and library supplier as, without their flexibility, craftsmanship, knowledge and dedication, none of this would have been possible.

During a six-week closure period, the building was completely gutted, scaffolded internally, painted, carpeted and put back together with no fuss, with everyone working together and around each other!

Consultation

As a Charter Mark holder Torbay Library Services prides itself on the fact that they will genuinely listen to staff and customers' suggestions. With this ethos it was important to us to not only consult and inform, but to also be prepared to adapt our plans in light of feedback.

At the outset we used existing consultation, such as comments from our most recent PLUS surveys. We also used information provided by staff and customers resulting from a consultation asking 'What would your perfect Torquay Library be like?'.

Prior to the library's closure we also put our plans and ideas on display and invited comments and suggestions. Equally importantly we fed back our responses.

Inevitably you cannot please all the people all of the time, and for me this was highlighted in the responses to our proposal to introduce an X-box 360 (funded by an e-learning grant). Comments for and against are illustrated below:

Against:

Whoever thought of putting in a play station should be moved to some child care job... spend the money on something useful.

Can't see how PC games link in with the library ethos of information literature and learning.

And pro

PS2 and Xboxes can be good for learning. It does not just have to be about books!
Forward thinking, well done.

It's a cultural hub. Libraries need to move with the times and be relevant to all.

One particularly contentious area was that of our existing wooden shelving,
prompted by the comment:

Why spoil this traditional library by removing lovely wooden shelving and installing
more computers?

We did remove one section of wooden shelving on the balcony and relocated
some of our existing computers to this area. We were conscious that the balcony
area is not the most accessible area of the building. To assist choice, we wanted to
locate something on the balcony that was also available elsewhere.

Figure 4.3 Torbay Library Service, Torquay Library, balcony
Source: Remploy

We also removed the remaining wooden 'original' shelving from the back wall in the main area of the library. Unfortunately, we were unable to afford wooden shelving throughout. We had hoped to re-use some of this in the reference library but, at one point, advice indicated that this would not be possible.

We were exceedingly fortunate not to abandon our wooden shelving, a subject dear to some of our customers', and indeed some of our members of staff's, hearts. We were also very fortunate to have craftsmen in the Direct Services team, and two highly skilled carpenters came to our rescue. The wooden shelving that could be reused was reconstructed to complete wooden shelving throughout the reference library.

Along the way – CC – cutting corners – or Best Value solutions?

To illustrate my point here I will use, what I feel to be, two of our most creative examples of best value solutions.

Storage

What are libraries' most precious assets? Staff, undoubtedly, but, of course there are the books themselves, our very reason for being. The problem with books and refurbishment is that you wish you didn't have so many when it comes to finding somewhere for them whilst the actual refurbishment is to take place! Obvious really, but one of those costs you would really rather not have to factor into the equation. We estimated that we would have to relocate approximately 45,000 books out of the building, as we had limited space to store them on the premises, and, with the central hub being completely gutted, leaving them where they were was not an option.

Upon receiving a removal and storage quotation that would severely 'eat' into the precious refurbishment budget, it was decided to seek alternative solutions. After considering a number of possible options (including the possibility of hiring a giant storage container), one stood out to be particularly cost effective. The Torbay Council depot at Aspen Way was able to offer a storage solution. With the assistance of several men, a van, thousands of green recycling skips (nice irony there) and a lot of goodwill and flexibility by all, a more cost-effective solution was obtained.

The real glass ceiling

One outstanding feature of the Torquay Library building is the amazing glass ceiling, a real period feature with bronze fret work. Sadly I will be the first to confess that I had not really taken any notice of it until I was summoned to the public floor to receive a complaint. Having a flat roof, in some need of repair, debris, mainly in the form of dead leaves, had accumulated for all to see through the glass. Upon investigation it was revealed that the cleaning bill ran into thousands and, inevitably, with a severely restricted repair and maintenance budget this was something we could ill afford on any form of regular basis. Not only did the debris render this feature an eyesore, it also affected the light entering the building.

Several members of the Torquay Group felt strongly that this feature should be highlighted, and money found from the budget to have the glass cleaned. One problem with this was that, inevitably we would be faced with a substantial cleaning bill for subsequent years, something we already knew we could not afford. The 'sustainable' solution was to paint the glass ceiling, removing the eyesore of the debris and need for annual cleaning bills.

What we have now is a real feature. Many coats had to be applied to achieve the pearlescent white finish, and with the fretwork repainted and correct levels of lighting, it can now be viewed with pride instead of as an eyesore.

Service arrangements for the closure period

The lending librarian at Torquay and a branch librarian worked on procedures for date stamping, overdue issues, fines and loan allocations prior to closure. Closure posters and bookmarks were produced, and information regarding the closure was posted on our website.

Working with our colleagues in Connections (Torbay Council's Advice and Benefits Office) we were able to offer a limited face-to-face service during the closure period, e.g. taking in returns, issuing reservations and inter-library loan items. A Galaxy-enabled terminal and phone line allowed us to offer as complete a service as we could.

What did we get wrong?

In many respects not a great deal! Following the re-opening of Torquay Library the biggest number of comments and complaints we received was not in relation to the refurbishment itself but to fiction categorization, which was introduced at the same time.

The introduction of fiction categorization had been 'on the cards' at Torquay for a number of years, and it was felt that the re-opening of the refurbished library would be the ideal time to introduce this.

The system itself was relatively straightforward, but our customers responded negatively in such numbers that we had to take note! To ensure we were not just hearing the views of a vociferous minority, a survey was undertaken to gauge customer reaction.

The results were as follows:

Table 4.1 Torquay Library: Fiction categorization survey

Total number of completed returns	762	
Total liked	205	26.90 %
Total disliked	557	73.10 %

Clearly we needed to look at returning the bulk of our fiction to an A–Z sequence. The books would still be labelled by type of book (genre) which should assist those who did like the categorization. Looking at the results of the survey, and bearing in mind the constraints of the building, there was also some scope to retain some categories. A small working group of Torquay staff was formed to consider the results, and come up with recommendations as to what should be changed, and how we implemented any changes. We let our customers know the results of the survey and the timescale for putting things right.

We also had a number of comments about the height of some of our shelving and, in response to staff problems getting to lower shelves, and some borrower comments, we raised the bottom shelf of large print by about 4 inches, and the top shelf went up by 1 inch.

Did we meet our targets?

Sadly no. We did not succeed in reaching our two main LPSA sub-targets and suffice it to say that, with the one exception of the stock target, the final results are very disappointing. We had fallen short, and would not achieve the reward grant we were striving for which would have enabled us to carry out further refurbishments across Torbay. Nevertheless, there have been significant benefits in having LPSA Target 4, including:

- a significant increase in library visits and borrowing for the first time in a generation;
- pump-priming money used to refurbish Torquay Library;
- increased resources made available to spend on library stock, resulting in greatly improved quality – acknowledged by library users and recorded in improved stock satisfaction rating;
- high satisfaction ratings – Torbay was one of only four out of the 15 south-west authorities to achieve the Public Library Service Standard (94 per cent) for adult library user satisfaction, and was one of only three out of the south-west authorities to achieve 90 per cent or more for under-16 library user satisfaction;
- introduction of a loyalty card which has proved highly popular with customers.

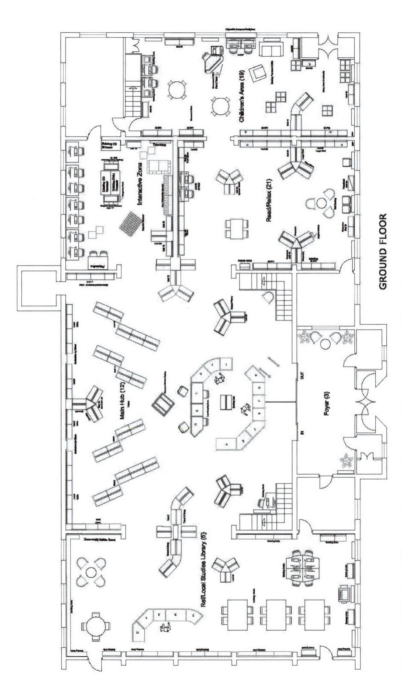

GROUND FLOOR

Figure 4.4 Torbay Library Service, Torquay Library, ground floor plan
Source: Remploy

Result

Along with the benefits mentioned above, including an increase in visitors and borrowing at Torquay, the library has been brought into the 21st century with more seating, lower shelves, a coffee machine, comfortable reading areas with shelving for more book stock and an interactive zone with graphic novels. We wanted to ensure the needs of library members were met without compromising the fabulous Art Deco features in the building. We felt we had achieved our vision.

And, in the words of some of our customers:

> This is so utterly civilized, inventive, open, light, forward looking, simple, clear, effective, up to date and most importantly personal and friendly, not to mention comprehensive.

> I learnt to read in this library and still have my 'Good Readers Circle' stuff from the 1970s. After uni, I moved around a lot and came back to Torquay eventually and came back to the library. I was worried that the redesign would be too commercial ... And I'd lose memories of a cosy place. But it's not – I really like it. Retains character but updates ... Great job – thanks.

Further information

http://www.remployfurniture.co.uk/pdf/solutions/libraries/casestudy_torquay.pdf

PART 2
New Styles of Provision –
Widening the Library Role

The Visitor Experience… is a major refurbishment exercise with some new
build to meet the expectations of the public, all of the public,
in the modern age.
– The National Library of Wales

Chapter 5

Winchester Discovery Centre, Hampshire: Discovery Centre and More

Richard Ward

Introduction

As the twenty-first century moves steadily through its first decade there is common agreement that library services are at a crossroads. There have been a number of dire predictions that unless radical measures are taken the service that has been steadily developed since the mid 19th century is doomed to extinction and will soon be viewed as a quaint development of the Victorians along with public baths and railway access to just about every town in the country.

In my view the debate facing libraries may be presented quite starkly: there are those who say that all the problems of the library world would be solved if library managers reverted to basics, filled their libraries full of well-chosen books, opened them long hours and gave them a modest makeover. The other side of the debate feels that the problems are more fundamental and libraries need to change radically in the ways that Hampshire, with its Discovery Centre programme, and Tower Hamlets in London, with its Idea Stores, are doing. A longer coverage of these issues including a discussion of the many reports and articles covering the debate may be found in the Public Libraries chapter I contributed to *British Librarianship and Information Work 2001–2005*.[1]

To summarize the position briefly: we believe in Hampshire that basing the future survival of the library service on trying to return to the years of mass issues of mainly undemanding literature, which peaked in the 1970s and 1980s, is doomed to failure. Readers interested in some of the academic research which helped lead to this view may like to read the paper published by Douglas Grindlay and Anne Morris entitled 'The decline in adult book lending in UK public libraries and its possible causes'.[2]

We do, however, believe that the public library service has a great future providing it is prepared to adapt and change and this chapter is about how we in Hampshire County Council have approached that necessary transformation. The building transformation work underlies this whole chapter but it should not be forgotten that actually what is being discussed is transforming the service: changing the buildings is only part of that. Without the service transformation building refurbishments – to adapt an old cliché – would be the same as painting the Titanic as it steamed towards the iceberg.

Background to Hampshire Libraries

Hampshire is a large, mainly rural, county on the south coast of England. It enjoys beautiful countryside, a network of pleasant small and medium-sized towns and has a great heritage with the home of the British Army at Aldershot, extensive aviation interests around Farnborough, much naval history at Gosport and the charming cathedral city of Winchester. Although the county is relatively prosperous, there are areas of deprivation in some rural parts and in some towns which suffered from cutbacks in defence spending. The two large cities of Portsmouth and Southampton have been unitary authorities, and thus responsible for their own library affairs, since 1997.

The library service is provided through 55 libraries. This is far fewer than in some other large counties but is compensated for by a recently modernized fleet of 19 mobiles.

For many years the county council has been proud of its library service. Hampshire maintains its own in-house architectural service and under the leadership of Colin Stansfield Smith, and latterly Andrew Smith, designed and built many library buildings, which for architectural excellence stand comparison with any in the world.

Libraries enjoy the political support of the county council but members were shocked by an adverse Audit Commission report which branded the service as one which was unlikely to improve. The leader of the council, Cllr Ken Thornber CBE, decided that matters had to change and in 2002 appointed Yinnon Ezra to lead the newly formed Recreation and Heritage Directorate. A few months later I was appointed as Head of the Library Service. Yinnon and I had worked together in Kent, where, with others, we had developed the Discovery Centre concept. Within a very few years the Audit Commission judgement on Hampshire's libraries had been turned round.

Discovery Centres

Discovery Centres are modernized town centre libraries. Each Discovery Centre has at its core a modernized library. Well-displayed book stocks carefully chosen to meet the needs of the local population, reference and local studies provision as appropriate, books and other materials and activities for children and young people, public access computers and photocopiers are all blended together in colourful and stylishly designed surroundings. Then to this mix is added whatever is appropriate locally from a range of activities and functions suited to the particular town being served. These activities or functions could include art galleries, archives, museums, teaching spaces, meeting rooms, restaurants, cafés or coffee facilities, museums, Citizen's Advice Bureaux, Tourist Information, council one-stop shops, or whatever is needed. The linking theme is that the Discovery Centre should work as a coherent whole: a non-threatening, non-commercial space in the city where people can come together – to read and browse, choose a book, borrow a DVD, look at an art exhibition, meet friends, study local history or research a family tree, or attend an adult education class.

Notwithstanding my earlier remarks about culture change being more important than buildings, the rest of this chapter will be devoted to our approach to one major scheme.

Winchester Discovery Centre

The need

The need to revitalize the library service has been addressed above – in Winchester there was also the opportunity. The public library in Winchester has a long and proud history – in fact, like several others, it can claim to be oldest public library in the country. The library operated from two sites – the lending, children's and local studies library was in a Grade 2* listed building on Jewry Street whilst the reference library was in part of the library service's HQ building a few minutes walk away on North Walls. The Jewry Street site was very shabby: although externally a fine building with a frontage copied by the architect Owen Carter from an Inigo Jones church in Covent Garden, internally it was no longer fit for purpose. The reference library was in a building with major structural faults, was of little architectural importance and, were it not for internal scaffolding, was in danger of collapsing. There was also the inconvenience to staff and customers of a service split across two locations.

The opportunity

The political will existed to provide Winchester with a library it deserved. The county council had been supportive of its library service and had invested large sums in Portsmouth and, particularly, Southampton, when they were part of the administrative county before the 1997 local government reorganization. When those two cities became unitary authorities a commitment was given that the County Council would provide the people of Hampshire with a flagship library of which they could be proud.

All that was lacking was a scheme. The county council owned a plot of land next to the new and admired Hampshire Record Office. For a city centre library this was at best a secondary location but nevertheless the county went ahead with an outline scheme, drew up sketch plans and started the public debate about the new library. It would be fair to say that whilst there was support for a new library nobody much wanted it on the proposed site.

Relationships between the city of Winchester and the county council had been problematic for some time but matters began to change. What came together was the city's understanding that the county was serious about developing a new library

– and crucially, as is so often the case, there was a change of personalities. After it became clear that there was little public support for the proposed site, the county asked for the city to consider allowing development on the car park in which the Jewry Street library stood. At the same time the city was grappling with how to deal with a bequest it had received some years before from the estate of Bapsy, Marchioness of Winchester. This bequest was to provide the people of Winchester with a civic community centre which could act rather as a village hall provides a focal point for a rural community. The bequest was to be spent at the Guildhall but nonetheless the city council was interested to see if providing a public hall in the new library would enable them to discharge their obligations under the terms of the bequest. In the event the Bapsy money was not used for this purpose but the city still decided to contribute to the scheme and gave the county council half the car park on which to build the extension, and £1 million towards the capital cost. As part of the arrangement between the two authorities the newly refurbished 'library' was to be a Discovery Centre with a multi-purpose, hall, an art gallery and a space to be programmed by the city council, as well as the teaching spaces and all the more conventional library improvements.

The funding package

Things were coming together – we had the need, we had the vision and we had a scheme. We next needed the funding. Perhaps I should say here that matters do not proceed smoothly from one element to the next: all get worked on in parallel and a degree of post-hoc rationalization is needed to make it all look so neat. That is true of the funding package itself. There are two basic ways of going ahead: either you say to the architects 'Build us a library of x thousand square metres' and they say 'That will cost you so much' or you say 'We have got a budget of £x million; how big a library will that get us?'

We knew that we needed a refurbished and extended library that would replace the existing lending, children's and reference libraries. We knew the size of the site we had, and we had an indication of the external funding from the City Council. We also knew that we could count on the capital receipt from the sale of the reference library and the old library HQ. Those items together gave us £4.5 million and the architects reckoned that a development of the size we wanted would cost about £7.5 million leaving a funding gap of about £3 million. This amount was within the funding capability of the county council's capital programme and authority to go move on to detailed planning was obtained.

The planning

As noted above we have in Hampshire a well-respected architectural service that offers a complete package to client departments. That service includes interior designers and the ability to call upon consulting engineers and other specialists not normally employed by county councils. This is paid for by an inclusive levy of 16 per cent of the project cost. It is worth understanding this point as it does alter the traditional client–architect relationship in that both parties are employed by the county council and share the same ends. Had there not been these in-house arrangements then the planning would have been far more detailed and a precise brief produced.

As it was, the brief we gave the architects was a high level statement of aspirations for the building. We then worked very closely with them in an iterative process commenting on their suggestions and refining their proposals, and they listened to our requirements and concerns so we jointly arrived at a solution we are all happy with.

The brief included a statement of values for the building:

- An inspirational building.
- Light and airy, with visibility in and out.
- Built as far as possible without internal walls and boundaries.
- An 'in-depth' service capability – the visitor progresses through the building, from popular, noisier facilities to more serious, quieter areas.
- Zones; some multi-use, some dedicated spaces.
- Built to encompass flexible use.
- DDA compatibility is essential.

We informed the architects of our key requirements for a Discovery Centre:

- Books – adult, children's, teen; reference and lending.
- Information in a variety of formats – books, periodicals.
- People's Network.
- Audiovisual stock; DVDs, videos, CD-ROMs, Playstation games.
- County music and drama service.
- Special collections.
- Business information.
- Reader development events.
- Requests service.
- Help points.

We also discussed with the architects the need for:
- An art gallery.
- A multi-purpose hall seating up to 200.
- Winchester City Council's 'City Space' (an exhibition gallery now focusing on Winchester's history and art).
- Flexible teaching spaces.
- Refreshments – licensed coffee bar.
- Public toilets.

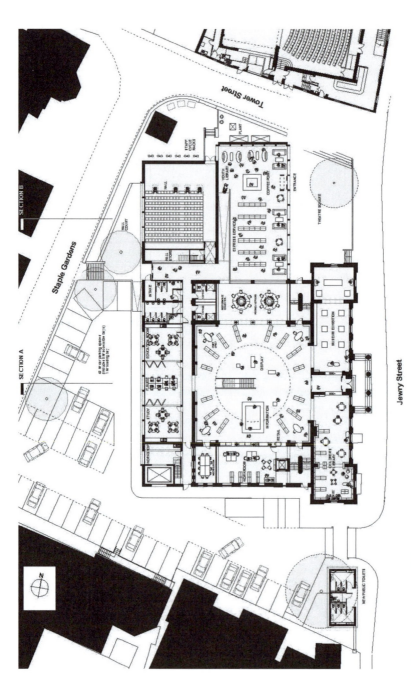

Figure 5.1 Plan of Winchester Discovery Centre, Hampshire

A key part of the talks was the relationship of the spaces to one another and how the building would work at different times of the day. We wanted the building to be multi-purpose and available for use outside of core library hours with different parts of the centre open late into the evening.

Figure 5.2 Winchester Discover Centre, Hampshire, library central space (CAD view)

For this approach to work there had to be complete confidence between the librarians and the architects. We arranged a fact-finding trip for the architects and the key librarians to visit the newest and best comparable schemes in the country. Each profession had to speak openly about the 'must haves' and the 'can't haves'. In our case this was aided by the fact that we had worked with the design team on a previous major project (the transformation of the Gosport Discovery Centre) and on several new-build libraries. Adopting this method does mean, however, that decisions are taken jointly, and although either side could play its 'professional card' that was not done lightly. Instead matters were talked through and one side convinced the other that their way should prevail – or a compromise was found. In practice what tends to happen is that the service professionals' view predominates in practical service delivery matters and the architects' view predominates in design and aesthetics. But our architects are practical people and fully espouse the 'form follows function' principle.

Whilst all these activities were going on there was in parallel a programme of public consultation with focus groups, telephone polling, street surveys, public meetings and questionnaires. All the information gained was fed into the planning and taken account of.

Whilst the library service was leading on consulting the end users the architects were carrying out their own consultations to ensure, for example, that their plans for the art gallery and multi-purpose hall would meet the requirements of the users, and that the necessary listed building consents would be obtained. This latter point is not a trivial matter and the need to be talking very early to the relevant bodies such as English Heritage should not be underestimated.

The design freeze, project appraisal and building works

At some stage the decision has to be taken to freeze the design, obtain the necessary approvals – both in-house to actually commit the budget and externally for planning permission – choose the contractor and start building.

Because the ground work had been carefully laid the approvals were obtained in relatively straightforward way and the contractor was chosen using the County Council's Major Framework Contract process. Two already approved contractors were invited to submit bids for a Best Value evaluation process. The successful contractor would then work closely with the design team before detailed matters were finalized. There would be full competitive tendering for all the subcontract works.

Before the building could actually start there had to be an archaeological survey. Winchester is a city with a distinguished history and the site was known to have been occupied in Roman times. There were also known to be some World War II underground air raid shelters. From the scheme's point of view, if not the historians', it was good that nothing of unexpected significance was discovered, and the building works could start in earnest.

Because the scheme involved completely refurbishing an 1838 building it was always to be expected that problems would arise – and they did. These included such matters as sections of untied brick walls and the uncovering of nineteenth-century cast iron beams still in place over the cast iron columns – which were known about and were being exposed as part of the refurbishment.

Apart from those matters the building works progressed well with all the many complications around such a complex scheme being solved. A last-minute problem was caused by the need to redesign the sprinkler system to incorporate a storage tank as the water company decided that the mains pressure was not sufficient. There were also complications caused by the next-door developer, whose scheme needed to encroach upon our site.

The building was passed back into the possession of the county council before all the work was complete. This was not ideal, but had to happen so that the specialist furniture and equipment could be delivered and installed. The library staff had to become experienced in managing a building site with all the attendant health and safety issues.

At the time of writing the Discovery Centre is almost ready to open. The shelving is all in place, the book stock is being arranged, the IT is mostly ready, the internal guiding has been designed and is about to be installed. Things remaining to be done include finishing of a long list of snags, installing the coffee bar equipment, installing the City Space exhibitions and a major textile artwork, and generally finishing things off.

Figure 5.3 Winchester Discovery Centre, Hampshire, express library
(CAD view)

Throughout the scheme the public have been kept informed as to what is going on via a regular newsboard in the temporary library, by local newspaper coverage and by their being able to observe the building site as they walked by. In the week before opening, when everything is almost ready, there will be a series of previews when large numbers of people will be shown round.

And finally

Had the deadline for this chapter been a month later I could have reported on the opening and the reaction to the new building by the users. Those of us involved in the scheme are convinced that we have jointly created a new style of service fit for the twenty-first century. The people of Winchester and the surrounding area will ultimately decide whether or not we are right.

I must acknowledge the work of Yinnon Ezra and Andrew Smith, the two directors who drove the scheme forward; Alec Gillies, Martin Hallum and Ian Noakes from the design team; and Chris Edwards, Philippa Harper and Jan Turner who very ably represented the library service.

Notes

1   Ward, R. (2007), 'Public libraries', in *British Librarianship and Information Work 2001–2005*, ed. J.H. Bowman (Aldershot: Ashgate), 14–28.
2   Grindlay, J.C. and Morris, A. (2004) 'The decline in adult book lending in UK public libraries and its possible causes', *Journal of Documentation*, **60** (6), 609–31.

Chapter 6

National Library of Wales:
The Visitor Experience Project

Mark Mainwaring

Reasons for refurbishment

Who can fail to be moved by the picture of Sisyphus, doomed to push his stone up to the top of the hill, only to see it roll back down in perpetuity? To those who know the magnificent setting of the National Library of Wales (NLW), set on high ground overlooking Aberystwyth and the sparkling waters of Cardigan Bay, the solution to his dilemma is plain: become a delivery person for a legal deposit library!

Following the grant of the original Royal Charter in 1907 (and the grant of legal deposit status in the Copyright Act of 1911) materials have arrived in West Wales and made their way up Penglais Hill with the specific intention that they be stored with care and made available for generations to come. The 2006 supplementary Royal Charter sets out the objects of the institution both for legal deposit and the wider collection context:

> To collect, preserve and give access to all kinds and forms of recorded knowledge, especially relating to Wales and the Welsh and other Celtic peoples, for the benefit of the public, including those engaged in research and learning.

The Visitor Experience project (VE) described hereafter is a major refurbishment exercise with some new build to meet the expectations of the public, all of the public, in the modern age.

Following the laying of the foundation stone in 1911, NLW developed physically to meet the needs of growing and varied collections by building towards the rear of its site. During the late 1980s, as a consequence of the continued pace of collection growth, it became apparent that the library would soon face a critical space problem. Failure to address the situation adequately could have endangered its capacity to operate as a legal deposit library and thus cause a major loss of facility and status to the people of Wales.

Time was bought by a grant from the then Welsh Office for a limited building extension to the north of the site. This enabled proper planning leading to a grant in 1992 of £11 million to construct 'The Third Library Building' (TLB): a major storage facility utilizing the remaining land to the rear of the earlier buildings. Capacity would be created estimated to cater for growth in collections over a quarter of a century and to provide specialized facilities for important parts of the existing collection. The six floors were designed for defined uses: Floor 1 providing cells for a variety of storage uses (incunabula, manuscripts, records, microfilm, phonograph recordings and a fully effective Faraday cage); Floor 2 comprising a floor for maps and some pictures; Floors 3 to 6 giving mass mobile shelving for books and bound newspapers.

Figure 6.1 National Library of Wales, Aberystwyth, the Drwm, rooftop view

As TLB construction was proceeding, prior to its opening in 1996, strategic thinking moved on to consider how older parts of the building might be better utilized following removal of a logjam on modernization facilitated by the departure of large parts of the collection into TLB from almost every corner of the earlier structure adjacent to public areas. The Citizen's Charter is a good symbol of the prevailing 1990s mood in which these planning deliberations were set: to put services to the public, defined as widely as possible, at the forefront of activities.

Hence, the 'Visitor Experience' project became the dominant strategic building thrust of NLW for subsequent years.

The planning and design process

Reports on the experience of visitors to NLW were prepared by the Director of Administration and Technical Services (a post currently entitled Director of Corporate Services in the NLW structure) and the then Chairman of the NLW Buildings Committee and submitted to the latter body for approval on 31 January 1994. They sought to inspire commitment to a more detailed study by setting out how the current experience could be transformed by a number of key developments.

A physical feasibility study was commissioned in 1995 by the Burgess Partnership (Cardiff). The report included the comment:

> So what is meant by 'The Visitor Experience'? In simple terms it relates to all aspects and parts of the Library that a member of the public might encounter. The brief to improve this Visitor Experience means addressing those environmental and cultural factors in a physical form to provide a focus. New or improved facilities should relate to the needs of all interest groups, age ranges, educational levels and cultural backgrounds.

This study highlighted the possibilities for building transformation through, amongst other suggestions, a new entrance, rationalizing the flow of people through the building, improving facilities for the disabled, upgrading exhibition and catering arrangements and establishing a shop.

Writing a decade onwards from those initial planning discussions, it is interesting to note there was little emphasis in the VE on the reading room facilities: most concentration was on other aspects of service save for those offered by the National Screen and Sound Archive (which at that time were almost non-existent). Those and other areas of NLW were, however, referred to in a wider internal ten-year Review of Buildings and Services. In more recent years the contrasting quality of the VE provision and advances in technological and security expectations have led to planning for significant improvements to the main reading rooms.

In 1997 L and R Consulting were appointed to produce a plan developing the concept outlined in the 1995 report in the context of the potential market, to review the capital proposals, analyse the revenue implications and prepare a document that would form the basis for an application by NLW to the Heritage

Lottery Fund. Their brief was to identify NLW key assets and long-term themes for interpretation and exhibition; prepare a market appraisal identifying important market segments leading to a projection of potential visitor numbers, suggesting the 'product concept' of NLW for the future; and prepare a five-year profit and loss account and a marketing plan. They were also asked to advise on the most appropriate management arrangements for the new facilities.

Planning was aided by a major strategic public consultation exercise in 1999, 'Choosing the Future', which confirmed the appropriateness of the intended improvements. The developing plans also received support in the Aberystwyth Resort Action Plan (Ceredigion County Council and Wales Tourist Board).

Other documents of planning relevance included a building fabric condition survey, a security report, outline design proposals for mechanical and electrical services, a full survey of heating and water systems and a survey of asbestos in underfloor ducts. A buildings conservation plan was prepared in 2001.

During the planning process NLW also sought input from local disabled groups.

A vital part of the TLB project had been the role of the ' Project Users Group' which met regularly under the chairmanship of the Director of Administration and Technical Services (the 'Project Sponsor') to sign off planning decisions at important stages. This internal group included those managers with a particular departmental interest in the new facility and made for clarity of decision-making that greatly aided efficient liaison with the architect and contractor, avoiding the danger of instructions going to the latter from different directions at uncontrolled cost, and ultimately delivered the project on time and to budget.

Throughout the VE project-planning process, the same positive approach was adopted with a 'Project Use Group' chaired by the librarian and attended by most senior managers with a functional interest in the success of the project. This group received regular reports on key project issues and was helpful in planning development, ensuring buy-in and facilitating an effective mesh between physical and service issues.

Whereas TLB had been essentially a major new-build project with specialized fitting out for internal use, the VE was a complex refurbishment exercise with some new build but a large number of public service issues, many related to fitting out. As a consequence, the responsibility for detailed planning and project achievement was divided between the Director of Corporate Services and the building facilities manager (in charge of enabling works, new build, structural, mechanical and engineering or mechanical and electrical, financial control and liaison with the Heritage Lottery Fund as principal funder) and the Director of Public Services (fitting-out of furniture and equipment, signage and marketing strategy).

NLW is a registered charity and, in accordance with legal responsibilities, regular reports were given to the Buildings Committee comprising trustees (and, through its minutes, the full Council of Trustees). Their input, detached from all the detail facing the paid staff, was a refreshing additional element of the planning process, particularly since NLW tries to have at least one trustee with an architectural background.

The VE design solution

Availability of financial resources was, of course, an important driver in the planning process and ultimately, for cost reasons, it was decided to put back certain elements of the original strategic thinking: the creation of a welcome/introduction area in a vacant front courtyard, the extension of conservation facilities and the installation of full air-conditioning in the main exhibition gallery.

However, significant funds were made available: £1 million from the National Assembly for Wales, £2.4 million from the Heritage Lottery Fund and £1.9 million from the NLW private funds given or left to it by generous private benefactors over the years (a tendency that we continue to encourage!).

This enabled the project to proceed in several stages between 2000 and 2004 and comprised the following:

1. Completion of enabling works was a preliminary phase to ensure that the services infrastructure was adequate for the new demands on the building. The works included replacement of the boiler plant, one refurbished and one new boiler house, new heating distribution mains with much improved control and expansion of the building management system. The work also included installing a new internal cold water main, new incoming electrical main and associated equipment with large areas of the extensive services duct needing asbestos removal before any works could be undertaken.

2. Refurbishment of former (mainly) storage areas to the front of the building to incorporate a wide range of public services: a reading room and offices for the National Screen and Sound Archive, an education suite, additional exhibition areas, a restaurant, a shop and new lavatory facilities in several locations. The project also included utilization of a former emergency escape door to create a new main entrance, with adjacent reception, that is both user friendly and more strategically located than the original entrance, now retained solely for ceremonial purposes. The operational effectiveness of NLW was much improved by including a central security control room in the refurbishment works and the commencement of an extensive CCTV installation programme.

3. Creation of a new conference/audiovisual viewing facility in a vacant rear courtyard with a room for the 'crown jewels' of the collection.

In addition to the project architect, specialist design consultants were engaged to assist in a range of fitting out issues: audiovisual and theatrical presentation needs, catering equipment, shop layout and signage.

Figure 6.2 National Library of Wales, Aberystwyth, the Drwm, the courtyard view

Perhaps the biggest challenge facing the delivery team was to maintain NLW as an operational body while these major developments were occurring in the heart of the building, continuing the services in the reading rooms by providing books, manuscripts, pictures, maps and audiovisual materials. It also had to continue to function as an operational home to nearly 300 staff, facilitate meetings and welcome casual visitors.

Coming onstream in stages, the formal opening ceremony of the library refurbishment took place on 12 June 2004 in the 'Drwm' ('drum' in English) that took its name from the innovative design shape finally chosen for the development. Rather than simply infilling a vacant rear courtyard, it was decided to construct an elliptical building within the area, thus permitting viewing of all the original architecture. Clad in stainless steel, this makes a fascinating architectural impact which is particularly appreciated from an atrium running the full four-floors' height of the building in one corner. The auditorium occupies the equivalent of the two lower floors while the services for much of the VE are located on the top floor. The latter lies above the sensitive materials ('crown jewels') floor which is accessed by connections from exhibition areas in the existing building. It is known as Hengwrt, a name rich in cultural significance for Wales. Floored with Welsh slate, it has almost a cathedral-like atmosphere of cultural reverence.

Figure 6.3 National Library of Wales, Aberystwyth, aerial view

Problems along the way

The greatest contextual problem NLW faced was, as indicated above, implementing all aspects of this multifaceted project within a living public building. This required, in particular, careful sealing of work areas, use of a tower crane, strict conditions for building workers and careful liaison with the public and staff.

Another underlying and inevitable challenge is posed by the location of the library itself: with a wonderful view over Cardigan Bay, surrounded by fine agricultural land and mountains, this is a place that few wish to leave. Unfortunately, arrival is the problem because Aberystwyth is some two to three hours from Cardiff and the Midlands with road and rail links far from ideal. The cost implications of this journey has to be built into financial planning together with the issue of availability of supplies and advice, particularly if these are required at short notice.

There is a distinction between challenges that one could reasonably have foreseen prior to a project and those that are unexpected. NLW has for some time now been committed to risk assessment and although the tools for this were not so widely available in the late 1990s when planning started, the approach adopted during the TLB work was maintained. This sought to either allow for known risk, with a significant budget contingency provision, or be alert to pick up problems at an early stage and create both technical and financial solutions. We were fortunate in maintaining assistance from an exceptional cost management consultant throughout both the TLB and VE projects.

It is probably true to say that the areas where we had the most difficulty maintaining this control were those with the least in-house expertise e.g. large-scale audiovisual implementation and provision of a significant catering operation.

The unexpected did happen: the early departure of a key staff member, the discovery of some asbestos, the evidently inadequate original specification for air-conditioning in the kitchen, the electrical changeover which damaged CCTV and other technical equipment, a small dust leakage into the building, problems with commissioning the audiovisual equipment, the inadequate appreciation of the effect of the limited site access, delays from subcontractors and other subcontractors going into liquidation, changes to regulations requiring major design changes after a critical point in construction and insufficient detail in some areas of design all had their impact.

Set high on a hill, NLW is very exposed to the south-westerly winds from the Irish Sea. In retrospect we could have spent more early design time on making the new main entrance more resistant to the prevailing wind conditions.

We also could have investigated more closely at an earlier stage the resources available to both the architect and the contractor in relation to the project.

However, notwithstanding the above, the opening ceremony ultimately took place at approximately the date envisaged during the planning process and the project was completed within budget.

Evaluation of the refurbishment

The VE project has been a great success and has lived up to all the hopes of those many people engaged with its various elements over the past 13 years: above all the building is much more alive.

Core services in the reading rooms have been maintained and expanded through the new facilities offered by the National Screen and Sound Archive. Building use has been broadened in an exciting way: children use the education suite (41 groups in 2006–2007); many more adult groups now visit (280 in 2006–2007); a wide range of events take place in the Drwm including lectures, film shows and staff events; a quality restaurant has been developed attracting the public in its own right; the successful shop has made a name selling items created in Wales; all visitors (including the disabled) get equal access through the new entrance and a wider range of exhibitions is on view.

Adjacent to the entrance is a comfortable reception area where visitors can obtain information or obtain readers' tickets.

Things that can be taken for granted such as vastly improved lavatory provision and signage have become embedded in the experience of visitors but there is also the imaginative use of plasma screens and Film and Sound Collection 'juke boxes' to surprise and delight. Signage itself is a subject of note because of the NLW policy to provide all such materials in both Welsh and English.

The original intention to improve the flow of visitors through the building has been realized and prompted other beneficial changes such as the relocation of a security control point to a more operationally effective position just outside the reading rooms.

Inspired by the quality and success of the VE project, NLW has undertaken a significant upgrading of its South Reading Room to better facilitate the study of delicate materials, with particularly high-security arrangements, in the western end, and family history resources to the east. A similar project is intended to modernize facilities in the North Reading Room, mainly for the study of printed monographs and journals.

The car park has been extended to cater for increased visitor numbers and initial plans have been laid to facilitate a greener approach to travel by easing the movement of park and ride buses from the town. It is hoped that the latter will be achieved by linking the road systems of NLW and the adjacent Aberystwyth University with a consequent easy loop for bus traffic movements.

On future visits to Aberystwyth it is our hope that Sisyphus would deliver his load with care and then stay in the building, take coffee and a cake after his journey, proceed to view an exhibition, comment with sadness that the shop does not currently sell *Myths of Ancient Greece*, listen to a talk in the Drwm and then be inspired to obtain a reader's ticket and research his genealogy. What a challenge to our helpdesk! In fact, he need not even come in to the building to do much of his research because of the great expansion in our online digitized resources in recent years.

But that, as they say, is another story …

PART 3
Remaking University Libraries – Creating Modern Learning and Research Environments

The library looks fabulous; it looks like someone has pushed the walls out to create more space.
– Comment on the Kendrick Library, Birmingham City University

Chapter 7

Kenrick Library, Birmingham City University: From Dismal to a Dynamic Refurbishment

Judith Andrews

Introduction

The Kenrick Library refurbishment project at Birmingham City University (previously the University of Central England) has been implemented over a period of four years from August 2003 to August 2007. The initial trigger for the project was twofold, i.e. the decision to relocate the university's directorate team out of the library building and to release the vacated space back to the library service and the announcement of the availability of HEFCE capital 3 funding in the summer of 2003.

The problem

The Kenrick Library was opened in 1984 and extended in 1991. It was designed before the major spurt in student numbers and before PCs became an essential element in library service delivery. There had been no major overhaul of decoration or facilities since the library had opened and there were a number of known problems. The main areas that the project set out to address were as follows:

- There were ongoing problems with the physical environment. These problems related to heating levels, ventilation, acoustics and lighting.
- One of the main challenges was the need to support the requirement for different types of study environment, i.e. silent and group work. The way the group study areas were organized created significant problems of noise. This was a major political issue and complaints were received on an ongoing basis.
- Access within the building for disabled users was an area of concern. A disabled access audit had identified three sets of heavy wooden doors as particular problems.
- The overall ambience of the library could be best described as dismal. The building had not been redecorated or refitted since it had been built. Areas

of the original orange carpet, the use of dark wood furniture and wooden sloping ceilings all contributed to a dated and dark environment.

The birth of the project

The first glimmering that something could be done was the decision to relocate the directorate team and the promise of £225,000 to spend on the associated relocation within the library. This was followed by the announcement of an internal bidding process within to decide which projects would be funded from the university's HEFCE capital 3 funding allocation. The Library Management Group made the decision to submit a bid to the vice chancellor for a more significant refurbishment project. The library budget funded an architectural feasibility study and the Estates Department funded an environmental survey in mid August 2003. As a result of these two studies two bids were submitted to the vice-chancellor, one a 'do minimal' project valued at £2.2 million and the other a major project valued at £3.3 million. An invitation to a meeting with the vice-chancellor and two pro-vice-chancellors was received shortly afterwards. The purpose of the meeting was to discuss how the initial £225,000 had grown to a multimillion pound project. In the end the findings of the environmental survey and an acknowledgment that the library looked very tired won the day and it was agreed that the project would receive some funding. Following the internal process and a successful bid to HEFCE the project was allocated a budget of £1.6 million.

Library preparation

While waiting for the final decision on the project we acknowledged that we needed advice from an expert on how the best possible result could be achieved. We contacted Andrew McDonald, then of the University of Sunderland and an acknowledged expert in library design, and he agreed to spend a day with the Library Management Group to discuss the issues that needed to be considered. Following this very positive day we set out to develop a detailed project brief which would be used to inform our Estates Department and the project team about what we wanted to achieve.

The brief was developed using input from a number of different sources. As many academic staff and students as possible were contacted for their comments. This included contacting everyone who had written to comment or complain about the Kenrick Library. A significant number of responses were received covering a broad spectrum of issues. Not surprisingly, knowing the problems of noise, the largest number of student responses was concerned with the type of study environment they wanted. The other main source of input came from library staff. All sections within the Kenrick Library were asked to consider what they would want in the new library irrespective of cost. The responses were collated and considered by the Library Management Group and all appropriate suggestions were included in the brief. The collated responses document was sent to all staff indicating what had been included in the brief and explaining why other suggestions had not been included.

The completed briefing document covered all aspects of the Kenrick Library highlighting the issues to be considered and establishing the main aims for the project. These were as follows:

- High-quality facilities that have the 'oomph' or 'wow! factor'.
- An environment that is conducive to study.
- An environment that is flexible enough to support different modes of study, i.e. individual and group with access to electronic information services.

Planning and design process

Following discussions with the Estates Department it was agreed that the library would be involved closely in all aspects of the project. This was very reassuring because in previous new-build projects, where a new library had been part of a larger project, library staff had not been able to achieve this level of involvement.

The first phase of the process was the selection of the project architects. This was organized by one of the assistant directors of Estates who was assigned to lead the project on behalf of the university. A procurement process, using the brief prepared by the library as a key element, was undertaken. The short listed companies were interviewed in January 2004. The interview panel was made up of an assistant director of Estates and the Library Management Group. The selection of the successful company was based on the quality of their responses and the level of fees submitted in the tender response. Once the architects were appointed they took the lead in selecting the quantity surveyors and mechanical and electrical engineers. Once the designs were in place the building contractors were brought on board (June 2004). The library was included in all of the selection interviews.

The full project team was as follows:

- University Estates Department
- Director of Library Services
- Robothams Architects (architect and lead consultant)
- Faithful and Gould (project manager, quantity surveyor and planning supervisor)
- Ove Arup & Partners Ltd (mechanical and electrical engineers)
- GTH Construction Limited
- the university health and safety officer.

Once the team were on board a series of actions were undertaken including the following:

- A full measured survey of the building was commissioned.
- Detailed discussions of the briefing document were held with the project team.
- The project architect spent a number of days in the library observing how it was used.
- The original environmental survey was reviewed by Arups.
- Visits were arranged for members of the project team to two other academic libraries, the Harrison Learning Centre at the University of Wolverhampton and the Adsetts Learning Centre at Sheffield Hallam University.

From there a set of initial designs were drawn up for consideration by the project team and the Library Management Group. The designs were discussed in detail and amendments made. The revised plans were considered by the Library Management Group and were shared in discussion sessions with all Kenrick Library staff. Feedback was shared with the project team and final amendments made before the design was frozen.

Once the design was frozen the project was costed. It had been acknowledged from the start of the project that the agreed budget allocation was modest in terms of the size of the project and the aspirations set out in the project brief. However, it had been agreed that the design should include everything included in the brief as it would be easier to remove things than to add them in later. Therefore it was no surprise that the costs were much higher than the budget would allow. A value engineering exercise was undertaken to bring the project within budget. From the library point of view this was a very difficult process, as it was hard to make compromises in the knowledge that they would reduce the quality of the final product.

Once this stage in the project had been reached the designs were shared with the vice chancellor. The overall scheme was considered in detail, the work to be included in the first phase was discussed and the impact of the value engineering exercise described. At that point the vice chancellor decided that he did not want the quality of the project to be affected adversely and he made additional funding available to reinstate much of what had been cut from the first phase. This commitment from the vice chancellor was evident through the rest of the project with the result that additional allocations from the university's capital budget brought the final project cost up to £3.4 million.

Design decisions

Some of the most important decisions taken by the team related to how the refurbished building was going to function. The proposal put forward by the architect was that the building should become quieter as a user progressed upwards. Therefore the entry level (Level 2) would be the group work area with the two floors above being quiet or silent. The next area of discussion related to the different types of study areas that could be provided. The final design provided

20 group study rooms based on Level 2, and a set of 14 individual study carrels located on Level 3. It was also decided that the study places on the two quiet floors would be provided by perimeter benching separated into individual working areas by perforated steel dividers.

Figure 7.1 Kenrick Library, Birmingham City University, group study rooms

In terms of the look and feel we wanted to achieve it was agreed that we needed something that was modern but not so modern that it would date quickly. The architect suggested the use of glass and light wood finishes and this was accepted by the project team. The design used glass partitions wherever possible, e.g. for the fronts of all the group and individual study rooms and for the front of the new IT area. Maple was used for the perimeter benching and new bay ends for all the shelving. It was also agreed that the sloped wooden ceilings located on two of the floors would be clad with acoustic panels and painted.

One of the suggestions made in the briefing document was that we could consider the use of different colours on each floor of the building to provide a different identity. The design interpreted this by using colour as an accent on each level with one feature wall and the columns on one side of the floor being painted in the chosen colour. The rest of the space was painted white. The benefit of this is that if a colour starts to look dated it is relatively easy to repaint the feature areas.

One aspect of the brief that exercised the project team significantly was how the 'oomph' or 'wow! factor' could be delivered on a modest budget. One proposal included in the original design was the enlargement of the void over the main foyer. This survived the value engineering exercise but concerns about the loss of floor space lead to its removal from the final design. The desired effect was achieved by a combination of lighting, the creation of a new balcony over the main stairs and the replacement of the old stair furniture with wonderful glass and steel balustrading.

Details of the phasing of the work

Phase 1 summer 2004
- Construction of individual study carrels on Level 3.
- Full refurbishment of the public areas of Level 4.
- Electrical upgrades (funded from Estates' maintenance budget).
- Minor roofing repairs.

Phase 2 summer 2005
- Completion of the public areas on Level 3, including the upgrade of lighting, redecoration, new carpet, installation of new study benching and shelving bay ends.
- Complete refurbishment of the public areas of Level 2 (excluding library foyer), including the construction of 20 group study rooms, the relocation of the enquiry desk down from Level 3, upgrade of lighting, redecoration, new carpet, and new shelving bay ends.
- Roof repairs.

Phase 3 summer 2006
- Total refurbishment of the library foyer and lending services.
- Refurbishment of the main staircase out of the foyer.
- Relocation of the Level 3 IT area into an enhanced area associated with the current computer rooms on Level 2 thereby bringing all the main IT provision together in one area with a dedicated air-conditioning system.
- Completion of remaining areas on Level 2 and Level 3.
- Creation of a High Demand Collection on Level 2 to provide student access to short-term loan material previously housed behind the desk. The short-term loan collection was little used and a review had recommended that a walk-in collection with a self-service issue/return unit would increase usage.
- Replacement of the air-handling plant.
- Further roof repairs.

Phase 4 summer 2007
- Refurbishment of lift.
- Sound insulation in individual study rooms.
- Minor work in the foyer area.
- Yet more roof repairs.

**Figure 7.2 Kenrick Library, Birmingham City University, Level 4
before refurbishment**

**Figure 7.3 Kenrick Library, Birmingham City University, Level 4
after refurbishment**

Challenges

It is inevitable that a project of this size will have unexpected challenges. Some of them were minor like pipes or ducting appearing in unexpected places during the strip-out phase of the work. These were considered as routine issues by the project team and addressed without any significant impact. The biggest impact on the project came as a result of a change of policy within the university. This was the decision *not* to move the directorate out of the Kenrick building. The loss of the promised additional space meant a major rethink and concerns about whether it would be possible to carry out any of the work scheduled for Phase 3. After some time alternative office space was identified elsewhere on the campus which allowed a relocation of staff out of the building. This opened the way for almost all the planned work to take place. The main loss to the project was that of a large additional training facility.

There were a range of other issues that emerged as the project progressed but they all fell into the category of lessons to be learnt. The first summer proved to be the most demanding of the project even though it was the smallest of the three phases. There were three elements to this. The first related to building a relationship with the construction contractors in terms of their learning about the oddities of a library and the library staff learning to live and work alongside a building site. The second was a learning experience for us in terms of how we managed the logistics of the book moves required to free up the area to be refurbished. It had all seemed sensible on paper but in the end it involved huge amounts of double handling of the stock. The third related to the contractors working with the architect to establish the quality of finish that would be required. These lessons were taken on board and stood us in good stead through the following two summers as the size and complexity of the subsequent phases increased.

In terms of design lessons learnt there were two specific issues, both relating to the individual study carrels. Within a short period of time after occupation the plasterboard walls started to acquire nasty marks. On investigation it became clear that these were caused by the metal chair backs. This was considered by the project team and solved by the addition of a Perspex covering extending halfway up the wall. The second issue related to the acoustics of the carrels. The carrels had a more generous space allocation than the few carrels that we had had before. This meant that they were immediately adopted as small group working rooms. As they had been designed as individual spaces the need for acoustic separation had not been considered. This meant that we received complaints about noise transfer between the carrels. The problem was considered and a solution was put in place in Phase 4.

The final challenge was the huge investment of time the project required. This included regular project team meetings, meetings to discuss specific issues, on-site meetings while the work was ongoing, work within the library to plan and supervise the logistics of the stock moves and the book retrieval services that we offered and the need to be on call to discuss problems that arose.

Outcomes/benefits

The refurbishment has delivered a number of operational benefits as well as an improved environment. They include:

- The new group study rooms are very well used and have contributed to a significant improvement in noise levels.
- The introduction of the new self-service High Demand Collection has seen a 700 per cent increase in the usage of the short-term loan material.
- The relocation of the self-service facilities away from the issue desk have led to increased usage.

Conclusion

For a significant period of time the project team and Kenrick Library staff literally lived and breathed this project. The work dominated the library over three summers and at no point did the library close. During these periods students and library staff lived cheek by jowl in a building site. Was the investment of time, effort and money worth it? Yes, absolutely: all involved are proud of what has been achieved. The library is light, attractive and welcoming and many of the noise-related problems have been addressed. Library staff are happy with the improved working environment and comments received from users are the final proof of a job well done:

> The library is amazing, I am so pleased with the way it looks.

> The library looks fabulous, it looks like someone has pushed the walls out to create more space.

> The setting of the layout is encouraging to attend regularly and spend hours a day in a relaxed environment. This promotes concentration, focus and minimal noise in the study areas.

Chapter 8
Glasgow University Library:
From Book Warehouse to Lighthouse for Study

Helen Durndell

This hilltop library tower has been at the heart of the campus, heavily used by students and staff since its construction in 1968. An iconic building, it stands on the highest point of the campus, and its towers dominate the view from many points of the city. However, cumulative wear and tear, and major changes in the volume and nature of use – increased student numbers (from just under 9000 in 1968 to just under 24,000 today), longer opening hours and increasingly pervasive IT – meant that it became uninviting and unsupportive of current and developing learning patterns.

Figure 8.1 Glasgow University Library, exterior

A process of redevelopment began in 1996 with the construction of a 12th level (custom-designed premises for special collections).

Overall design

The overarching aim has been to provide a high-quality environment for study and research, offering a significant degree of choice and flexibility.

Improved environment, new lighting (including different types of lights in study and stock areas), ceiling and floor finishes, varied furniture – these combine with other elements, such as refurbished toilets, water coolers and automatic solar blinds for glare reduction, to create an attractive environment conducive to study and research.

A wide range of study areas has been provided to suit different types of study and individual needs, as the phased project has progressed. Some seating areas have open desking, some have centre screens, and some have centre and side screens to create carrels. There are also clusters of desktop PCs, while other areas have power and data sockets to increase flexibility, and to enable laptop use. Other areas have no power or data provision (although all are wireless enabled) to create a different local ambience. There are also other types of seating: tub chairs with writing tablets; sofas with low tables; high stools and tables; and horseshoe-shaped booths.

Growing demand for group study has been accommodated with the provision of group study rooms. Support for research has been provided with the creation of two research rooms – each with four individual desks, bookable for up to 12 weeks at a time, with lockable drawer units, and power and data provision.

Design impact

As the refurbishment has progressed, user reaction has been clear and positive, particularly evident from annual LibQUAL+ surveys. Sample quotes include 'The wireless internet access and the refurbishment of Levels 6 and 7 is fantastic. I really enjoy working in the library now', and 'The floors of the library that have been recently renovated are practical, modern, comfortable and really well-suited to group or individual study. Can't praise them highly enough'. The University of Glasgow's recent nomination in the 'Best Student Experience' category of the 2007 Times Higher Awards mentions the improvements to the library building. The refurbishment programme was a winner of the British Building Maintenance Award for 2006 from the Institute of Maintenance and Building Management.

Environmental issues, efficiency and sustainability

The new building services have been designed to improve efficiency, achieving overall reductions in energy consumption, together with improvements in the building's environmental emissions. This is achieved by combining high-efficiency equipment with sophisticated control and monitoring systems, with service delivery closely matched to demand. The monitoring systems also increase efficiency in maintenance, for example by allowing 'just in time' rather than extensive routine maintenance. This philosophy is also applied in the new lighting which uses a combination of presence detectors and timers.

Historical overview

The University of Glasgow was founded in 1451 by the Bull of the humanist pope Nicholas V. From the beginning, the university was undoubtedly furnished with some books for teaching, which took place initially within the cathedral church of St Mungo.

The first explicit mention of the library is dated November 1475 when the first donations by the university's chancellor, Bishop John Laing, were recorded – a manuscript compendium of Aristotle and Pseudo-Aristotelian texts, and a paper volume of 'quaestiones'. The next gift noted is that of Duncan Bunch, the first principal of the 'Auld Pedagogy' as the Arts Faculty was then called.

In 1633 a general subscription began to build a 'common librarie within the Colledge of Glasgow'. King Charles I granted £200, although this sum was not paid until 1654 (by Oliver Cromwell). When it was visited by Sir William Brereton, in about 1636, he found it 'a very little room not twice so large as my old closet'.

The manuscript catalogue of the library compiled in 1691 shows a library of some 3000 volumes arranged on the shelves by subject in 64 lettered presses (cupboards).

The plans for a library building were prepared by William Adam, and Adam's 'New Library' was completed in 1743. Then, as part of the move of the whole university to the west end of the city in 1870, the books were moved to the mock-gothic Gilbert Scott Building at Gilmorehill. The library occupied the north front of the Arts Quadrangle and is described as being 'well lighted and commodious, and contains provision probably sufficient at the present rate of increase for the next fifty years'.

The 1968 library tower

Dominating Glasgow's west end skyline, a tall concrete and glass edifice now vies for attention with the university's late 19th century neo-gothic tower. The 12-storey university library, evocative of the towers in San Gimignano in Italy or a Scottish baronial castle, opened its doors in 1968.

The architect was William Whitfield whose design method has been characterized as dependent on separating function (e.g. 'served' and 'serving' areas) expressing them as architectural forms. The library building is a series of powerful verticals finished in rectilinear bush-hammered concrete. The librarian at the time, R.O. MacKenna, was among the early advocates of developing reader services in university libraries and this influenced his 1962 brief to the architects. He specified that 'the emphasis must be on bringing books and readers together with the library staff acting as intermediaries in the process, and this should make itself evident as the keynote of the design'. The confined site meant that the new library was a high-rise building and MacKenna made a special feature of this by organizing the library as a series of carefully coordinated subject libraries.

The main part of the building consists of eight 'paired floors', now Levels 4-11, with four atria allowing an illusion of light and space on the mezzanine floor while maximizing the space for shelving in the middle of both floors and naturally lit reader spaces on the perimeter of each floor. The circulated staircases and lifts are separated from the floors.

A large extension project, a reduced version of the original library plan which had been to achieve a mirror version of the 1968 build, was completed in 1986. This saw a doubling of floor size on Levels 3-6 and an increase by a lesser amount on the upper floors, tapering to Level 11. This northern annexe was firmly devoted to book stacks, and at this stage in its history the 1968 building could fairly be described as a tall warehouse for books. It was probably the peak of the open access print-based research library.

The need for change

Over the past decade, the University of Glasgow has invested in a major redevelopment and expansion of the library building designed to meet the needs of students in the 21st century. By the 1990s, high usage had taken its toll through general wear and tear, and there was a need for new services to match developments in teaching, learning and technology. Parts of the internal layout were inappropriate while the lack of group study and interactive areas was increasingly problematic. Each of the main floors were decorated in matt beige and brown colours interspersed with exposed aggregate concrete panels in the circulation areas. The ceilings had experienced colour degradation and the floor finishes were a mixture of vinyl and brown carpeting in both the stack and study areas.

As part of the assessment for this project, a full options appraisal was carried out to evaluate a range of options ranging from 'status quo' to brand new library building. The outcome of this process was an endorsement of the existing building as still having the potential to match current requirements, and that the location was still optimal for the university campus development. From the perspective of today, it can also be seen that this decision had a significant low-carbon use impact.

Figure 8.2 Glasgow University Library, library levels

A new floor for rare books and manuscripts

The redevelopment programme, based initially on Follett funding, began in 1996 with the addition of a new floor onto the original building. This 12th level allowed the creation of environmentally controlled premises custom-built to house the Special Collections Department (and stopped the roof leaking!).

Designed to a high specification by the Holmes Partnership of Glasgow, the new facility tops the concrete and glass façade of William Whitfield's 1968 building with an elegantly contrasting curved roof under which the supervised reading room (24 places) offers spectacular views to the north over the Campsie Hills and beyond, while a dense-stacked store offers secure housing for the rare books and manuscripts. Improvements in environmental control are included, and a 50-seat seminar room allowing material from the collections to be used for group teaching in conditions of security and seclusion.

A new landmark entrance to the building was created and the space vacated in the basement was refurbished to bring the undergraduate collections together, create a new service desk and provide general computer clusters on Levels 2 and 3. Improved access for wheelchair users was another important element in the project.

The increased concentration of computers in the library, which became the primary location of networked services for students on campus, quickly exposed the poor environmental conditions and an upgrade with air-conditioning was carried out on Levels 2 and 3.

With the library effectively at capacity, the integration of the Education Faculty library could only happen with the provision of a remote library store. A leased building only a few miles from campus in Hamiltonhill, was opened in mid 2003. This off-campus Library Research Annexe offers excellent environmental conditions in high-density shelving for low-use print research materials and has been an essential element in relocating stock from each subject floor to allow a more effective use of space.

Project brief

The brief for the project evolved through broad consultation with the library staff, academic staff and Estates and Buildings staff. This allowed a wide view of the project to be taken with a number of expansive requirements including:

- Internal environment brought up to current standards.
- Application of new and emerging technologies.
- Environmental improvements made.
- Reductions in toxic emissions achieved.
- Internal ambience of the library provides a quality learning environment.

The brief created well-defined requirements including the implementation of services to sustain current and pending IT applications, such as wireless communications, and an enhancement of the temperature and humidity control to provide improved internal comfort conditions.

The ventilation system had shown signs of nearing the end of its life expectancy. Some characteristics which had been experienced include increasing air leakage, valve seizing and motor defects. Changes in teaching methods, learning patterns and the all-pervasive IT had put pressure on the building and its services.

Expected standards and quality of lighting had also increased significantly over the life of the building and rapid changes in both the use of the library and the advance in computer technology have meant that the lighting system also faced wholesale obsolescence. A new approach to provide better general illumination, reduced glare and improved uniformity in both the book stacks and study areas was required.

Phased refurbishment – scope and logistics

From the outset it was recognized that it was impractical to undertake such a major refurbishment in a single operation due to the disruption it would cause to the functioning of the library and the intrusion into the study cycles of the university. The best window of opportunity for undertaking major works has traditionally been the summer vacation when the numbers using the library are significantly reduced. This creates a window of approximately 17 weeks for all planned works to be undertaken.

A further factor in the programming of works was the availability of funds. Phasing the works over a number of years has allowed a manageable funding stream to be established and the works to be financially planned in advance.

The physical constraints of the building are key drivers in defining the scope of each refurbishment phase, in particular the linking of pairs of floors through double atria spaces. This fact singularly determined the maximum extent of a phase of work. The principle elements of work which have been included in the project cover:

- removal of asbestos from structural, architectural and services elements
- renewal of the internal floor and ceiling spaces, with redecoration of the entire space
- full air-conditioning and installation of daylight/temperature-controlled automatic window blinds to control solar heat gain and glare
- new lighting to allow extensive use of PCs and to improve illumination within the book stacks/study areas
- renewal of the electrical power system to allow extensive use of electrical power.

The logistics of working round a facility which was used for up to 18 hours a day, seven days a week, required significant forward planning to ensure that a safe and secure working environment was created during each stage of the works while disruption to normal library operations was minimized. On the lower levels establishment of site boundaries and restrictions was relatively straightforward with the use of independent access and defined ground-level routes for the movement of materials and site operatives. As the works progressed, the logistics issues increased as work moved up the building requiring increasingly more complex planning and reviews. Access was restricted to external routes only with dual hoisting for materials, personnel and minimal cross-flow of people between library users, staff and construction site operatives. Eventually the only shared routes were a common emergency means of escape running the full height of the building.

Environmental impact

Each of the annual phases was procured through a competitive tender with the engineering services contractor acting as the main and principal contractor; this was due to the high level of services renewal that typically comprised 60 per cent of the total construction cost.

A key driver in refurbishing many of the services is to improve the overall system efficiencies through the application of higher efficiency equipment for generating heating and cooling, use of variable speed technology on the motor drive systems to allow the close matching of the demands with the service delivery, and the application of distributed digital controls and associated energy efficient software to deliver overall reductions in energy consumption and energy bills together with improvements in environmental emissions.

The original air-handling systems were based on a high-pressure constant air-flow rate supply and extract system distributing air through nozzle diffusers. This system was used on each floor and was inherently high in energy use. On each pair of floors these systems have been replaced with a combination of variable air volume and displacement supply systems to reduce energy use and significantly improve space temperature control. Thyristor drive technology has been used to ensure close control of delivery air requirements to match space temperature and humidity demands which can vary significantly due to the exposure of the perimeter study areas to solar gain and to respond to fluctuations in occupancy and internal gains both on a daily basis and in periods of high study demand linked to examination periods.

Further energy reductions have been incorporated through the use of high-efficiency light sources and the use of presence detection lighting control replacing the original manual pull cords in the book stack aisles and the simple central switched control of the study areas.

The project works including the replacement of the centralized cooling system which included the use of cooling towers to reject waste hear from the building. The new chillers are both air-cooled units incorporating heat recovery to improve overall operating efficiency. In addition, systematic asbestos removal has been achieved throughout the building.

Each phase has included a renewal of the smoke detection and fire alarm system to enhance compliance with modern standards and practices, by using a fully addressable system capable of highlighting an incident to a single sensor location. The new system allows easier routine testing and maintenance improving the facilities costs of running the building. Further health and safety features include the renewal of the fire-rated doors to conform to current standards. Disabled toilets have been created by reconfiguring existing user facilities on each level.

Design outcomes

The building interior has been remodelled to a modern, contemporary standard. The study spaces in the library allow the maximum benefit of daylight to be delivered with appropriate glare control. The building now offers a high level of flexible IT-enabled study areas, with a broad availability of printed material. Varied learning spaces range from casual seating areas to silent study carrels, and wireless zones are in place, complemented by powered study desking.

Figure 8.3 Glasgow University Library, study area

The floors are coupled together through four atria-style spaces which allows extensive introduction of daylight into the reading areas. With the height of the building these features offer a stimulating backdrop for library readers. New turnstiles were installed in 2006 as part of a a remodelling of the entrance area, giving students a more rapid entry with an extra turnstile and faster card reading. At the same time, the original 1968 lifts were completely replaced to conform to current safety and accessiblity legislation.

With additional funding from the Wolfson Foundation, two existing rooms on Level 11 have been converted to created a new facility to meet the aim of improving the preservation environment of important historic photographs by the creation of a state-of-the-art photographic store.

The future

Supporting collaborative learning requires an increase in, and more varied, group study spaces. Students appreciate more comfortable seating for extended periods of reading but need desks and power for intensive study. As collections and services become increasingly networked, the library continues to offer a neutral space which is neither home nor office but offers a range of options to support research and learning, from social gathering space to individual study carrels.

Extensive capital investment by the university in electronic backfiles covering many print backruns of journals in science, technology and medicine is allowing further redevelopment of space. Library staff have carried out an audit to identify where print stock can be relegated, liberating space for learning.

Opening hours have been increased by 37 per cent as the internal environment can now sustain that level of activity. The library building remains a beacon of learning and a hive of activity in the centre of campus.

Architect, engineer and client

Architect on the main redevelopment project: Eric Watson, William Nimmo & Partners, 7 Fitzroy Place, Glasgow G3 7RH
(The original 1968 architect was William Whitfield; the architect in 1996 was Holmes Partnership, Glasgow.)

M&E engineers: Douglas Blair and Ken Douglas from Jacobs Babtie, 95 Bothwell St., Glasgow G2 7HX
Structural engineers: Rab McQueen from Jacobs Babtie
Lead consultants/contract administrators: Jerry McGregor and David Thirlwell from Jacobs Babtie

Hartley Library, University of Southampton: From Accretion to Integration, 2002–2007

Mark Brown and Richard Wake

Context

The University of Southampton has its origins in the Hartley Institution, founded in 1862 from the bequest of a local merchant, Henry Robinson Hartley. Part of the original foundation was a library, which formed a nucleus for later developments, and which in 1919 moved from a building on Southampton's High Street to a new building, constructed of red brick, which still forms the front of the present Hartley Library. Today the Hartley Library serves as the main library to the university, housing the collections in humanities, science and social science, the special collections of printed books, and the archive collections. The library has five floors, identified for the purposes of orientation as Levels 1–5.

Between 1935 and 1978 the library was extended four times. In 1959 a rear extension to the existing building opened with additional floors, followed by new build to accommodate expanding special collections in 1970. A major remodelling including a large extension of the special collections facilities opened in 1988, and the south wing of the original 1914 building was integrated in 1998. All these extensions extended accommodation for stock and improved and extended the range of seating available, and from the early 1990s significant attention started being paid to developing the workstation and IT provision in the library. As part of the small 1998 project, supported by Follett funding and the Wolfson Foundation, workstation provision doubled and a new IT training suite was created. These services were located in part of the original building, making use of structures dating from before the First World War and unsuitable for book stacks.

Print collections grew steadily throughout the 1990s. By 2001 the Hartley Library was effectively full in terms of stock, and the fabric and overall presentation of the library were looking increasingly outdated. In the period since the last major extension and refurbishment in the 1980s the university had grown very considerably, with a student body now touching 20,000. Patterns of learning and teaching, particularly in the integration of print and electronic materials, and support for students' learning, had been completely transformed. Electronic materials had been growing in importance, but as a research library the holding of significant print and archive collections remain core to the university's mission. The focus, therefore, was on complementary, hybrid collections. In the area of

Figure 9.1 Hartley Library, University of Southampton, exterior
Source: Stephen Shrimpton

special collections, where the Anglo/Jewish archive was growing exponentially, and for scholars and students visiting the library to use the political and Jewish collections, the facilities were inadequate.

The sense of a building no longer fit for modern purpose grew stronger towards the end of 1990s. The demand on shelving space had led to widespread use of narrow gangways and shelving units over seven shelves in height. Dark wooden furniture, particularly large tables seating six or eight, appeared increasingly old fashioned, and the extensive use of wooden panelling, which had given the building a sense of gravitas in the 1980s, now looked outdated. There was a growing mismatch between the way the library wished to present its physical environment and its services.

Making the case

Lead times for achieving new build and refurbishment projects in universities are often lengthy. At Southampton the demands on the university's capital programme were already significant, and the potential for endowment income was low. It took two years, and more than one feasibility study, to convince the university that investment in its main library was a priority. Three things were instrumental in achieving the political and financial support needed for a major extension and refurbishment project.

Firstly the university's developing education strategy made student-centred services a priority for investment. The library was the first of a series of projects funded between 2003 and 2007, which have included sports facilities, a new student services centre, modernized halls of residence and student union services. Secondly there were opportunities to attract external funding from a variety of sources which were successfully marshalled together just at the right time. Although a key driver was the improving facilities for students, one of the most significant elements in the programme was a major extension of special collections, which was supported with a grant of £951,000 from the Heritage Lottery Fund and £25,000 from the Jewish Claims Conference. To underline the role of the library in research, and by extension research-led teaching, external funding was also gained both from the HEFCE learning and teaching fund and the Strategic Research Infrastructure Fund (SRIF), the latter being scheduled only for work associated with Science and Social Science. The third element was the level of political support within the community. Although there was a lot of support, it is fair to say that the project was not without its detractors.

In the event the debate helped focus attention on key principles. Looking back on this period it is clear that the emphasis on a renewal of the research and learning environment was a key driver for change. By the time planning started in earnest during 2001 the overall rationale had shifted away from a need for more space for growing collections and updated study space to the idea of a total renewal of the environment, which would absorb the different phases of the post-1935 building into an integrated service environment reflecting the university's research-led mission.

The result was a series of three linked projects which have increased the overall area of the library by one third, adding an additional 3600m^2 and refurbishing a further 5400m^2 at a total cost of around £12 million.

Vision and design principles

Our vision was for a modern research-orientated library welcoming both undergraduates and researchers which would promote the values of the university strategy for learning and teaching, and for research. Central to the vision was the creation of a high-quality, flexible study environment, with good quality seating, small study rooms and distributed access to network connectivity. Underpinning this was a complete rationalization of the distribution of the stock throughout the library based on the principle of integration of collections and services, but with an eye to the future shift in the balance of print and electronic materials.

The brief for the design of the extension and refurbishment therefore emphasized the need for clarity, coherence and integration based on the following principles:

- Library collections are a diverse but complimentary mix of print and electronic resources which are continually dynamic. Collections will be partly electronic, partly print with a strong emphasis on moving towards electronic delivery in key areas, particularly research periodical literature. The library will support the best fit strategies for collection and will provide printed, manuscript and electronic collections in a way that makes them appear interdependent.
- There should be a range of study environments, providing both for individual and group study. The study places should be wired up to allow access to the network and space will be defined flexibly to allow a change of use. In addition the facilities for networked access group study rooms and small IT teaching rooms should be provided to allow students to be tutored in small groups and to practise presentations.
- The configuration of space should offer a sense of natural zoning to allow quiet study space, social space and group space to function effectively.
- Services should be provided flexibly to help users find material quickly, reducing the amount of out of sequence and difficult to find material. The environment will facilitate academic liaison librarians to expand their role in supporting the delivery of the curriculum by working directly with staff and students through information skills teaching, small group tutorials, one-to-one advice and point of need support.
- The library should reflect the requirements of disability legislation and improvements in health and safety by installing a fire safe lift, re-spacing

shelving to allow for wheelchair access and reducing the height of the stacking from seven shelves to six.

- This transformation should be managed in such a way that we could continue to operate the full range of services of a working library with the minimum acceptable disruption to users.

Planning the vision

Having established the guiding principles for design, library staff then began to plan more specifically. Developments were identified which enabled these principles to be realized.

- The configuration of stock was changed radically from a subject arrangement to an arrangement based on the type of material. All periodicals (with the exception of law titles) were placed on Level 1 of the newly refurbished library, with books then arranged on the remaining floors. Previously, books and periodicals had been shelved together, with science and engineering subjects on Level 1, social sciences on Level 3 and arts and humanities on Levels 4 and 5. Besides being a major change in the way resources were offered to the library users, this change was to prove enormously complicated to implement during the project. However, the view was taken that this was a 'once-in-a-lifetime' opportunity to make the change.

  The change was made not only to realize the goals of providing appropriate study environments and services (because books and journals have somewhat different requirements) and natural zoning, but also to offer flexibility in the future. Space planning was done on the assumption that the number of printed journals would decline over the period following completion of the project, and that existing printed journals would be replaced by electronic access to titles, whereas the migration to e-books would be slower and would be concentrated on acquisition and not on replacement of existing titles. Gathering periodicals in one part of the library would enable to space made available to be consolidated and thus easier to utilize.

- Enquiry services were also significantly reconfigured. The previous service had been based on subject divisions, reflecting the layout of the building, but whilst various arrangements had been tried over previous years, none had proved totally satisfactory. It was decided to offer services particularly tailored to the type of material available in the location of the service. The enquiry service on Level 1 was redesigned as a journal support service, encompassing print and electronic resources and document delivery. Whilst all library users will use these services, we anticipated that those engaged in research and those in their final year of undergraduate courses or on masters' courses would be the predominant users of this material. On Level

3, a subject support service was offered, which was designed with the needs of students particularly in mind, although of course all library users are welcome to, and indeed do use, the service.

- The 'look and feel' of the space was considered carefully, with an interior designer closely involved. A great deal of care was given to the choice of both décor and furniture, and both were used to signal the intended use of particular spaces. It was important that the furniture looked attractive besides offering both functionality and flexibility, and we eventually paid a premium to achieve these ends. However, as almost every visitor to the library has requested the contact details of the supplier, we feel justified in the choice we made.

- The redesign of the entrance hall enabled a significant change in the service offered to anyone entering the library. The new design incorporates turnstiles and enables access to the library to be restricted to university card holders and requires other visitors to identify themselves (although this measure was not introduced immediately). More significantly, the new reception desk enabled staff to face towards the entrance, where previously there had only been a security role and the staff faced those leaving the library. This led to the ability to offer much more effective welcome and orientation services, and staff have been recruited specifically to play this role.

- The entrance hall was designed as a learning centre and incorporated a number of elements which might not be associated with a traditional research library but which contributed to achieving the guiding principles of the project. The introduction of a café was identified as an important addition to the facilities available to those using the library, and an area including casual seating and Internet café type computers offered an environment not found elsewhere in the building. Small consultation rooms for one-to-one meetings enabled colleagues from other departments to meet students, particularly those with learning differences, and offer support in any number of areas including study skills and the use of library materials, and the seminar room offers an informal communal area used by a variety of groups from outside the library.

Maintaining a working library

Although initially designed as a single project including the whole building, the work was in fact carried out in three stages. The main part of the work began in June 2002 and was substantially complete by the end of 2003, encompassing Levels 1, 3 and 4 (which is where special collections are located). Phase 2 was the entrance hall, which was refurbished over the summer of 2004. During Phase 3, Level 5 was extended and refurbished between June 2006 and May 2007. One small area of Level 4 remains in its pre-2002 condition.

Figure 9.2 Hartley Library, University of Southampton, reception desk
Source: Stephen Shrimpton

Before reviewing the finished project, it is worth noting that throughout building and refurbishing, the library remained open. This led to significant costs. Throughout summer 2003 much of the stock was inaccessible to readers, and this continued throughout the autumn term for some parts of the collection. Instead of retrieving materials directly, readers had to list their requirement for library staff to collect at advertised times. This led to a certain amount of frustration, but readers also appreciated that the material remained on campus and was still accessible. The disruption caused by the building work to those studying in the library was also a difficulty, particularly but not only at examination periods. When Level 5 was refurbished in 2006–2007, a similar situation existed for some parts of the stock, but once again readers appear to have appreciated the efforts made to ensure that the restrictions to access were kept to a minimum.

During the period around 30km of printed material were moved, sometimes more than once, without leaving the building.

Reflections

Given the opportunity to plan again, we would almost certainly design a very similar building to the one we now have. There has been continuous pressure on group study space, and it may be that more study rooms should have been included. Particularly at busy times the zoning can break down as the areas where quiet interaction is permitted are insufficient. There have been occasional difficulties with heating in some of the large reading areas and with ventilation. The main difficulty has resulted from the closure of a university site in summer 2006, requiring the relocation of about 45,000 items into the Hartley Library, using shelving which, in the initial projections, had been expected to accommodate stock acquisition. The firesafe lift has also been a disappointment, and it is only in late 2007 that all requirements have been met to enable it to fulfil its function. However, most of the original goals have been accomplished:

- The full range of study environments envisaged now exists and at busy times to library is now full. Laptop access has been so successful that there are now laptop-free areas to meet the complaints of those who find tapping at keyboards distracting, the quiet areas are (on the whole) quiet and there is a range of facilities. The consultation rooms have been only partially successful and the number has been reduced.
- The rearrangement of stock appears popular with library readers, and certainly the redesigned enquiry services which accompany it have proved very popular. The concentration of journals has already enabled more effective use of space. We have removed printed editions which can also be read electronically and re-used the space, a process which is accelerating as the library is now part of the UK Research Reserve project. The new arrangement also enables much clearer signing and guiding and orientation.
- The reconfigured entrance hall has created an entirely new ambience in the library. Visitors can now be welcomed and directed immediately they enter the building, and even those familiar with the library have a point for information and direction. The café has been so successful that it has expanded and is reportedly one of the busiest catering outlets on campus. The area is full throughout the day and is a popular meeting place. However, the greatest advantage is perhaps at weekends and in the evening, when the ability to enjoy a break and some refreshment meets a need which, when absent, was a source of frequent negative feedback.
- The configuration has proved flexible. We have already installed a new range of mobile shelving on Level 1, and have plans to replace some shelving with seating in summer 2008 to accommodate incoming students from the site closing in 2009.
- The facilities available to special collections have been revolutionized. Besides improved storage and state of the art equipment for conservation,

the reading room is not only larger, but has enabled seminar-type use of special collections material, and postgraduate courses have benefited from this greatly improved access. Several popular exhibitions, some in conjunction with major academic events, have been mounted, which would simply not have been possible previously. The exhibition areas have also led to the development of links with local groups outside the university.

This account has not dwelt in detail upon the practicalities of living through the changes, and especially in 2002 and 2003 library staff and library users lived through a great deal of disruption. It was certainly true in this instance that there was 'no gain without pain', but it is undoubtedly also true that the library in 2007 is not only much improved in every respect on the library in 2002, but also much better equipped to cope with the changes which the future will bring.

Figure 9.3 Hartley Library, University of Southampton, open area

Source: Stephen Shrimpton

PART 4
Extending the Library –
Modernizing and Adding Space

Lack of space also limited the number and range of IT facilities we could
provide for members ... or, indeed, anywhere for members to talk or have
a cup of coffee. Even basic facilities such as cloakrooms ... had
become inadequate.
– The London Library

Chapter 10

Dublin City Library and Archive: From Concept to Reality

Deirdre Ellis-King

Provided by Dublin City Council, the Dublin City Public Libraries and Archive system serves the citizens of Dublin, Ireland's capital city, and visitors to the city. With a network of local branch libraries, central lending and reference library, services to primary schools and prisons, and with mobile halts, specialist reference services for business, music and Dublin studies, the Dublin City Public Library system is the largest in the Republic of Ireland. The library and archive facility at Pearse Street, the focus of this case study, is part of the Dublin City Public Library system.[1] The building, designed by the then city architect C.J. McCarthy, originally opened in 1909 with some support from the Carnegie United Kingdom Trust and functioned at various stages as branch library, headquarters and focus for Dublin studies research before closing and reopening following extensive refurbishment in July 2003.

Set mid-terrace, the library dominates its immediate neighbours, giving it a status as a landmark building on Pearse Street, a major access route into the city centre. As a case study it presents all the ingredients necessary to engage and excite professional interest revealed through development challenges related to all the elements of conservation, refurbishment and new build. Professional challenges of resolution, focused on delivering library services appropriate to the 21st century, within the framework of an old building in need of total refurbishment, are equally critical to consideration of Pearse Street as a case study of contemporary and future value.

Librarians and architects will be familiar with the arguments related to requirements for complementarities of form and function. They will also recognize the potential conflict inherent in conserving a building which must also satisfy the functionality requirements of a service housed within it. Happily in the Dublin context, complementarities of form and function have enabled a modern public service library focus to be achieved within the framework of an early 20th century building. Before moving to consider the project overall, readers will find it useful to know something of the forces which drove the library development.

By the 1990s the building at Pearse Street was in need of refurbishment, the architect's report to city council in 1994 describing its condition as requiring major intervention. However, the driving force for development arose in the first instance, not from the requirements of the building, but from library service needs related to access and storage of the specialist library collections housed there, and from additional external forces related to local government re-organization.

Figure 10.1 Dublin City Library and Archive, exterior (original building)
Source: Barry Mason Photography

Goals and objectives

Changes, for example, arising from local government reorganization in the greater
Dublin area in 1993 altered the 1985 plan which was based on an assumption of
continuity in respect of integrated local government library service provision in the
Dublin area. These changes led to the city librarian developing a greatly enhanced
brief for architectural services within the city which aimed to address not only the
storage and public access requirements of the library's special collections but also
a number of additional service requirements which would enable sustainability
at a broader city-wide management level into the 21st century. In line with
the evolutionary approach to design which characterized the project proposal
throughout the planning stage, the brief became the functional requirement's basis
for a feasibility study and ultimately the plan to address the storage and public
access needs not only of the Dublin and Irish studies research service but also
those of the city council archive which needed to be re-housed as a consequence of
changed views with regard to an appropriate location for this facility. Additionally,
in a context of growing realization of the potential offered within the building
envelope of the entire site, the requirement's brief also sought to address the

feasibility of incorporating the headquarters of the Dublin City Council Library and Archive Services within the new structure.

Key requirements therefore as presented in the library brief for architectural services included the elements noted, affording seating for up to 40 persons, a public reading room with 100 seats, storage space for special collections and archive, a conference facility capable of seating 80 persons, an exhibition/multi-function room, a branch library and a public café and, critically, a requirement for a headquarters management suite allied to administration offices, work areas, meeting rooms and public rest-room facilities. With account taken of the need for circulation and for electrical and mechanical plant needs, the total space requirements involved an increase from an existing 1920m^2 to a new total of 3450m^2.

Ultimately, achievement of the requirements would require demolition of all later additions to the original building and new build, refurbishment and conservation as appropriate. The inclusion into the project equation of two adjoining domestic-scale houses in the ownership of the city library system for many decades and recently unlocked for library use, proved critical to realization of a positive feasibility study outcome. Indeed, this availability also led to a greatly enhanced visionary solution to all requirements, given that the original library building, recognized to be of historical and architectural significance as indicated by its status as a 'listed' building for preservation purposes, offered limited re-use of the original building. This factor had been recognized equally by the city librarian and the city council project architect as presenting challenges in its re-creation as a library building of the future.

Pearse Street Library closed in 2000 as a prelude to re-development and renewal in a 21st century context. Thereafter, realization of the new facility involved a time-span of three years and a considerable degree of planning and logistical effort by architect, librarian and a team of specialists. Its realization also required a considerable degree of advance lobbying which was integral to the process of decision-making and approval to proceed.

Case for development

The case for refurbishment, conservation and new construction was developed and presented in the first instance by the city librarian to more senior management within the city council. Support at this level resulted in a key decision to retain the headquarters management functions of the city library system within the city centre. This was central to an overall plan which involved exiting completely from the then headquarters building in the south city at Fenian Street and moving bibliographical services to a new facility to be developed in the north city suburb of Cabra, some three miles from the city centre, in association with a new branch library. The decision paved the way for allowing management services, including the office of the city librarian, to be retained within the Pearse Street facility. This strategy, essential to realization of the overall requirements plan for headquarter functions, necessitated a high-level parallel approach to project and process management involving the three buildings, two in the city centre and one in the north suburbs, in order that the interdependent exit and transfer strategies related to all three would dovetail with each other. Critically, the bibliographical services centre, incorporated in a new 1858m^2 facility which also housed a branch library and mobile library base, opened on target in 2001, enabling the plan for bibliographical services, until then allied to management services, to be transferred from the old HQ building in Fenian Street.

Concept to realization: process

The process in bringing the project from concept to reality originated with the brief prepared by the city librarian. This led to an excited and enthusiastic response from the project architect who came up with a preliminary schematic design which evolved through a process of continuing development and refinement into a design concept which brought acceptance from key stakeholders. Critically, the key to moving forward lay in achieving a broad base of support from both senior administrative staff and from elected representatives who adopted the concept, and with it the implications of capital and revenue funding, following a presentation made by librarian and architect in December 1995. Their support was essential in enabling the project to proceed, as was the support of central government which contributed financially to the project. With finance secured, the process of project delivery commenced, the key objective being to develop a facility which would complement the functional requirements as set out in the requirements brief in a 21st century context.

Conservation, condition and design challenges

Issues of concern arose, the key one being that the building was 'listed' as being of historic significance both externally and internally. This factor entailed development of a retention and conservation strategy and ensured from the outset that relevant expertise was applied to the process of refurbishment and a conservation focus became an integral part of the building project. Some positive outcomes ensued including the retention of early 20th century ceiling height in the original building, a condition which enables a 'wow factor' by way of contrast to library buildings in Dublin of the later 20th century which were more domestic in scale. Some other conservation issues, involving retention of existing glazing and timber floors, offered challenges and a most satisfying resolution was achieved in respect of both whereby maximum retention of original features have ensured that visitors are enabled to appreciate the 'bubble' effect easily identifiable in the early

20th century glazing and to note the restored marks, probably the result of 1960s stiletto heels, in the original timber floors.

The condition of the building generally was poor with significant evidence of wet rot being apparent. More significant structural issues also presented themselves, including, for example, a need for resolution of a structural design fault in the limestone entrance portico. The façade, comprised of Mount Charles sandstone, also required attention, as was evident in the state of erosion of the stone which had deteriorated in substance. Its colour had changed from a soft yellow into a dirty black, the damage exacerbated by the effect of decades of traffic driving by the library doors.

Enabling the principle of universal access also proved to an architectural challenge in a building which had no lift, only one almost vertical stairway and an on-street frontage inhibiting provision of a wheelchair-friendly ramp. Significantly, the building was also entirely 'land-locked' sharing adjoining walls with buildings on either side and being located to the rear in close proximity to a terrace of small dwelling houses from which it is separated only by a narrow laneway. These factors ensured restrictive physical limitations and construction difficulties. The latter issue in fact led to a significant level of consultation aimed at meeting the concerns of local residents throughout the project construction phase. Additionally, in a list of factors affording particular design challenges, lay the existence of a lower ground floor which was 0.7m below the nearby River Liffey water table. There was a history of flooding in the lower floor of the building, the subject of temporary and generally unsatisfactory resolution over many years, and this was exacerbated by the building foundations lying on dense gravel. From an architectural perspective, however, if the requirements of the brief were to be met, issues affording design challenges, additional to those previously noted, needed to be resolved. This crystallized itself in finding a unique approach to 'marrying' or linking the original 'listed' old building with a proposed new construction and also in seamlessly integrating the adjoining terraced houses into an overall cohesive structure.

Design

The design was carried out entirely within the Dublin City Council Architects Department, with the project architect Bernard Grimes being responsible for design and completion of the building project. To quote Grimes: 'The design rationale adopted for this brief separated and defined old and new: maintaining the architectural integrity of the original building and matching appropriate uses to these spaces, while redeveloping the remaining rear section to cater for the more functionally demanding users'.[2] This principle of separation has in fact informed the design rationale, resulting in the library and archive stack floors being incorporated in a new encased rear extension, its exterior being relieved by the headquarters situated on the top floor with views facing out over the adjacent railway line and station. The more public functions including the reading room, branch library and exhibition room are incorporated in the original building. The design principles in essence have resulted in the 'rear brick wall of the original building [providing] a boundary line between the two approaches…'.[3] Capturing the implementation process, Grimes notes: 'The twin walls of a new linear service core allow the floors to cantilever against the old library wall. This structural separation is mirrored in a spatial separation which sees original and new spaces divided by corridors on all levels and is expressed externally by continuous glazing at roof level'.[4] From a library user perspective, this continuous corridor expresses itself as a new internal street which links the main reading room, part of the main building with its original windows intact, to public access facilities including the café and rest-rooms. These are part of the new-build element of the facility on the other side of the internal street. From a user perspective therefore, the inner streetscape in effect provides a window from which the non-intrusive shadow of passers-by may be noted. Equally, those using the library facilities during a break from research may note the interior of the reading room, as if viewing it from the High Street, a feeling which is assisted by the natural light which filters in from overhead and from a linking glazed wall. The urban street effect is further accentuated by the continuous lighting at roof level which percolates down into the new street and washes through into the refurbished reading room. Overall, the impact of the building is one of total transparency, a perspective which is reflected in all the public areas including the glazed lift from which library users have a view into the branch library and into the 'Dublin' exhibition room.

Figure 10.2 Dublin City Library and Archive, reading room

Viewed externally, the building is a model of interest on the streetscape; its front exterior restored to its original classical simplicity has regained its landmark and iconic status on the street. Its rear, remarkable by contrast in expressing a contemporary architectural dominance, is in keeping with the dynamic of its surroundings. This latter is achieved not least through the use of a curved plan form which reflects the curved industrial roof of the nearby railway station. The contemporary look and contrast with the original is further developed by the use of new materials such as steel, metal decking and curtain walling. These distinguish it from the restored original but in a way which suggests complementarities of vision and purpose, allied to its function as a library and archive. As Grimes notes: 'The combination of restoration and new build, each clearly defined and contrasting one to the other, has provided the solution to the complex requirements of brief and site. This approach retains, conserves and reinstates the principal historical and architectural features, secures their future and celebrates their unique value, making them accessible to the public, while providing modern, efficient repository systems and research facilities and a fitting headquarters for the city's library service'.[5]

Figure 10.3 Dublin City Library and Archive, library extension

The quality of the building, as it currently stands, in effect reflects the fact that the challenges faced in making it a library fitted for the 21st century, particularly those challenges presented by conservation, refurbishment and new build on a land-locked site, were overcome. To quote the city librarian, who acted as client on behalf of the city council: 'The quality of the new facility reflects the creativity of the architect and the expertise of the many expert engineers, skilled masons and crafts workers who have completed the building. They have effectively translated the combined vision of architect and librarian into a reality, where form and function fuse to serve public interest.'[6] In essence, the partnership of architect and librarian managed to achieve in Pearse Street a unique business solution in what was a complex set of functional requirements.

Implementation and management

An implementation plan and appropriate management process were of course critical to an effective and efficient project, with delivery expressed in management tools and methodologies used in accordance with standard professional practice and applied to building construction, functional design and issues of operational management. Critical, also, was the process of engaging in these requirements in parallel with a process of library-led consultation and information provision with neighbouring home owners, involving management and local elected politicians, and in a process of discussion and ultimately negotiation with staff trades unions. The project steering group included architectural, library, administrative and financial expertise. Operational sub-groups were formed as required and the various complex tasks, all requiring management attention at different stages of development, involved library and archive staff, architects, builder, engineers and a variety of subcontractors and individual experts. The process overall, of course required precision planning, dealing with schedules and dependent tasks, ordering equipment, identifying and specifying shelving and furnishing. It involved detailing specifications, assessing and negotiating tenders, and above all it involved meetings, minutes and reports to council, and to those with funding interest. The issues addressed, therefore, in bringing the project to completion were focused on an end result which would afford the best design and build outcome, culminating in an effective integrated library and archive facility. In effect the building had to meet user needs – form meeting with function in a fusion of professionally driven and led expertise.

Delivery of a building for public service

Opened in July 2003, the Dublin City Library and Archive offers Dublin's citizens and visitors to the city the opportunity to engage for the first time in research related to Dublin as a city of learning in a purpose-designed facility. Standing as an icon of architectural form and effective function, the result is a landmark building which makes a civic, cultural and architectural statement. It is on a major access route into the city, contributing to urban regeneration and maintenance of the city core. The building functions as a major public research and lifelong educational facility focused on Dublin studies, with all the dimensions of a quality service facility as detailed in the library requirements brief. Additionally, a constant stream of programmed activity related to Dublin, its history and heritage, gives it a public profile consistent with it being the headquarters of the Dublin City Council Libraries and Archive system.

Conclusion

As a case study, the Dublin City Library and Archive building offers some lessons of value, among which I would identify the importance of establishing a sense of common project ownership with key decision-makers who are vital to ensuring funding of any building project. Equally important is the availability to the steering team of project management skills and other appropriate professional and technical skills. In this particular context, architectural conservation and structural engineering can be singled out as critical to realization of the project. But overall, as viewed from the perspective of the professional librarian, the project brief was the catalyst for development. Coupled with ensuring the complementarity of form and function, expressed through awareness of the role of the librarian as client, the brief represents the single most important contribution to the delivery of a triumphant restoration project. As architect Arthur Gibney notes: 'Both the old library and the new building have been handled with considerable flair.'[7] In essence, contemporary techniques have rendered the original building as it would have been in 1909 – a truly wonderful landmark building worthy of the value conferred on it by Dublin's City Council as a library and archive of the future.

Notes

1   Ellis-King, Deirdre (1989), 'Dublin Public Libraries: an overview' in *Libraries of Dublin, Proceedings of a Conference held on 14–16 October 1988, as part of the City's Millennium Celebrations* (Dublin, The Library Association of Ireland), 24–33.
2   Grimes, Bernard (2003), 'Pearse Street library development', *Irish Architect, the Journal of the Royal Institute of Architects of Ireland*, July/August, 20.
3   ibid.
4   ibid.
5   ibid.
6   Ellis-King, 22.
7   Gibney, Arthur (2003), 'Pearse Street Library redevelopment, Dublin', *Irish Architect: the Journal of the Royal Institute of the Architects of Ireland*, July/August, 18–24.

Chapter 11

The London Library:
Changing to Stay the Same but Expansion and Renewal

Inez T.P.A. Lynn

A good friend does not change; nor does the London Library
– David Cecil[1]

Introduction

The London Library is an independent lending library founded by Thomas Carlyle in 1841. In October 2006, it embarked upon the first phase of the most radical redevelopment and renewal of its premises in over a century.[2] The library operates from a Grade 2 listed building in St James's Square in central London and now has a collection of over one million volumes covering all aspects of the arts and humanities, with over 95 per cent arranged on shelves to which members have unrestricted access for browsing. It is a registered charity with the aim of advancing education, learning and knowledge and is governed by a committee of members elected as trustees. Our much-prized independence enables us to decide for ourselves what our priorities should be, while also requiring us to ensure that the library remains entirely self-financing, supported by membership subscriptions, investment income, fundraising and bequests.

Membership is open to all (a trust fund exists to assist members unable to afford the full annual fee) and there are currently just over 8000 members. About 97 per cent of the collection is available for borrowing; loan periods are generous and flexible to meet readers' needs. Members have a strong sense of ownership of the library and find its distinctive working environment conducive to reading, learning and scholarship. Their affection for the library is often expressed as a desire that it should not change, but it has, in fact, been through a continuous process of change and development in order to continue meeting the needs of its users in every age.

Reasons for redevelopment

For the library to be sustainable in the 21st century, it needed to meet a number of key challenges, particularly those of accommodating and preserving its collections, while extending its ability to attract new members and ongoing revenue.

Space for the collections

The London Library has made a policy of retaining its older works alongside the newly acquired ones, resisting the impulse to discard what no longer seems 'relevant'. Browsers can thereby see the works of today in the context of the works of the past and each acquires deeper significance from the company it keeps. This means that the collection routinely requires about 1km of additional shelf space every three years. A thorough survey of shelf space in 2000 and an analysis of the growth rate of each subject revealed that shelving accommodating large parts of the collection had already been full for up to six years. Space was therefore urgently needed to accommodate the existing collections, to reunite subject sections which had been scattered through temporary book moves designed to relieve the worst areas of overcrowding, and to provide for carefully controlled growth in future.

Preserving the collections

The library's books date from the 16th to the 21st centuries and need to be maintained in a usable condition despite being both well travelled and well used. Extreme pressure on staff accommodation meant that conservation work on individual volumes could only be carried out in a makeshift fashion for lack of a properly equipped workspace. Furthermore, wide variations in temperature and relative humidity, unfiltered fluorescent lighting and an absence of ventilation in many parts of the library have created environmental conditions which contribute significantly to the physical deterioration of the collections and need to be resolved.

Space for members

The gradual addition of extra book stacks to the library over 150 years has resulted in a series of interlinked buildings best described as 'labyrinthine'. Improvements to basic navigation and way-finding signage were clearly needed for members to benefit fully from access to the shelves. Other facilities for members had long been much more limited than we would have liked. Daily usage varies according to the time of year (150–225 visits per day in the quieter months; 250–350 per day at busier times) but with just 55 reading spaces available, members often struggled to find a seat. Lack of space also limited the number and range of IT facilities we could provide for members and precluded provision of improved photocopying facilities, the introduction of scanning equipment or, indeed, anywhere for members to talk or have a cup of coffee. Even basic facilities such as cloakrooms for storing members' coats and bags had become inadequate.

Planning and design process

Acquisition of site

In 2003, a comprehensive membership survey which attracted a 50 per cent response rate, indicated overwhelming support for the acquisition of additional premises in which to expand in the immediate vicinity. The search for suitable premises came to fruition in June 2004 with the purchase of an adjoining building, 'Duchess House' at 17–22 Mason's Yard. This is arranged on basement, ground and four upper floors and was constructed by a developer between 1979 and 1981 for mixed use, with residential apartments, offices, a wine bar, a small commercial gallery and three garages. It offered an additional 1475m^2 to the library's existing 4700m^2.

Preparation of outline brief

Before seeking a design team, a detailed project brief was prepared. This covered the purpose and values of the library; a description of its needs and the objectives and scope of the project; the funding basis; indicators of success; a brief history and heritage status of both the library's existing site at 14 St James's Square and of Duchess House; an outline design brief specifying what the redeveloped library should include in terms of book storage, member and visitor facilities, and staff facilities; and an overview of design constraints including the presence of tenants, site access, structural considerations and the need to keep the library operational. It focused deliberately on describing the library's needs as clearly as possible rather than prescribing any particular solutions. As librarian, I took personal responsibility for writing this brief but it drew heavily on earlier work preparing the library's Strategic Plan, 2002–2007, which had involved all of the library's staff. At this stage we also engaged the services of a project management consultant with extensive experience of construction projects in arts organizations to test the brief and help us to identify potential architects with an appropriate track record. With his advice we also engaged a suitably experienced cost consultant. The brief was agreed by the trustees of the library and permission granted to proceed with the selection of architects.

Selection of architects

Six architectural practices were invited to provide conceptual responses to the outline brief. They included established experts in the field of library design, but also architects with relevant experience of sensitive intervention in existing buildings or in renovating historic buildings, or in producing 'iconic' buildings for arts organizations. We were looking for a sympathetic understanding of the library's ethos (and of the fact that members are fiercely protective not only of the building's real virtues but also of its defects and eccentricities); a willingness to listen to librarians to the point of really understanding our needs; and the ability to produce a design solution which would prove attractive to potential donors while also satisfying in detail the library's functional needs and economic constraints. It was also important that the chosen practice should be able and willing to participate effectively where appropriate in events arranged to interest potential donors in the project.

All six practices were interviewed by a subcommittee of trustees, who were to form the Building Project Steering Committee (BPSC), along with the library's senior management team (consisting of librarian, deputy librarian, head of fundraising and head of finance), the project management consultant and the cost consultant. Responses to the brief were very varied and Haworth Tompkins were appointed not for any previous experience of building libraries (they had none) but for their evident understanding of the character of the library and intellectually rigorous approach to getting to grips with its needs. They were then invited to propose both mechanical and electrical engineers and structural engineers to complete the design team.[3]

A period of intense briefing followed during which staff explained requirements in detail, introducing the design team to the meaning of library terminology (octavo, quarto, rolling cases, etc.) and helping them to familiarize themselves with the complex layout of the historic buildings and the required adjacencies of staff departments, reader facilities and book stacks. From this, a practice developed of weekly meetings between the design team and what came to be called the 'client review group' made up of one of the trustees from the BPSC, the librarian, head of fundraising and any other staff relevant to the subject of the meeting. This group provided a forum for rapid, informal review of design ideas and quickly became an effective and creative part of the design process, enabling significant progress to be made between monthly meetings of the full BPSC. In this way, the design was taken from an initial options study to a feasibility study, outline design, detail design and the production of information for construction.[4]

Affecting a listed building in a conservation area, the library's plans were always going to be of close interest to the planning authorities and the design team made a point of involving the relevant planning and heritage officers from Westminster City Council at an early stage. A full 'Historic Building Impact Assessment' report was prepared for them showing the history of the building and how the proposed alterations would be in keeping with that history. This attention to detail paid off and full planning consent was granted in November 2005; indeed, the scheme was specially commended by the conservation groups invited to comment on it.

While we were still at the feasibility study stage, consideration was also given to the form of contract under which the construction might take place. Apart from Duchess House, most of the future construction work will occur within the heart of the library complex, requiring materials to be moved to the various sites of work, preferably without being taken through the building. The need to remain operational throughout and to safeguard the book stock, members and staff from the potentially damaging impact of noise and dust would require careful sequencing of work and selection of methodology, and a high degree of cooperation between trade contractors and staff. Even Duchess House presented challenges, with the sole vehicular access restricted in height and the presence of residents on the top floor and at one side of the building. It was therefore decided to take the 'construction management' route whereby a construction manager (CM) is engaged as part of the professional team during the design stage and advises on buildability, methodology and programme. The CM then packages up the construction work trade by trade, lets the trade contracts in the client's name and manages the site, the interface with the contractors and the construction costs to completion. Unlike a traditional construction contract, where the work is tendered in competition on a lump sum basis, the risk of unexpected costs remains with the client and it is therefore important that the client be 'expert'. In our case, this expertise was provided by our project management consultant.

Design solutions and outcomes

By the time of its completion, the project will have renewed every part of the St James's Square site, joining it to Duchess House on five levels. The initial options study identified which parts of the enlarged site were best suited to additional book stacks, reader facilities or staff accommodation. This enabled the various elements of the project brief to be addressed in the most appropriate location. Thus, Duchess House – originally designed and built mainly as an office block, and now known as T.S. Eliot House – has been transformed into a combination of book stacks and staff offices, thereby releasing space elsewhere for additional reading rooms and other member facilities. Overall, the project will deliver all the requirements of the brief including the following main benefits:

Book storage

Additional open-access shelving to accommodate the collections for at least 25 years will be created by the conversion of the basement area of the whole, extended site to rolling cases and the construction of a new, three-storey book stack on top of the existing Victorian stacks.

Environmental conditions throughout the book stacks will be improved through a 'passive' solution involving upgrading insulation, treating glazing to control heat gain and UV damage, and installing mechanical ventilation to enable control of overheating in summer. This stops short of full air-conditioning with its associated environmental impact and increased running costs; however, full air-conditioning to achieve storage conditions in line with BS 5454 will be installed in the Anstruther Wing rare book stacks and the conservation studio.[5] Re-wiring and removal of water pipes from the stacks in the older parts of the building will reduce the risk of significant loss through flood or fire.

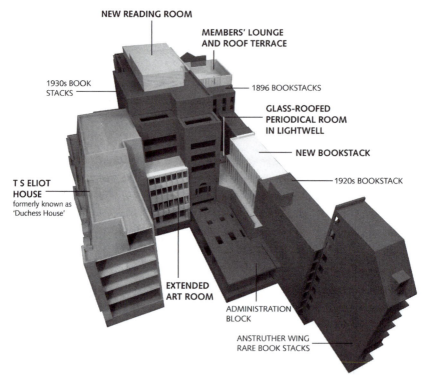

NEW READING ROOM

MEMBERS' LOUNGE
AND ROOF TERRACE

1930s BOOK
STACKS

1896 BOOKSTACKS

GLASS-ROOFED
PERIODICAL ROOM
IN LIGHTWELL

NEW BOOKSTACK

T S ELIOT
HOUSE
formerly known as
'Duchess House'

1920s BOOKSTACK

EXTENDED
ART ROOM

ADMINISTRATION
BLOCK

ANSTRUTHER WING
RARE BOOK STACKS

Figure 11.1 The London Library, model showing old and new elements
Source: Andy Chopping/Kandor Modelmakers

Member and visitor facilities

Reader spaces will be more than doubled with 120 purpose-designed desks available, each equipped with power sockets, wifi and task lighting. These will be located, as at present, amongst the stacks and in the historic first-floor reading room (which will be fully restored) but also in a new reading room on the sixth floor of the building with a more contemporary design, a lantern roof and views over Westminster, and in a periodical room at the foot of a glass-roofed lightwell at the heart of the building. While priority has been given in the design to the daytime function of these spaces as reading rooms, each has also been designed to be easily convertible into a reception or lecture space for revenue-generating activities out of hours. Similarly a small members' lounge which opens onto a roof terrace will also earn its keep through evening functions.

Access to the building will be considerably improved with a new members' entrance to the side of the main entrance hall providing level access for wheelchairs for the first time. An enlarged lift is also planned to enable easier access to those parts of the stacks where historic design does not preclude wheelchair access. A new stair running through the whole building will facilitate navigation and improve fire exit provision. Locker and cloakroom facilities will be doubled and a secure cycle store provided. The relocation of 'back room' staff offices (cataloguing, acquisitions, IT etc.) from the main entrance hall will allow for increased provision of IT and other facilities for members in this area.

Current status of project

Phase 1, involving works to Duchess House, has just been completed in late summer 2007, on time and on budget. There will now be a pause until fundraising for the next piece of work reaches its target; some parts of Duchess House have therefore been fitted out for interim use rather than for what will be their final function once works to the St James's Square building are complete. Thus, the book stacks on Floors 1 and 2 of Duchess House, which will eventually provide expansion space for the art history collections, will be used in the interim to provide decanting space for further building work. The new office space permanently re-houses the acquisitions and cataloguing departments (allowing the former to be accommodated together rather than scattered over six floors as previously) and provides an IT office with a separate server room, enabling IT staff to avoid for the first time being chilled summer and winter along with the hardware. A purpose-designed conservation studio has been created on Floor 3 and there is also a meeting/training room equipped for IT training and flexibly configured for meetings of up to 16 people. Staff rest rooms, a new post room and other administrative offices have all freed up space in the St James's Square building which will be used to expand member facilities in a temporary condition until the final design solution can be funded.

Challenges along the way

The need to raise the funds for the project at the same time as developing the design posed quite a challenge. Our chosen design process placed a high priority on getting the functional detail right before considering aesthetics; while this was undoubtedly the right approach, it made things very difficult for our fundraising team who needed convincing visual images to 'sell' the project to potential donors as early as possible. Their plight was eased to some extent by commissioning a large model of the entire site (funded by a donor) which enabled them to show the sheer scale and complexity of the project in a direct way.

Once work on Duchess House began, the difficulties of the site became apparent. Services to the six residential apartments proved to be interlinked with those of the remaining parts of the building in wholly unforeseeable ways. The construction management approach here proved its worth as our construction manager was extremely successful in keeping the residents on our side despite the inevitable mishaps when telephone connections were cut, their lift lost its power and so on. Indeed one of the notable successes of the project has been the way in which all involved – from the design team to the trade contractors – managed to maintain a spirit of cooperation with each other and avoided relations between the various parties becoming adversarial.

Overseeing the project on behalf of the library also offered challenges. It is really a full-time job in itself and doing it on top of the day job means long hours and never quite achieving as much as one would wish. Keeping staff up-to-date on what was happening and involving them appropriately was essential but at times required more time than was really available.

Design style

Haworth Tompkins have developed a strong reputation for their ability to intervene effectively in existing buildings.[6] They feel that above all this requires 'recognizing the difference between respect and sentimentality, respecting the strengths and primary character of the existing, without becoming overtly sentimental about elements that actually have little intrinsic value'. Working therefore with the proportions of each space and the quality of natural light, they have retained strong existing features and set them against new interventions which have integrity and are sympathetic to the existing setting without resorting to pastiche.[7] Thus new spaces, such as the enclosed lightwell, the attic reading room and the members' room and terrace do not attempt to imitate the Victorian spaces; rather they are clearly contemporary in design but refer to the older parts in their choice of materials: 'We have chosen materials which are slow-burn rather than slick . . . It's not hi tech, rather the tradition of the blacksmith and metal-basher – because that's how the building was originally made.'[8]

Duchess House posed a different kind of challenge. The building had little character and its external façade was dated and undistinguished. Externally the building has been transformed by replacement of the windows and the creation of a strong ground floor façade, contributing significantly to the regeneration of Mason's Yard which began with the completion of the new White Cube Gallery in 2006. Internally, the textures and materials of the older buildings have been carried through in a contemporary style, giving the spaces a character that is different yet somehow comparable to the rest of the library.[9]

Conclusion

With Phase 1 completed and coming into use, we are just beginning to benefit from the extra space available. We will shortly be conducting a project review workshop to capture all that has been learnt from the experience of the first phase to the benefit of Phase 2. We look forward to completing the project to ensure the library is set fair for its next 165 years of service to the readers and writers of the future.

Notes

1   Cecil, D. (1977), 'The library that never changes', *ADAM International Review*, **40** (397–400), 31–2.

2   For an architectural history of the library, *see* McIntyre, T. (2006), *Library Book: an architectural journey through the London Library* (London: The London Library).

3   Professional team: Haworth Tompkins (architects); Mace (construction management); Price & Myers (structural engineers); Max Fordham Partnership (services engineers); Gardiner & Theobald (cost consultants/quantity surveyors); John Fairclough (project management adviser).

4   An unusual feature of the project was the involvement of an artist in the creative process. Haworth Tompkins had worked successfully with artists previously at both the Royal Court Theatre and the Hayward Gallery and were keen to do so again at the London Library. Martin Creed (Turner Prize winner in 2001) was therefore appointed. *See further* Cripps, C. (2007) 'In praise of the cistern', *The Independent*, 20 September (Extra), 14–15 and Lorenz, T. (2007), 'Bookish charm', *Design Week*, **22** (42), 19.

5   Much thought was given to the optimum environment for the book stacks given the huge range of age, binding and paper types of the volumes shelved together and the fact that they leave the library while on loan. It was decided that BS 5454 which was devised primarily for a closed stack environment was less appropriate for the majority of the library's open-access stacks. It was also necessary to keep the amount of additional duct-work and bulky air-handling equipment to a minimum in order not to impact on space available for shelving.

6   The practice was recently short-listed for the RIBA Stirling Prize 2007 for its work on the Young Vic. *See also* Powell, K. (2001), *New London Architecture* (London: Merrell), 108–109, 118–19, 166–7, and Powell, K. with Strongman, C. (2007), *New London Architecture 2* (London: Merrell), 58–9 (London Library extension), 76–7, 184–5; www.haworthtompkins.com/ 31 October 2007.

7   *See* Pearman, H. (2006), 'A novel approach to book-keeping', *Sunday Times* 5 February; www.hughpearman.com/2006/03/1 November 2007.

8   Graham Haworth. *See* Lyall, S. (2007), 'London Library extension', *AJ Specification*, September, 14–23.

9   *See further*, Lorenz, T. (2007), 'Bookish charm', *Design Week*, **22** (42), 19.

Chapter 12

Malmö City Library, Sweden: Beauty vs. Efficiency – Planning for User and Staff Needs

Gunilla Petterson

The central library of Malmö was housed in seven rooms in a hotel building from 1905 until 1946, and after that in a refurbished museum. It was once again refurbished and inaugurated in 1999, two years after the new connecting buildings were opened. The final result is one of the most beautiful and technically advanced libraries in Scandinavia. The prolonged planning process, which began in the 1980s, allowed the staff the opportunity to carefully consider what services the library should offer. They came to realize that a never-ending cycle of planning and replanning is necessary, centred towards the users' needs.

A contributing factor to the planning of the library was of course that this took place in a very creative period of change in the library world with new library media and the rapid development of information technology. This was also the time when the necessity for a good work environment became obvious, both for the staff and the visitors. Flexibility and self-service became guiding stars.

The buildings

The distinguished Danish architect Henning Larsen won the architectural competition that took place in 1992 to design the library. Two new buildings were to be connected to the old building. This was originally built in 1901 as a museum, refurbished in 1946 as a library, and was a four-floor high square building with an open yard in the middle. The four towers, each with a different design, were copied from four castles in Denmark and South Sweden, a region that was once Danish territory.

In 1946 the open yard was built over and replaced by a book hall with an elegant gallery, and with staff workrooms and book stacks on five floors around this centre. The children's library occupied half the first floor with an entrance of its own, and on the fourth floor were an auditorium and a room for studying local history. The library entrance was placed in a glass-walled extension facing north and connecting with a small building just outside. The extension housed the reception, loans and returns, periodicals and a room for music.

Now Henning Larsens Tegnestue wanted to restore the building to its original design. The extension and the small building were pulled down and the original four floors were restored. There is a reminder of the open yard since this space is now, from the second to the fourth floor, a big lofty 11m-high stairwell with galleries at every floor. A glass roof has replaced the open sky. The galleries, birch-panelled with built-in bookshelves, have entrances to stock rooms, and the further into those rooms you walk, and the higher up in the building you go, the more old details you find, such as windows, bay windows and roof stucco.

The two new buildings can be described as an extension to the old one. On the second floor there is a 101m-long open passage between the east wall of the old building and the west wall of the new. The two entrances to the library are placed in a cylinder-shaped austere stone building in which light pours down from windows high up.

Figure 12.1 Malmö City Library, perspective of three library buildings
Source: Johan Kalén

The bigger of the new buildings is a magnificent square building, corresponding to the shape of the old one, but contrasting to the latter's enclosed appearance with two enormous 18m-high glass walls facing north and west and opening the room to the surrounding park. Facing east and west the building is an L-shaped stone building with ordinary windows. Since one of these walls with windows, sills and all, is facing the large hall, you also get an impression of being outside in the park from inside the room. This part of the building is five floors high and contains most of the staff's working areas, situated on floors four and five. The first floor is occupied by the returns machines, staff rooms and the public auditorium.

Four big massive pillars lift the roof of the hall above the L-shape. The visitors can pass from the old building to the new using connecting passages on the second and third floor. These passages open in the entrance building to small balconies and in the new hall to a large gallery.

Facing west is 'the Shelf', two galleries inside the glass wall with small divisions containing shelves and facing the hall. Looking for books up there is like walking inside a huge shelf.

Entering the library from the park you have the newspaper and periodicals room and the auditorium to the right and the children's library to the left. Two large stone stairs on each side lead to the halls. There are lifts in all the buildings.

The different ways the daylight enters these three buildings are of great importance for the impression visitors get. Henning Larsen called his competition entry 'The Calendar of Light' and that is now the name of the big glass hall in which you can observe the light from morning to evening, and through the seasons of the year. The entrance building is called 'the Cylinder' and the old building 'the Castle', not to be confused with the real Malmöhus Castle nearby.

The construction work started in 1994, but came to a long halt the year after, due to budget overdraft. The politicians demanded a cost cut, and it took almost a year to sort this out. Cheaper materials in the stone walls and floors, and the loss of stock area under the Castle, as well as an underground parking lot, were the most important changes that had to be made. This was one of many unlucky events that accompanied the project. Another was that Henning Larsens Tegnestue did not participate in the first stage of the work.

Beauty vs. efficiency

How to react as a staff member to the new buildings? It was not easy. In the library programme planning there was a great wish for as much open access to stacks as possible, since the staff had worked so many decades collecting books from stock rooms within and outside the library. And now, in the biggest hall, there were hardly any walls to put shelves against, only an open floor, a couple of small galleries and – air.

Short distances between stacks and departments were also desirable for an efficient managing of the materials, and here was a 101m-long wall-to-wall distance. What use could be made of the Shelf and the balconies? How to get an efficient lighting and a sign system legible for all without disturbing the architectural beauty? A welcoming atmosphere to greet visitors, especially the elderly, disabled and new ones, seemed impossible in this austere library.

The wind blew constantly between the two entrances facing north and south and caused severe climate problems for the staff, who sometimes could be seen working dressed in caps and woollen gloves. The architect had wished for an entrance hall with only a small reception and a café, but the staff did not want to force the users to take the stairs up to the second floor in order to return a loan or pick up a reservation. They believed that visitors wished to go through these dull routines as fast as possible. How to arrange a safe security system for the materials was another problem in these very open spaces.

The library's programme planning

The first real planning began in the 1980s, and was centred on looking over the library routines in order to make these easier and faster for the users. Malmö City Library was the first library in Sweden to discuss for instance getting rid of the big desks for loans and returns near the entrance, where the visitors would queue up, and instead combine these functions with the information services at smaller desks placed among the stacks, and later also self-service loan and return machines. Due to the long political decision-making process many of these ideas were carried out in other libraries before they were a reality in Malmö.

In the next phase different studies were made. In one of them the visitors' behaviour in the library was studied: where they went, what they were doing and how long they were occupied with different activities. The outcome was that not only the information desks but also chairs and tables ought to be placed among the stacks since the visitors moved frequently between browsing the shelves, sitting down reading and asking for help at the information desks. It was also decided from the beginning that all kind of materials within a subject should be stacked together.

Hard work was put into the task of obtaining ergonomically adapted desks, worktables, trolleys and other tools of assistance. The information desks and worktables were constructed in cooperation with the Faculty of Engineering LTH in Lund, where tests were made with full-scale models.

In cooperation with a physiotherapist, the library examined the work routines and the logistic processes to avoid too many heavy reloadings of the materials. The tables and desks were to be vertically adjustable, and most importantly very easy to adjust. A very important finding from these studies was the importance of changing work positions often, a finding that became important in reorganizing the work units.

While the equipment was being planned, IT development exploded and every routine became computerized, so it was important to carefully plan the computer desks for both the staff and the visitors. At the same time 'the paperless office' and flexible staff units began to be discussed. These ideas gave priority to large working areas with a shelving system as walls to promote cooperation within and between the departments.

The new library required more staff at the desks than the old one, and since the new staff budget was only marginally increased, the solution became working units in which librarians and library assistants worked together in a new way. The reception and the returns desk in the entrance hall were staffed from every library department, and it was considered important that librarians also worked there, answering questions and guiding the visitors upwards in the library.

As it became

'History and Future, Fantasy and Knowledge' became the motto of the new library.

The Calendar of Light, with most of the non-fiction materials, represented Future and Knowledge, the furnishing corresponding to the big hall with shelves in grey steel and glass gables with many computers for the visitors, and reading places along the large glass walls and up on the Shelf.

Figure 12.2 Malmö City Library, The Calendar of Light

Source: Johan Kalén

The Castle became the place for Fantasy and History with the children's/young adults' library, fiction, arts and music, the local materials, and the department for talking books. In Sweden talking books are available only for people with defective vision. Commercially produced books on tape, available for all, are stacked mostly in the fiction department. The department for talking books also has an assistive technology corner and 'word shop' for those who cannot read written texts, as well as books in large print, easy readers, and books on hard of hearing, including tapes in sign language.

Figure 12.3 Malmö City Library, The Castle

Source: Johan Kalén

The same light birch wood from the stairwell is used for shelving and furniture. It is combined with leather in the same colour in the chairs.

The children's library is furnished more colourfully, but the stone floor that had to be placed there because of too high a level of humidity in the ground has made these rooms more austere than desired.

The Calendar of Light and the Cylinder were inaugurated in 1997, the refurbished Castle in 1999. All library services had to be squashed into the new buildings during the refurbishing time.

Besides the stone floor in the children's library other changes had to be made to the plans: the grand doors in the main entrance from the park had to be replaced with a longer airlock which ended in rotating doors in order to raise the temperature indoors during winter, and the work rooms placed in the public area had to be moved and soundproofed.

Flexibility and self-service

In the Calendar of Light, and in most staff working areas, the floor is a double floor which carries electric wiring, computer cables and ventilation. In the Castle these installations are kept behind the wall panels.

The triangular information desks allow the visitors and the staff to meet without barriers, mostly in front of a computer. The self-help automats for loans and returns were an immediate success. Since the return and sorting machines available on the market could not handle all the loans in Malmö City Library, a special system was constructed with two industrial robots, sorting the books directly to the trolleys of the different departments. One of the architects designed an assembly line under the floor level with glass above, taking the books from the returns section to the robots behind the doors to the staff area. Both the line and the robots became huge attractions, especially among children.

Lighting

It was a difficult task to get a good enough lighting over shelves and tables that did not disturb the effect of the beautiful general lighting. Here readability won over beauty. In some rooms in the Castle one kind of lighting fittings on the shelves came too close to another kind in the roofs, due to the shelves being higher than those with a more accessible height originally planned.

Signs

Several experts were consulted to design a sign system that did not disturb the architectural interiors. Here beauty won over readability, the signs being placed too high and with too small letters. In the entrance hall the staff carried out signs with more detailed information than the architect found necessary, knowing that the visitors want to know directly where the different subjects are placed in the buildings.

Adaptations for the disabled

Good lighting, a good colour contrast in lettering and background, and large enough letters placed at eye height are important elements of signs for persons with defective vision, and these elements did not appear in this library's signage. The interiors almost entirely lack colour contrasts. This is one example of the problems of adapting the library to disabled persons.

It cannot be stressed enough how important it is that adaptations for the disabled are carefully calculated and a part of the budget from the beginning. This was not so in Malmö, but in planning the refurbishment of the Castle the library cooperated with representatives from the major disability organizations, and they influenced the designs of toilets, ramps – needed because of a height difference between the buildings and within the children's library – the distances between shelves, door openings, staircase markings and button panelling in lifts.

Most discussed was the need for self-help for the very disabled. Wheelchair-bound visitors must of course have access to self-service machines and computers, but how many floor markings can be placed in such a vast library without their losing clarity, and how much will a map in relief or a speech synthezizer linked to the queueing system be used? Is asking for help always a negative thing? In this library almost every new visitor has to ask for guidance when entering for the first time, and guidance was a library priority to staff in the entrance hall, with many persons available to help.

The library was more successful in enabling visitors' access to databases and materials through assistive technology than it was in enabling self-help access to the buildings.

Staff workrooms

It was a very good idea to place the staff workrooms in the Calendar of Light in the public area, near the information desks. It will thus be easier to adapt the staffing of the desks to the needs of visitors. However, this arrangement did not work out well at the beginning owing to the use of the same flexible wall system as that in the other staff work areas. These walls, or rather sets of shelves, neither reach the roof nor the floor and thus noise is carried around them. The staff working in the public areas could not work in this high sound level, and even the visitors complained of having to hear staff discussing and making business calls. The rooms had to be moved and furbished with ordinary walls and doors. They functioned much better after that, although they were still too small.

In other working areas the ability to move the walls has been frequently used, but no one is satisfied with the high sound level coming from colleagues around and from the double flooring. It is possible that the shielding should be either low enough to permit one to see over it; alternatively, the flexible walls could be abandoned altogether and replaced with real walls in closed rooms. The latter option is most often preferred by staff working long hours. This experience resulted in closed-in and larger workrooms in the Castle than was originally planned. The doors were carefully isolated, and the head of the departments got her/his own closed-in room.

Public opinion during the years of construction and refurbishing

The new library was eagerly awaited and the public followed the progress with great interest. Visitors to the half-ready library were very patient during the long period of refurbishing.

The first negative reaction came when a couple of trees had to be cut down. Protesters had to be taken down from the trees by policemen. Today most people regard the library as a real asset to the park, mirrored in the big glass windows.

More negative opinions came when it was known that the big wall paintings in the children's library with motifs from well-known fairy tales had to be destroyed because the walls had to be reinforced or moved. Worse still was that the storytelling cave was to be replaced by a new one. Parents and grandparents remembered the roof lit up by star constellations and the little fly among the big animals on the wall painting, and they wanted their children and grandchildren to have the same experience. But the protests stopped when the new storytelling cave was presented. On the outside it is a big pillar in the middle of a room with shelving all around it, on the inside there is a closed round room with a lofty ceiling, and today's children find this room as exciting as the older generations did their story-telling cave.

And the unique excitement in this library is still there; access is allowed only when a child knocks three times on a bookshelf, which then opens itself, showing a low-ceilinged pathway into the cave.

The lack of a silent reading room was also disputed. One reason for Malmö City Library's decision not to include such a room was that a new university library was to be built within a few years.

Marketing the new library

To encourage the inhabitants of Malmö to visit their new library was no problem at all, the visitors queued up to see the library that had already attracted so much attention. Almost every association and organization in Malmö and the surrounding region booked a guided tour. Sightseeing buses lined up outside every day for a long time. Librarians and architects came from all over Scandinavia, and even from further away. Still today the library has more foreign visitors than other municipal services in Malmö.

The library became at once the most popular meeting-place in Malmö, especially among young people, and the staff could during the daily guided tours make new connections and renew old ones.

Of course all of the written information about the library had to be altered, and the almost daily guided tours during the first years had to be administered and carried out. This created an immense workload for a couple of years, but the outcome made it really worthwhile.

Today, in 2007, the library has developed more than could be foreseen in 1999. The 24/7 library is here. It must be noted, however, that the library attracts as many visitors now as before, even if the library users can renew their loans, ask questions and do many other things online at home.

The robots have been replaced by a more advanced return and sorting system. New media and new user needs have caused stack transfers. Fewer library routines are handled in the entrance hall due to more self-service systems. The entrance facing the north is now permanently closed, giving more space to the café.

The architect may have underestimated many of the users' needs, and the staff the importance of beautiful surroundings for the library visit, but the clashes and compromises that did occur created a library which is loved by the inhabitants of Malmö, a pride of the city of Malmö, and in itself still ready to meet new challenges.

Table 12.1 Malmö City Library: Facts and figures

Malmö's population: 276,244	
Malmö City Library Floor space	15 300m2
Public area:	9 300m2
Building costs:	236 million SEK
Fitting costs:	46 million SEK
Building period:	1992–9 including the architectural competition and refurbishment of the old building
Architects:	Original building 1901: John Smedberg Extension and rebuilding: Henning Larsen Tegnestue A/S
Designed for	1.5 million visitors and loans per year
Collections 2006:	600 000 media
Visitors 2006:	840 000
Glass facade:	(Calendar of Light) 1400m^2
Awards:	Sweden's most prestigious architect award The Kasper Salin Prize The Malmö City Architecture Award

Chapter 13

Waterford Central Library: A Space For All

Jane Cantwell

Introduction

Situated in the centre of the historical and vibrant port city of Waterford in the south-east of Ireland, the original Waterford Municipal Library (built in 1905 and originally named the Carnegie Library) was an imposing but compact building symbolizing in its structure much of the character and personality of the city itself.

History

0n the 19 October 1903, the philanthropist Andrew Carnegie laid the foundation stone for the Carnegie Library in Waterford, following his pledge of a grant of £5000 for the building. He received the freedom of the City of Waterford on that date.

The library was completed by February 1905 and included a reference room, reading room, ladies room, book stores, art room and caretaker's accommodation.

It was an impressive building, with an external cladding of limestone, extending to two floors and an attic space comprising of c. 700m^2 in total.

Brendan Grimes in his book *Irish Carnegie Libraries* (1998) refers to a teacher's guide, which states that 'the vestibule floor had beautiful fan-shaped designs in mosaic and gigantic patent revolving swing doors between the porch and the vestibule'.[1] A significant feature of the old building was a magnificent atrium in the centre of the building. This has been repaired and preserved in the new building.

Reasons for refurbishment

Waterford was a growing city in the 1990s, and it was clear that the Carnegie Library could neither accommodate the book stock nor facilitate the expansion of services, including IT services and new media.

The building had been superficially renovated in the 1980s and was both cramped and overstocked. In spite of high windows and an atrium providing light in the building, it lacked adequate space for basic comfort and for service development.

Figure 13.1 Waterford Central Library, exterior

Source: Joe Evans, photographer, Waterford News and Star, Waterford

Time for renewal

In August 1995, Waterford Corporation (now Waterford City Council) advertised for a consultant architect to submit plans for the design and construction of an extension to the Carnegie Library.

The only space available for this extension was a small site adjacent to the library. A simple brief was provided requesting ideas for the extension of the library to a 195m² site. The requirement to create a library of at least 1900m² would not have been achieved by this original brief.

Initially when plans were drawn up for the development of the adjoining site, they included a basement in order to maximize available space. However, following a full archaeological investigation, retaining a medieval wall, bern and ditch would have occupied over one-third of the basement space. Although thse finds were historically significant, such usage of the valuable space in an already restricted development footprint would have been both illogical and expensive.

In October 2000, McCullough Mulvin, Architects, provided new plans excluding the basement. The 12th-century city wall was incorporated on view under a glass floor on the ground floor in the building.

The plans provided for a building of c.2000m² stretching over four floors, three for public use; the top floor was to include administrative space, a canteen, an IT communications room and storage space.

Planning and design

The specification for the extension and renovation of the library building required that some of the original features of the library be retained so, unlike a green field site, the challenge from the librarian's perspective, was to identify how existing and proposed new services could be incorporated into the architect's plans.

At the planning and design stage it was necessary to combine the objectives, priorities and ambitions of both the architects and the librarians in order to achieve a building that would be architecturally interesting, practically workable and within budget!

The following section summarizes the priorities identified by the architect's design team and the librarian's project team. Essentially, the final result for both librarians and architects was to produce a new 21st-century city library. This was achieved through the assimilation of these priorities. A combination of close cooperation between the librarians and architects and mutual trust in the combined vision for the building was needed to achieve this outcome.

The architect's vision

After identifying the elements of the old building requiring conservation – the red brick underbelly of the building, the atrium, the limestone façade and, of course, the excavated city wall – the architect produced design solutions which allowed for maximum expression of these older elements and also allowed the materials used in the newer sections of the building to be influenced by these elements.

The architect's main priorities were:

- Site strategy
    Integration of old and new fabric, appreciation of urban context.
- Conservation strategy
    Planning the incorporation of new interventions into the old building.
- Light and circulation
    Creating routes within the building and providing light throughout building.
- Integration of building and furniture
    Choice of furniture to enhance and supplement the lines of the building.

The underlying themes for the design of the building required the original building to be stripped back to a shell and redesigned from the ground up.

These themes included:

- Visual intrigue – glimpses from floor to floor and one area to another.
- Flow and movement from one section to the next.

- Height and impact of vertical space.
- Changing levels on floors, windows and shelving.
- Combination of old and new materials.
- Creative use of light, both vertically and horizontally.

Externally, the new building was clad in limestone to provide a seamless appearance with the older structure and internally, the atrium formed a central point of light with new internal windows acting as reflections allowing light to emanate throughout the building.

The exposed city wall underground was illuminated and revealed through a glass floor and the stripped-back, red-brick arches contrasted strongly with the atrium and modern steel beams.

Board-marked concrete was used in large quantities throughout the building. Black American walnut cladding was chosen for its richness and depth of colour. The decision on furniture later in the project was strongly influenced by the original choice of cladding and the darker furniture provided a modern finish to the building.

As the site for the expansion of the library was landlocked and small, with only minimal street frontage, its potential was maximized by using natural ventilation, new light shafts and white walls which contrasted with the concrete and wood panelling and reflected the light, making optimum use of natural resources.

The most dramatic of these light shafts was a large, concrete void stretching up to the top of the building. The architects viewed the circulation pattern in the building as a journey linking distinct places within the building and with views from one place to the next.

The entrance is deliberately large, accommodating a suspended, overhanging mezzanine which seems to just hang unsupported over the space. Because of the existing, preserved arches and the light flowing through the atrium, the user is drawn into the heart of the ground floor area and the information desk.

This movement created on the ground floor is repeated on the first floor by a glass-sided bridge overlooking the central information desk on the ground floor and leading to the local history and study areas, each of which have large, internal windows allowing views overlooking the ground floor and up through the atrium to parts of the second floor.

On the second floor, there is a similar natural flow through the space. Wide steps, another glass-sided bridge and internal windows reveal new spaces and invite the user to explore deeper and discover the glass-roofed audio listening area and the reference/meeting room.

Furniture and interior design were crucial to the final outcomes and included varying unit heights, unique bespoke furniture, beanbags, soft cube seats and interesting, coloured chairs provide a range of choices for users. Casual leather sofas and low tables placed directly beneath the atrium, provide a well-lit, attractive space for meeting, drinking coffee, reading and browsing newspapers.

Figure 13.2 Waterford Central Library, information desk

Source: Joe Evans, photographer, Waterford News and Star, Waterford

Angled study desks, individually lit, provide privacy and peace for serious research. Round tables for discussions, group work and meetings are available in both the local studies and reference areas. These are contrasted with the long bank of computer desks placed in a snake-like pattern on the second floor.

The solid, open seating with bright red leather cushions in the audio listening area defines this space as an attractive place to browse, listen, chat and meet. It is particularly inviting to young people and always bright and welcoming due to both the glass roof and the floor-to-ceiling windows.

Furniture is integrated into other pieces of the buildings so tables become shelves and seats can be used as steps.

The architect's objective was to allow the user of the space to do so in a multifunctional manner, with each area of the library allowing glimpses into other areas, perhaps tempting the user and leading them on a journey of discovery in the same way that reading one book leads to another and one website links to another.

The librarian's vision

The librarian needed to identify how the new spaces, as designed, could be utilized throughout the building in order to create a user-friendly building that would have universal appeal.

Broadly, the ground floor was to be a welcoming, vibrant, busy space (including teenage and children's spaces and also space for adults to meet, chat, read, browse and drink coffee). The first floor was envisaged as a quieter space for serious research, classes or reading and the second floor was to contain multi-purpose areas ranging from spaces for serious work to areas for fun and entertainment (including Internet access, an audio learning/listening area, a business library, non-fiction materials and a reference library/meeting room).

Whereas the spaces were outlined in terms of function, the librarian's need for adaptability, flexibility and interactive spaces combined well with the architect's vision of flow and movement through the building, in that spaces were created which could be utilized in accordance with user and library needs.

The main priorities from a librarian's perspective were:

- Accessibility
    External access, circulation through the building, signage, etc.
- Flexibility
    Shelves, IT provision, moveable furniture.
- Security
    Security gates, CCTV, tagging all materials.
- Ambience
    Light throughout the building, use of furniture, soft seating, colours, flooring, etc.
- Value for money
    Durable materials, multifunctional spaces.

As a public space, the library needed to be welcoming and accessible to all. It needed to be a knowledge resource, a leisure facility, a play/fun space and an exhibition/meeting place, all combined in the one building.

As a working space, the height and light juxtaposed with comfortable, secure areas for study, research, reading, listening and leisure.

In designing and planning the new building, both physical and cultural accessibility were high on the priority list. Not only did the building need to be fully compliant with all relevant legislation and building regulations but also the services offered needed to be as inclusive as possible.

Measures to facilitate physical and cultural access included:

- Fully automated access at street level.
- Accessibility proofed signs, which included braille.
- Disabled parking spaces outside the library.
- Two lifts (including a platform lift) with lift buttons marked in braille and lift announcements.
- Public toilets available on all levels with accessible toilets including rails and emergency alerts.
- Main information desk on two levels to facilitate wheelchair access.

- An induction loop.
- Free movement through the building and around shelves.
- Baby-changing facilities.
- Self-issue machine.
- Optical scanning facilities on ground floor.
- Free Internet access on 35+ PCs.
- Large print and audio stock.
- Online access to 250+ newspapers.
- Audio listening posts and seating area.
- Screen magnifiers.
- Information brochures available in eight languages.

Measures to ensure maximum flexibility included:

- Varying unit heights for shelves.
- Bespoke designed storage, shelving and display furniture.
- Moveable furniture and shelving (on castors where possible).
- Folding screen to allow the meeting room to be divided into two rooms.
- Modern, durable materials used to prevent the rapid dating of library.
- A variety of chairs, small tables, display units transferable throughout the building.
- Centralized management of public IT service providing efficient control and ease of use for customer.

Security measures included:

- CCTV cameras covering all floors of the building.
- Security gates at main entrance.
- Internal security-coded doors and electronic fob access for staff.
- Security strips on all stock and valuable equipment.

How ambience was created:

- Furniture, colours and strong layout were used to create a certain atmosphere on each floor e.g. studious or busy/noisy depending on use.
- Modern light fittings with lighting in alcoves and up lighters were used throughout the building.
- Neutral colours on walls and flooring were offset by splashes of vibrant colours in furniture.

Value for money:

- Ongoing value for money exercises were carried out during the building project.

- Solid, durable materials were used on all surfaces.
- Multifunctional spaces allow the public to use the building in many different ways.
- Networking of public IT provision allows for ongoing economies.

Challenges during the building project

Controlling capital costs

The budget for the renovated and extended central library amounted to c.€5 million. Over-runs in some areas were unavoidable, particularly in automation costs and the provision of additional technological features.

Time delays in commencing the building project meant that, before the library building even started, it was necessary to compromise on certain aspects of the project. Fortunately, it was possible to do this without sacrificing on quality, particularly in the public area of the building.

Throughout the project, additional costs needed to be factored in and once the project team had left the site and the snag list had been completed, additional adjustments and repairs are an ongoing aspect of revenue expenditure.

Project management

When working on a capital building project, the librarian is part of a team of architects, builders, mechanical and electrical engineers, IT specialists, quantity surveyors, etc. and each have their own priorities. The process requires good project management and negotiation skills and the librarian has a responsibility to ensure that decisions are not made that ultimately limit the scope of the building. These decisions can range from important decisions regarding overall size and layout of spaces to relatively minor decisions, such as the location of sockets, but they can all impact on the potential services that can be made available to the public.

Crisis management

Inevitably, throughout the project there will be some major and minor crises. The following points are worth remembering:

- Develop good working relationships with the project team.
- Don't be intimidated by technical jargon.
- Be as specific as possible in the initial brief to the architects.
- Keep library priorities to the forefront throughout the project.
- Learn when to make demands and when to compromise.
- Small details do matter!

Has the library renovation been successful?

The building has been transformed from a traditional library focusing, to a large extent, on lending and standard services, into a modern and architecturally impressive building offering a wide range of services.

The large entrance foyer and mezzanine provide ample space for exhibitions, launches, etc. and there are a number of options available throughout the building for meetings, classes, debates, seminars and concerts.

The rubber-floored children's area adjoins the main foyer of the library. It is a bright, double roofed space surrounded by arches and both acoustically and visually is as successful as a place for children's play and storytelling as it is for concerts and TV/radio shows.

Figure 13.3 Waterford Central Library, children's library
Source: John Power, Power Photography, Waterford

In summary, the library now has:

- adequate space for classes, talks, exhibitions, seminars, dance, bands, TV and radio shows, etc.
- scope to put collection development policies in place through, for example, the expansion of non-book material and the development of newer collections e.g. teenage, parent, literacy, business, etc.

- good display space for newspapers/magazines/journals
- extended access to historical materials e.g. microfilms, maps, etc.
- sophisticated online and IT services
- large, bright spaces for children and teenagers to make their own.

Awards achieved

This success has also been demonstrated through the number of awards received by Waterford City Council Central Library, including:

- an Opus Building Award, 2004
- a Royal Institute of Architects in Ireland Award, 2005
- a CILIP Public Library Building Award 2005 – Winner 'Heart of the Community' category
- short-listed for Best Public Building Category LAMA Award 2007

Impact on the community

Waterford Central Library had an estimated 216,836 visitors in 2006, averaging at 716 visitors per open day.

A total of 1741 users joined central library for the first time in 2006. Of these, 517 were foreign nationals, representing almost 30 per cent of the total. People from a total of 68 countries (including Ireland) joined the library. Users who joined the library in 2006 speak over 50 languages.

Not only are our services increasing but our users are becoming more diverse. With the motto 'access for all' the newly refurbished library is building on its traditional role as a 'library for the people'.

Through ongoing consultation – including meeting with residents from the nearby hostel and older people's accommodation; outreach to schools and other young adult meeting places; consultation with multicultural groups; formal alliances with literacy, social welfare, educational groups and informal feedback from events, launches, exhibitions and day-to-day library users – the library service continues to use the space provided to facilitate the changing requirements of its users.

A new Public Library User Survey (PLUS) was carried out in September 2007 and will provide further insight into these library requirements.

In summary, architecturally, the design of the library was based on a holistic concept of flowing sequences of space and complex visual links, which translates on a practical level to provide a sense of harmony and security to users throughout the building. We believe that it works and continues to work in the way a public building in the centre of a busy city should work.

PART 5
Library Refurbishment Programmes – Forging Templates for Building Renewal

From the initial project we drew up a standard fitting-out brief ... with this brief we were able to save time by not having to re-invent the wheel for every library.
– Leicestershire Libraries

Chapter 14

Barnsley Central Library:
There and Back – Remaking Libraries

Kathryn Green, Jane Lee and Wendy Mann

Libraries review – Re-making Libraries

In external assessments, Barnsley library service had consistently been rated as 'Fair' (in the BV Inspection 2001 and the Comprehensive Performance Assessment or CPA of 2003) and was a CPA Improvement Priority for the authority. In light of this, in 2004 a libraries review (*Re-making Libraries*) was undertaken in order to make recommendations for the future improvement of the library service in Barnsley. It analysed the main drivers of the service and strategies to take libraries forward. The resulting cabinet report in November 2005 approved an investment in revenue funding for one year of £200,000 for books and £25,000 for ICT equipment, and a capital sum of £2.122 million for both the central library and the branch library network. A condition of the allocation of capital funding was that further cabinet approval was received for the final refurbishment scheme.

In July 2006 cabinet approved a light refurbishment of the public areas of the central library, including ventilation work, work to meet DDA requirements and maintenance and refurbishment works to bring the library up to modern standards and make it more inviting and attractive to visit. The report also approved the introduction of RFID (Radio Frequency Identification) at the central library as a means to improve access and customer service. RFID also provided the option to extend opening hours without investing in additional staffing and it was also acknowledged that in line with *Framework for the Future* staff could devote more time to serving customers and helping them with their book choices, as well as offering customers the option of privacy on borrowing items of a sensitive nature (e.g. medical books). The technology also provided a new security system and in addition, funding was approved to replace the People's Network equipment. In total, cabinet approval was given for capital expenditure at the central library of £1.665 million.

Background to building

The central library was purpose built and opened in 1975; it is a four-storey, flat-roofed, reinforced concrete frame construction with brick-clad infill walls and elevations, and covers an internal area of 3588m^2. The architect, Victor Lee Son, described the building as 'a deep plan near cube form'. Natural light is provided via full floor-to-ceiling-height windows that are located either side of each external supporting column. Internally the library has solid floors, plastered and painted walls, suspended ceilings, fluorescent strip lighting and a public lift and a staff lift. The original Integrated Environmental Design for heating and ventilation was intended to recover, condition and redistribute the electrical energy expended by the lighting via slot diffusers in the ceilings.

Internally, areas consist of lending and reference facilities, audiovisual materials, a children's library, ICT suites, the archives and local studies department, study support, reserve stacks, meeting rooms, a coffee bar and offices for managers and administration staff.

In 2003, an asset management assessment rated the roof, walls, windows, doors, electrical services and fixed furniture and fittings as 'poor'. There were annual complaints from the public relating to the excessive heat in the building during the summer months, which had increased since the introduction of computers into the building. The condition of the original 1975 shelving which was prone to collapse also presented serious health and safety risks.

In the Adult PLUS survey in 2003–04, only 34 per cent of users rated the interior of the central library as 'very good'; in 2005–06, 60.4 per cent of children rated it 'good'. The central library had also been closed on Thursdays for several years following budget cuts and this was also a cause for complaint, with only 17.2 per cent of users rating the opening hours as 'very good'.

The location of the central library is on a hill, away from the main pedestrian shopping centre and transport interchange. Since it opened in 1975, retail businesses and utility companies have moved away from the street and the library is now relatively isolated in an area consisting mostly of bars and bistros. The result was a steady decline in visitors, and therefore usage, between 2000 and 2004. Book issues declined significantly from 387,187 in 2000–01 to 269,230 in 2005–06.

Visits to other libraries

In preparation for the refurbishment work, the BMBC architect, David Mate, the chief libraries officer and the lending services officer visited other libraries which had recently been refurbished or were new builds attracting positive comment in the professional literature. Visits were made to Brighton, Sutton, Swiss Cottage and Tower Hamlets' Idea Stores. The visits were invaluable for enabling both the architect and library managers to see new designs and layouts and discuss with colleagues in these authorities how the designs worked in practice, the ideas behind the concepts and the issues which had been faced during the contract period.

Design

Following the visit, the findings were shared with other library managers and frontline staff representing all aspects of the service within the central library. This group became the team who looked at design proposals, discussed the implications of changes for service operation and delivery, fed back comments from other staff and highlighted comments previously raised by members of the public, which included:

Air conditioning for the summer.

A more relaxing reading area.

Comfy chair area in café.

Bigger lift to accommodate pushchairs/wheelchairs.

More computers, a place for people to read quietly.

Open Thursdays.

Figure 14.1 Barnsley Central Library, ground floor

The overall remit was to create a modern public library, fit for the 21st century, which would be attractive and encourage more people to visit. In particular the library needed to appear less cluttered, whilst retaining the capacity for the stock, and create definite zones for different aspects of service or user groups (e.g. Sound and Vision, Young Adults).

Particular features of the design were:

- adult non-fiction stock to be located on one floor – previously this was split over two floors
- a quiet study area to be created following complaints about noise travelling through an open plan building
- the central balcony area to be enclosed with a glazed screen
- People's Network PCs to be brought together into a single suite adjacent to the staff enquiry desk
- display areas to be created on the staircases – which were previously open – thus eliminating the risk of injury or antisocial behaviour
- an additional People's Network suite to be created on the ground floor – this was previously used by study support in the children's library
- a study support area to be created on the ground floor alongside the young adults' collection and the sound and vision section – young adult stock has seen an increase in issues of 152.9 per cent
- the children's library to be opened up by removing a wall, and a spectacular seating area created providing a versatile space to be used by children, families, groups or school classes
- the coffee bar to be relocated to increase visibility and re-branded as Café FullStop. Again, a wall would be removed to double the seating area and create a modern bistro-style space
- the lecture theatre to have increased flexibility with the introduction of a second partition allowing the space to be subdivided into smaller seminar rooms, whilst still retaining the capacity to seat 100 for events
- all the meeting rooms to have the latest whiteboard and sympodium technology for presentations
- two new lifts, complying fully with DDA standards with mirrors, Braille panel, sensors and voice alerts for floors to be installed
- ramps, an additional disabled toilet and a new advanced sensory fire alarm system with both voice and flashing light alerts to be introduced to improve the building's access and safety features
- air-conditioning to be installed throughout the building and general repairs made to the roof.

Figure 14.2 Barnsley Central Library, coffee bar

Planning and logistics

The planning process began in March 2006 when a team of staff came together to discuss what would be involved in the whole refurbishment process. The team consisted of three core managers who would eventually see the project through to its conclusion, representatives from each department and other library staff.

From this meeting a logistics document was produced which covered various aspects of the process and the tasks involved. Each person was assigned a number of these tasks. Meetings were held frequently as a very tight timescale was involved. Consideration had to be given to the following topics:

Temporary accommodation for staff

- Where would staff work during the closure period?
- Could staff be utilized at other service points?
- How much space and what facilities would need to be in place – ICT, telephones, toilet facilities, etc.?
- Would the premises be secure?
- What work would staff need to take for the four months?
- What items could be left behind in offices and stacks?
- Could we take advantage of the closure period to offer training or to encourage staff to take annual leave?

After considering several options including a recently closed school, branch library and council offices, the decision was taken to move into a resource centre approximately seven miles away from the central library. Within the centre was an existing branch library which was due to be relocated, office space and storage units. The branch library was relocated to its new home in June 2006 leaving behind a large empty room with toilet and kitchen facilities, phone and ICT connections and alarm. The storage units were alarmed and within a locked compound. Each member of staff was asked to provide a list of what they required to take with them and what ICT they would need. Staff were encouraged to take leave during the closure period and some staff were used to cover holiday absences in other service points. After consultation with the contractors it was decided that any items, which were not needed, could be left in offices and that the books in the stack would be covered over.

Services

- Electricity, water, telephones, post, newspapers, inter library loans, Securicor cash collections, deliveries, cleaners, contracted services, etc. would all need to be disconnected, diverted or temporarily suspended.
- Meters would need to be read.
- Where would we keep cash during this period?
- Where would our delivery van be based?
- How would stationery and supplies be issued to other service points?
- Where would new book deliveries be made and how would these be processed?

A list of all suppliers and services was compiled and each one was contacted to inform them of our temporary relocation. Also all telephones were diverted and arrangements made for staff email accounts to be transferred. The resource centre had its own safe so we were able to utilize that. Our delivery van was temporarily based at another service point and the routes slightly rearranged to make the centre its first and last stop each day. Deliveries of new books were diverted to the centre and as we had ICT access these could be processed and sent out as normal.

Public services and publicity

- How long would we need to close for the work and to empty and refill the shelves etc.?
- Could we provide an alternative location to deliver a public service?
- What would need to be in place in order to do this?
- If this was not possible, what else could we offer?
- Could we offer the home delivery service to the elderly and borrowers unable to travel to other service points?

- How would we provide a requests and archives service, and also answer reference enquiries?
- How would we run the Summer Reading Challenge for children who used the central library?
- What would happen to classes held in the library?
- Could we continue to run our study support sessions in another location?
- What would happen to our regular room-hire and coffee bar customers?
- How and where would we advertise all this to the public?
- Did we have enough time to consult with the public beforehand on designs etc. and then display proposed plans?

The estimated contract period was 14 weeks starting 7 August 2006, and the library closed two weeks prior to this to pack all the books. Originally the central library was due to re-open on 8 January 2007, but due to an extension to the contract period this became 22 January, and staff had approximately three weeks to tag and return 68,000 items to the shelves. Several options were looked at to deliver an alternative service within the town centre but due to the logistics of finding a suitable space and providing the necessary ICT access, as well as health and safety considerations, it was decided to have book drop-off points at town centre locations and encourage borrowers to temporarily use branch, mobile libraries or the home delivery service instead. Archives and local history material would be in storage therefore an 'Out of Office' response was added to the archives e-mail address informing people of the closure and giving details of alternative locations to direct their enquiries. Reference staff were relocated to an office in a large branch library and used reference works and directories to operate an e-mail and telephone enquiry service. Young people were encouraged to participate in the Summer Reading Challenge at branches and study support signposted them to other centres. Regular room-hire customers and classes were informed of our closure and given details of alternative locations which they could use on a temporary basis, one of which was adjacent to the central library and we provided the caretaking support. Publicity material, press releases and radio interviews were used to give information about the temporary arrangements and details of alternative service points for books, ICT access and new facilities. Leaflets were distributed via all branch libraries, health, community, resource and sports centres and other public locations across the borough.

Book stock

- Where and how would we store all the books from the building, including thousands of new, uncatalogued books from an end-of-year buy?
- Could we edit the bookstock before moving?
- Where would we store valuable and irreplaceable archive material?
- Insurance cover would be needed for items in storage.

- How, when and where would we get stock tagged for the new RFID system?
- How, where and when could we train staff on the new RFID system?

All book stock was benchmarked in the weeks leading up to closure so that unwanted material didn't have to be packed and stored, and a book sale was held. As the book stock was stored on site at the resource centre, staff had access in order to catalogue, repair and tag the books for the new RFID system. The majority of tagging and training for RFID wasn't able to take place until we moved back into the central library. Archive material was also stored in a secure unit. For insurance purposes, a value had to be given for all the book stock and furniture in storage.

Removal logistics

- Who would do the removal?
- How would we choose a company?
- Who would empty and re-fill the shelves?
- What furniture could be used, stored or discarded?
- How would we ensure everything reached the correct destination?
- Could we use unwanted furniture in good condition elsewhere within the service?

Quotes were obtained from several removal companies. These were a mixture of local general removals and nationwide companies specializing in business removals. Each one had a tour of the building and a list of locations and items to be moved. A matrix was drawn up so that the quotes could be evaluated and the company chosen then looked at the process in greater detail and visited the three sites. They provided approximately 2200 crates in which to pack the books, bubble wrap for fragile items and special boxes for PCs and also gave advice on packing such as how many books per crate, how high to stack crates and how best to transfer archive material. Each location and category of books was assigned a colour-coded label so that everything reached their intended destination. A schedule was devised for the two-week moving out period and all items were moved in order of priority based on usage. A plan of the room we were moving into was drawn showing location of staff so that ICT, files and personal items could be placed in the correct areas. The move took eight days in total. Prior to the move an inventory of furniture was undertaken. Furniture was either to be kept, re-allocated or discarded. Re-usable items were offered to other service points and then to other council departments. The contractor disposed of discarded furniture. The furniture we needed to keep was moved by the removal company and temporarily stored in another location until the move back.

The interim period

Working with the furnishing company

Three major library furnishing companies were invited to provide a quote based on a design brief produced by the architect. Presentations were held, a scoring matrix was compiled and each submission was examined in detail against the evaluation criteria. Demco Interiors was selected and several design meetings were held. We needed to select colour schemes and confirm furniture for each service area, whilst trying to create a unified look throughout the building. Demco suggested that we select a signature colour for each floor, which we adopted. They were very helpful in making suggestions on colour coordination, carpets, fabrics, furniture, graphics, signage and bespoke items. DDA considerations had to be paramount when choosing colours, especially in relation to access issues and visibility. The library service's display assistant took photographs of local landmarks and these were used as a focal point on hanging banners. During the development of the furnishing scheme our original intention to have a themed children's library was changed to create an area with visual impact without limiting it to a narrow age range. We were especially pleased with the design for a bespoke, tiered, soft seating area with shoe rack and the coloured shelving.

Figure 14.3 Barnsley Central Library, children's seating area

ICT

By 2006, the ICT equipment purchased as part of the NOF Public Libraries ICT programme (People's Network) was becoming slow and giving rise to complaints. The refurbishment was an opportune time to replace the existing kit. Demco suggested the introduction of new 'Sawtooth' IT desks to be used for both the People's Network and study support PCs. As we already had ICAM as the PC management system, this was extended to cover all 30 public access PCs on the ground and first floor. We are pleased to say that these machines are now in use for a large percentage of our opening hours.

RFID

During the time we were in our alternative premises we also needed to look at acquiring the new RFID system. Prior to drawing up the specification library managers had attended the CILIP RFID Conference and also had presentations by potential providers. Fortunately, in the library world colleagues are quite often willing to share their work and expertise and we were able to draw on information shared by other library services in drawing up our specification. At one point in the process it was thought that the implementation of RFID could be included in the general refurbishment contract, but unfortunately this wasn't the case and it had to be managed separately. The tender documents were prepared in conjunction with the strategic IT team and signed-off in August 2006 and evaluation of the tenders took place in September. Site visits to other libraries were arranged during October and the tender evaluation was completed with recommendations in the first week of November. We received the go-ahead to place the order on 16 November and once this was finalized our initial meeting with the chosen supplier, Intellident, took place eight days later. Now we were finally able to start tagging the stock. Intellident worked very closely with us to ensure we met our very tight deadline and despite one or two setbacks, primarily with the integration of the new RFID technology and our existing library management system (Dynix Classic), we are pleased to say that we did have the stock tagged and the RFID system in place for the re-opening. The RFID hardware, software and training was delivered in early December and the staff worked furiously to tag and convert the 62,000 books which had to go back onto the open shelves for when the central library re-opened.

Issues

During the course of the refurbishment, fortnightly site meetings were held with the contractors (George Hurst Ltd) and the other council departments involved. These were facilitated by the architect and it was here that clarity was sought, progress reported and issues and delays raised. Several major issues did arise which included:

- Asbestos was found in some areas which it was not possible to survey whilst the library was still open. This had to be safely encapsulated.
- Due to the installation of air-conditioning and new fire alarm systems, the ceilings in staff areas had to be replaced. Originally these were to be repaired, but the damage was prohibitively extensive.
- The lift shafts needed a good deal more work in terms of strengthening than was originally anticipated and resulted in the lifts not being commissioned until after Christmas, with the subsequent effect on the return of stock.
- Several elements of the design and colour scheme had to be amended at short notice due to the unavailability of certain items, particularly the carpets, and requirements of DDA.
- In addition to the central library refurbishment, our largest and busiest branch was also refurbished between October 2006 and February 2007, so there were also design and planning meetings around this. During December 2006 work at a further branch, involving a new counter area, carpet and decoration, was undertaken.

The move back

No sooner had we moved out of the building than it seemed it was time to start planning the whole process in reverse. The return journey was slightly easier as it was just a case of getting everything back to one central location rather than three different ones. The colour coded label system was used again but instead of different locations the colours were used to reflect different floors within the library. Staff, ICT and files were labelled with the owner's names and the relevant floor and we had to ensure that there was someone on each floor during the moving back period to direct the removal company to the correct offices.

Snags and problems

Once back in the central library, we had only two weeks to start unpacking, continue tagging, reshelve the books and put furniture and other items away. This is when snags and problems came to light such as damage to some items, wrong furniture being supplied, insufficient data and telephone points on one desk and faulty plasma screen connections.

Over the following months a snags list was compiled and items rectified within the 12-month defect period.

Impact and evaluation

The central library re-opened on 22 January 2007 preceded by publicity in the local press and on the radio. The library was officially reopened by the mayor and cabinet spokesperson for children, young people and families on 1 March 2007 (World Book Day) and was celebrated with visits by local authors.

As the figures below reveal, the overall issue figures for the central library show an increase of 10.7 per cent. Comparisons beyond July 2007 are not available as the library closed in August 2006. Most categories of stock show an increase in usage due to the refurbishment, increase in new members and the addition of new stock. The decreases within the fiction paperback category are probably best explained by the reduction in the number of paperback stands (which will be addressed in the future); and talking books which did not receive any significant amount of new stock prior to the re-opening.

Table 14.1 Barnsley Central Library: Comparative issue and membership statistics 2006 and 2007

Category	2006 (Feb–July)	2007 (Feb–July)	Variation
Foreign language	288	239	-17%
Adult non-fiction	33 955	36 106	+6.3%
Fiction	36 458	36 548	+0.2%
Fiction paperback	2 133	1 449	-32.1%
Graphic novels	189	596	+215.%
Large print	3 262	4 228	+29.%
Young adult	382	966	+152.9%
Children's	21 883	29 469	+34.7%
Parent's collection	484	691	+42.8%
Music CDs	1 944	2 465	+26.8%
Talking books	1 218	772	-36.65%
Children's CDs	96	228	+137.5%
DVDs	1 885	2 475	+31.3%
Overall issues	107 220	118 730	+10.7%
New members	855	1 686	+97.2%

Feedback from the public has been positive regarding the fresh look of the revamped interior, the spacious feel and modern décor. The children's library in particular has received very favourable comments and the café has achieved the desired impact with its relocation, comfortable leather sofas, chairs and new bistro style menu. Negative comments were mostly related to the new shelving, which has a low-level bottom shelf whereas the original shelving started at knee height. We are attempting to rectify this by using the bottom shelves as face-on display.

The Barnsley Coalition of Disabled People was invited to tour the building and comment on difficult areas prior to the refurbishment. Following a return visit the group nominated the central library for an Access for All Award specifically for enabling independent access to information and resources. The citation read 'Our audit process shows that since the refurbishment, it is considered by our committee that your premises has achieved a Gold Standard and is accessible for most types of disability'.

The central library has been visited by colleagues from library authorities throughout the country and received positive feedback. Any authority planning a refurbishment is welcome to visit and discuss our experience in more detail.

Notes

Barnsley Central Library (1975) Official opening pamphlet, Barnsley, Barnsley Metropolitan Borough Council.

Barnsley Metropolitan Borough Council (2001) *Libraries, Best Value Inspection.* London, Best Value Inspection Service (September).

BMBC, Children and Young Peoples Services Spokesperson (2006) *Refurbishment of the Central Library* (Cab.19.7.2006/11.1), Barnsley, Barnsley Metropolitan Borough Council.

BMBC, Education Spokesperson (2005) *Libraries Review: Remaking Libraries* (Cab.30.11.2005/9).

Institute of Public Finance, Barnsley Metropolitan Borough Council PLUS Survey (2003) *Combined Weighted Authority and Service Point Report* (November), London, The Chartered Institute of Public Finance and Accountancy.

Institute of Public Finance (2005) *Barnsley MBC Children's PLUS Survey Combined Weighted Authority and Service Point Report* (October), London, The Chartered Institute of Public Finance and Accountancy.

Chapter 15

Coalville, Birstall and Enderby Libraries, Leicestershire: Case Studies in Renewal

Margaret Bellamy

Background

Leicestershire is a mainly rural county which has 54 static libraries. They are organized into three levels: seven major, eight shopping centre and 39 community or village libraries.

After several years of little investment in the library buildings, a review panel of elected members found that 'the network of buildings, many temporary, many too small and all under resourced, is substandard'. This was reinforced by an Audit Commission Best Value inspection in 2002 which identified that 'A number of library buildings are in poor condition, too small, badly-located or housed in temporary premises'. As a result of this, the County Council set a capital budget of £5 million to rebuild or renovate 40 of the libraries from 2002 to 2008. The county council recognized the role that a revitalized library service could play in helping to meet its corporate objectives. In its Medium Term Corporate Strategy it gave a commitment to 'Improve the access to and the quality of libraries'. Criteria were devised to identify the priority buildings and a programme devised. Priority for rebuilding was given to those temporary buildings which were in a poor physical state, and most have now been replaced with purpose-built libraries. Other criteria used were: usage, suitability of the building, state of the building and its décor, cost-effectiveness, potential for partnership working, and location.

As at March 2008, 34 have been completed, and another 10 are in the pipeline. It is expected that the programme will continue after that date.

Funding

As well as funding from the Medium Term Corporate Strategy, capital has been obtained from:

- the local Leicester Shire Economic Partnership, to create access centres in five libraries
- cooperation with parish and other local councils
- partnership with developers

- contributions from other county council departments which recognize the role which libraries play in delivering their priorities
- funding to improve the disabled access to buildings
- money from VAT refund
- Section 106 (developer contribution) money.

Planning for change

We had to be clear of our objectives before starting the programme and what we wanted from the end result. The two reports published by CABE (*Better Public Libraries* and *21st Century Libraries*) gave us a good starting point from a non-library perspective. We had the results of the Public Library Users Survey which highlighted what our customers wanted from a library service. We also held discussions with staff at all levels and visited other authorities.

With the first library which we refurbished we employed a consultancy which brought in outside experience, which helped to modify and improve our ideas.

The overall objective was to create a library which people would be attracted to use, one in which there was space to browse and meet and chat to friends. The library needed to create enough space for a really good children's area in which activities could take place without disrupting the service. We wanted to create a 'wow' factor on entering.

There needed to be zones in the larger libraries so that people using the library for different purposes could do so without impinging on other users. The design needed to create two main areas: quiet for study and browsing, and noisy for activities. If the library was large enough, we wanted to create a separate teenage space. The basic concept is that a user enters the library into an open space, which has the quick choice books and a browser area. Beyond that is the rest of the adult fiction. Talking books, large print and newspapers are put near to each other with tables and chairs. The reference, local studies and adult non-fiction are placed beyond the counter along with the PCs. The children's area is the opposite side of the library from this area and linked to the adult fiction. The teenage area is located near to the DVDs and sound recordings and where possible is a defined separate space.

A crucial element in the design was to create an open and informal look when first entering the library, so counters are moved away from the door whenever possible. At Ashby de la Zouch Library we moved the counter from immediately inside the door to the back of the library, which opened up the whole area so much that one regular reader was convinced that a wall had been removed.

Some of the buildings have been adapted from other uses, like schools and factories, and so can be awkward shapes or be on two levels, so one aim for these was to offer a cohesive whole.

How we did it

Library services are part of the Community Services Department, which has a facilities team of four. We work with them and with the staff of the County Council's Property Section. Outside architects are employed for the new builds but all the refurbishments are managed in-house. A capital programme project board manages the overall programme and every project has its own project team which consists of a member of the facilities team and local staff.

From the initial project we drew up a standard fitting-out brief which covers colours to use, standard furnishings, space allocation, lighting levels, overall layout and design. With this brief we are able to save time by not having to re-invent the wheel for every library. Cost-effectiveness is ensured by bulk purchasing such items as shelving, by recycling materials and furnishings between libraries, and having standard designs for furniture.

The initial brief was to produce a scheme which would not date so we went for a classical blue and white, with an accent colour of yellow in the children's area. The shelving was kept to white metal and the furniture in beech, with soft furnishings in blue. The colour scheme has helped to give the libraries a much lighter and brighter look than before and makes the space look larger. One advantage of the project brief is that by keeping to it we are creating a corporate look for all the libraries. Several of our borrowers use more than one library and they can identify where or how to find what they want. Another key element in the design is a deliberate lack of clutter; posters and leaflets are kept to minimum with most being kept in folders, not on the notice boards.

The final crucial factor is the lighting. This is upgraded to lux levels of between 400 and 600 with additional wall or spot lights to add atmosphere.

We employ a local firm of shop fitters who are very cost-effective and also bring in new ideas for furniture and layouts. As they worked with us on the projects, their knowledge has developed and has added to the final finish.

The key elements of the look are:

- a browser area with soft furnishings
- a larger children's area which is bright and attractive and large enough for activities
- improved disabled access, into and inside the buildings
- additional PCs
- zoned areas for different users and activities
- a more open and spacious feeling
- improved levels of lighting
- a different atmosphere from that of the older-style libraries.

Post-refurbishment reviews

After every project there is a debrief meeting and from this the best practice is identified and used to update the design brief. After six to eight weeks the library is reviewed and any changes made if necessary. An 18-month review assesses the success of the project by looking at users' comments, performance statistics and staff comments and again reviews the overall layout of the library. At this stage a final report is produced which includes an evaluation of the cost-effectiveness of the project.

Results

Leicestershire County Council has a standard look for its libraries, which the public can recognize.

> They look modern and welcoming and the ambience has changed to be more relaxed (and noisier!).

> Issues and visitors have increased the last 12 months, by 3.82 per cent for issues and by 11 per cent for visitors. These are being maintained 18 months later at the initial libraries to be changed. One community library increased its issues by over 350 per cent.

> We are attracting new users who are not traditional library customers.

> Other organizations are seeing the library service as a good partner to work with.

> Customer comments overall are very positive about the new look libraries and people tend to stay longer.

> In the latest Public Library User Survey (PLUS) overall user satisfaction with the service has increased to 96 per cent.

Case studies

Whilst the principles which we use are the same for the three levels of library, in practice there are differences in scope so the case studies highlight one library for each tier.

Case study 1: Coalville Library

Coalville is one of seven major libraries in the county servicing a population of approximately 33,000. It is 625m² and was opened in 1971. The building is a large rectangle with windows down one side, a set of small rooms which could be used for private study and a larger meeting room.

Figure 15.1 Leicestershire County Library Service, Coalville Library

Coalville was selected as it had had no major work done to it since it opened in 1971 and was very dowdy, outdated in its layout and visually unappealing. The whole appearance was off-putting and gloomy with a brown carpet and shelves. The layout was rigid with the shelves arranged in long rows down the library and no comfortable areas provided for sitting. The computers for the People's Network had been slotted in to where space could be found, which was not the best place for them. The centre was dominated by a large reader's advisory (RA) desk and the counter was situated in a dark entrance hall which was very difficult to access by anyone in a wheelchair or with a pushchair. The local studies were divided between two different rooms and, as one was the meeting room, sometimes not open for use.

Coalville was performing below the average for the major libraries on all its performance measures, especially for stock, and its visitors and issues were continuing to decline.

Money became available from a VAT refund, and also from a successful bid, to open an access centre in the library.

Coalville was the second library to be refurbished and the principles used in the initial project were applied to create a light and open feeling.

Meetings were held between the head of library services, the in-house facilities team and the local library manager and staff to work out the general appearance and layout. The project went smoothly, helped by the staff remaining on site in the workroom area so they could deal quickly with any queries from the builders and fitters.

The library was only closed for two months and an alternative service offered from a local museum.

The design brief was to improve the access, make the layout more user-friendly, improve the lighting levels and rationalize the layout, especially the use of the study rooms. Major internal works were the removal of the screen which created the entrance hall, taking out all the internal partitions and creating new rooms and moving the counter and RA desk. This allowed users to come straight into the library without any barriers. New interior rooms were created which brought local studies together in one room and created a separate room for the access centre.

The library was rearranged with the children's area being moved from a dark corner into the window area, a browser area created with sofas, low tables and a coffee machine immediately inside the entrance. The RA desk and the counter were put together to make one point of contact for the public.

The final layout has given a more spacious look, areas of use have been zoned with the busier and noisier areas at the front and the study areas at the back. The children's area has been made bigger, allowing for more activities to take place. A separate teenager area was also created.

The response from the public has been good. In the latest PLUS over 90 per cent of the users rated the interior attractiveness as good or very good. Visitor numbers have increased by 40 per cent and issues are still continuing to rise by 2 per cent per annum. A wider range of people now use the library and tend to stay for longer, the browser area especially has proved popular.

The first review of the access centre noted that it had met the majority of its three-year targets in the first year. In the initial months after re-opening the new access centre did create difficulties, with large numbers of disruptive teenagers using it and driving away families and older users. By working with other agencies, and by banning the use of chatrooms, this has been resolved.

At the 18-month review minor changes were made to the layout, in the light of experience gained from other projects and to keep the library looking interesting.

Case study 2: Birstall Library

Birstall Library is a shopping centre library, serving a population of 12,000. It is in a rapidly growing commuter town.

It is a two-storey building, built in 1980 and covering 470m². The space was difficult due to the number of pillars, the position of a staircase, the arrangement of the rooms upstairs and the odd shape of the building. The original design for the upstairs included a staff workroom, community meeting space and children's library. Access from the lift to the children's area was through the meeting space which over the years had become the library storage area. On the ground floor about half had a low, dark wooden ceiling which housed the lending stock on high metal shelves, creating a cave-like atmosphere. The more open parts of the library were used for the PCs, reference and local studies stock. Entrance was made difficult by double doors on a lobby area.

Its performance was below average for a shopping centre library and, although it is situated next door to a primary school, it was underused by children and parents. There were problems with the use of the children's area in the evening when all the staff were downstairs.

The design brief was to make the library more user-friendly, create more library space, improve the children's area and improve the staff working area. Several ideas were discussed including bringing the children's library downstairs and putting the adult non-fiction, reference, local studies and PCs upstairs; filling in some of the odd corners and building out under the upstairs overhang; and removing the entrance lobby. However, due to the constraints on usable space and the costs associated with the building work most of the ideas were proved to be impractical which meant that the layout of adult's area downstairs and children's area upstairs had to remain. The gain in space from altering the footprint of the building was too expensive to be cost effective. The only building work which was undertaken was the removal of the lobby.

The major changes were upstairs where the junior area was completely remodelled and all internal walls removed. The children's area was made larger and re-sited next to the lift and the staff workroom and a community room rebuilt at the other end.

Downstairs the ceiling was painted to lighten it and new lower-level white shelving used. The computers were moved and the entrance area became a browser area with quick choice fiction, sound recordings and DVDs. The lending area was changed so that it had the advantage of the more open space.

This was one of the more difficult projects due to its internal layout. Several ideas had to be abandoned, either because of cost or the physical constraints of the building. As the project progressed, ideas and solutions had to be found quickly to overcome the unexpected; for example, when the lobby was removed the ceiling was discovered to be a different height to the rest of the building so a way had to be found to disguise the join.

Since re-opening, Birstall Library's overall issues have increased by 48 per cent and those for children by 66 per cent; visitors have increased by 16 per cent. In the Public Library Users Survey over 95 per cent rated the library's attractiveness as good or very good. It has also attracted more community use, such as a regular Internet training course.

Figure 15.2 Leicestershire County Library Service, Birstall Library, children's area

Case study 3: Enderby Library

Enderby is one of 39 community libraries; it serves a village with a population of 6000. The library is 218m^2 and is situated in part of a community complex. It is a good size and shape for its purpose. It was opened in 1986 and the walls were decorated in orange hessian, with brown carpet and shelves; it has not been decorated since its opening. The layout was traditional with long rows of parallel shelving. A major drawback of the layout was that the PCs were in the centre of the library and the teenagers using them caused disruption to borrowers. However, a good feature was the size and position of the children's area. The library was well used by children and teenagers, especially the PCs.

The brief was to modernize the library in the new style, create a teenage area with its own PCs and break up the formal layout. The staff were involved in the brief and worked with a group of local teenagers to design this area.

Access centre funding was obtained for the project, providing that it could be completed within three months. This created difficulties in getting contractors on site and in ordering materials. The library closed for one month for the work to take place and it was completed on time. The library reopened in April 2007 and to date it has been impossible to assess the long-term impact. However, comments from users have been positive and more teenagers are using the library but with less disruption to other users.

Figure 15.3 Leicestershire County Library Service, Enderby Library

Chapter 16

North Yorkshire Libraries: Creating a New Library Brand

Julie Blaisdale

In 2001, the future of the library and information service in North Yorkshire looked relatively uncertain. As in many other local authorities' services, book and audiovisual issues, income and visitor numbers were declining.

In order to identify why customers were not using the service, an external market research company Market Profiles were commissioned to survey non-library users in key locations throughout the county in 2002. Their brief was to:

- determine why people were not making use of library facilities
- explore attitudes and perceptions of libraries amongst non-users
- identify levels of awareness of services and facilities currently offered by the library service
- identify services which are required to encourage greater usage in the future.

Six focus groups were convened across the county. Some of the reasons for not using libraries that were identified as part of the survey included:

- uncomfortable/unappealing buildings
- staff attitudes
- out-of-date, old-fashioned stock
- high charges
- unsuitable opening times.

When respondents to the survey were asked to describe their image of a library 34 per cent said 'quiet'. It was difficult to ascertain precisely whether this was a positive or negative image, except that it was often accompanied by other negative descriptions, such as dull, boring and old-fashioned.

Comments about the fabric of buildings included

It's horrible, you couldn't settle down in a comfy chair and read a book in there.

I know it needs to be functional but it could be more comfortable.

It's a small room with one big table and plastic chairs. Everybody stares at you when you walk in.

Libraries have to grow with the times; it's just stuck in the Dark Ages.

When asked for suggestions about how to make the library service more appealing respondents replied:

It needs to be bright and inviting with lots of daylight and easy parking.

Somewhere more inviting, so you don't just walk past thinking it's another office.

Bulldoze it down and build another one.

Suggestions about possible internal layouts included:

Have separate sections to allow for kids to be in there as well as for people to study.

Allow us to have some personal space.

Table 16.1 Refurbished libraries in North Yorkshire

Library	Opened
Selby	September 2003
Scarborough	October 2003
Gargrave	January 2004
Northallerton	February 2004
Sherburn	April 2004
Crosshills	July 2004
Ayton	August 2004
Colburn	August 2004
Tadcaster	October 2004
Scalby	November 2004
Easingwold	November 2004
Hawes	April 2005
Stokesley	September 2005
Pickering	September 2005
Boroughbridge	December 2005
Eastfield	October 2005
Knaresborough	June 2006
Whitby	December 2006

From a corporate perspective, the library service had begun to be regarded as an important means of delivering the council's Public Access Strategy, a method of providing access to a range of services including those of the county and district councils as well as those of other partners.

In order to deliver the Public Access Strategy, £6.2 million was invested in a programme of refurbishments which would transform the overall look and feel of the libraries. Opening hours were revisited and the consultation with customers and non-users was used to inform how services would be designed and developed and many were extended and changed to reflect customer demand. Every member of staff also received customer care training.

Planning and design

Selby was the first library to be partially refurbished to accommodate a new visitor information function. Interestingly the 'library' part of the building remained untouched and as a result, library performance did not improve. The visitor information centre was a success and now manages over 2000 enquiries per year.

Scarborough Library and Information Centre was the first of the new fully refurbished sites. At the outset it was clear that the library, which had been largely untouched since its opening in 1934, had to look like a library fit for the 21st century. The interior of the building consisted of a number of separate areas, most of which would need to be opened up if a range of services were to be delivered.

Once the design and layout for this library had been agreed, they formed the template for other sites in the refurbishment programme. Design company 'Indigo 6' were commissioned to come up with a range of design options and colour schemes based around a corporate colour scheme, effectively a new 'brand' for the library service in North Yorkshire. All libraries would have the same colour scheme throughout, shelving and furniture would be from the same ranges, the counters would all have a fluid look, external signage and internal guiding would be the same (even down to the wording used) and staff uniforms would be introduced. As well as looking professional and providing a very definite image, branding also made sense in practical terms. Shelving layouts, guiding and signage and additional items could be altered and exchanged with other sites in the knowledge that this would have no effect on the aesthetic of the interior. We wanted customers to be able to immediately recognize that they were in a 'North Yorkshire Library' and to feel instantly familiar with the surroundings.

The branding of the new libraries in North Yorkshire took away the need to consider colour schemes for every site and left library staff free to focus on public consultation, staff training, stock acquisition and the design of internal layouts.

**Figure 16.1 North Yorkshire County Libraries, Knaresborough
Library, exterior**

Each of the projects went out to tender, involving a variety of architects and
contractors with each redesign. All were provided with a specification on which to
base their tender, which had to be sympathetic to the needs of the service with an
understanding of what the end product had to deliver.

Each of the refurbishments was led by a service head, support services manager
and a local area manager. The service head was the main point of contact with the
contractor and architect, with a brief to ensure that the specification was adhered

to and that the branding was applied effectively and consistently across every site. Operational issues associated with the project and the local manager and links liaison as required with the local contractor was dealt with by the support services manager. The architect or designer provided a schedule before work began so that everyone knew what was happening when.

Some of the key issues that were identified as part of the refurbishment programme included the following. How do you continue to provide a service whilst a library is being refurbished? This is particularly important if there are no other local libraries to absorb some of the business. If you do provide an alternative service where is it provided from and how? All our refurbished sites have offered an alternative service, either from spare mobile vehicles parked on or near the existing library or on alternative sites – local schools and vacant buildings for example. How will items be issued? What stock will be taken to the alternative site? Will the service be pared down (generally just book loans)? Will staff need to be relocated to other libraries?

Consultation

Consultation with existing and potential customers covered a range of methods such as working parties, focus groups and straightforward questionnaires. At some sites customers (selected by a competition) were also involved in buying stock for refurbished sites. It was not always possible to include everything customers wanted and it is important to acknowledge this as part of the consultation.

When the building is handed over

Once the building work had been completed, it was handed over to the library service. Prior to this shelving plans had been devised and ordered. Front-line staff were involved in the process which also incorporated comments received from the public consultation – both groups were knowledgeable and had valuable opinions on effective layouts.

Additional items were also ordered – display stands, seating, desks etc., and extras that improve the overall finish of refurbished sites including:

- high-quality drinks machines (which we use with cups and saucers, not plastic cups) to create café areas
- dishwashers for staff which maintain high standards of hygiene, and save staff time
- bespoke counters
- teenage areas with games consoles
- spaces that are fully DDA compliant, including toilets and baby-changing facilities

- display cabinets selling goods and products by local designers and craftsmen.

Figure 16.2 North Yorkshire County Libraries, Knaresborough Library, interior

Once the libraries actually opened, there were programmes of events and marketing promotions that usually lasted for at least one month. These included author visits, open days for local organizations and information days for families, as well as IT sessions for customers and visits by local schools.

In the light of the Market Profiles research, opening hours had to be reconsidered. Were libraries open when people wanted them to be? As a result of North Yorkshire's refurbishment programme, four sites at Knaresborough, Pickering, Scarborough and Selby now open on a Sunday. Fifteen out of eighteen refurbished sites have seen their opening hours increased, with the majority of these being outside 9am – 5pm.

Effect and outcomes

It is clear that the refurbishment projects have had a dramatic impact on the quality and delivery of services. They have not simply represented cosmetic change but fundamental transformational change throughout the service. For the programme to have succeeded in the way that it has, it is important to have committed staff willing to embrace change, and a corporate vision that is supported at the highest levels by both officers and elected members.

We have transformed libraries into spaces where whole sectors of communities can regularly meet, with meeting and interview rooms of various sizes and comfortable waiting areas, which can also be used when customers need to use the service of one of our many partner agencies.

The library service is marketed – as 'New Look, No Shush' to external organizations in an attempt to alter preconceptions and challenge stereotypes. This has helped raise our profile when working with partners such as district and parish councils, job centres, and the police. We actively market all our services through regular press releases and enjoy a close working relationship with the internal communications unit.

Figure 16.3 North Yorkshire County Libraries, Eastfield Library, interior

The outcomes from our refurbishment programme have exceeded all our expectations. Issue figures, income and visitor numbers have all increased. On average, book issues increased by 25 per cent. At some of our 'older' refurbishments this trend has continued during 2006–07. Children's book issues have risen a further 16 per cent. The additional revenue funding put into stock and opening hours also supports staff when promoting the library service to schools and other visiting groups.

Staff feel they now have the right 'look and feel' to promote the service, finding it easier to promote a service they believe in and we are now proud to invite any organization to share use of our buildings.

The service looks more professional, is challenging perceptions and as a result external agencies are now working with us in increasing numbers. The library service in North Yorkshire is seen as a forward-thinking organization that embraces change with some agencies now co-located within our buildings. For example a number of libraries offer services such as payment facilities for council tax, housing advice centres, registration services, Business Link and Tourist Information.

In addition, our willingness to deliver non-traditional library services alongside existing ones means that the library service remains at the heart of the council's corporate vision for its frontline services, and is able to engage more effectively for local communities.

Table 16.2 North Yorkshire libraries: Evaluation of refurbishments

Library		Date closed		Date opened		Closure period
Scarborough		25 June 2003		10 October 2003		107 days
Gross capital budget	Net capital budget	Total capital spend	Total revenue spend	Stock expenditure	Staffing (extra hours)	Total cost of project
£619 700	£514 700	£575 491	£178 000	£100 000	173 staff hours to extend opening by 18 hours per week	£753 491
		November 2001 – October 2002		November 2003 – October 2004		% change
Total book issues						
Total income generated		£55 451		£86 593		£31 141 (56%)
Total number of AV issues		240 154		258 660		+8%
Total number of new members		1 584		3 150		+99%
Total number of computer sessions		Not available		59 245		N/A
Total number of visitors		Not available		393 640		N/A

Library		Date closed		Date opened		Closure period
Northallerton		1 November 2003		20 February 2004		79 days
Gross capital budget	Net capital budget	Total capital spend	Total revenue spend	Stock expenditure	Staffing (extra hours)	Total cost of project
£493 000	£393 000	£450 979	£60 000	£60 000	No increase in staffing but opening hours increased by 4 per week	£510 979
		March 2002 – February 2003		March 2004 – February 2005		% change
Total book issues		144 741		152 390		+5%
Total income generated		£25 696		£29 737		+£4 0410 (16%)
Total number of AV issues		13 071		15 393		+15%
Total number of new members		1 391		1 609		+16%
Total number of computer sessions		2 633		17 291		+557%
Total number of visitors		149 812		152 816		+2%

Library		Date closed		Date opened		Closure period
Colburn		29 November 2003		11 August 2004		256 days
Gross capital budget	Net capital budget	Total capital spend	Total revenue spend	Stock expenditure	Staffing (extra hours)	Total cost of project
£815 000	£100 000	£100 000	£23 600	£20 000	8 hours per week added to extend opening hours by 7 hours per week	£123 600
		September 2002 – February 2003		September 2004 – February 2005		% change
Total book issues		11 859		14 828		+25%
Total income generated		£1 035.60		£1 920.58		+85%
Total number of AV issues		417		646		+55%
Total number of new members		179		419		+134%
Total number of computer sessions		367		2 197		+499%
Total number of visitors		Not available		11 875		N/A

Library		Date closed		Date opened		Closure period
Sherburn		29 January 2004		8 April 2004		70 days
Gross capital budget	Net capital budget	Total capital spend	Total revenue spend	Stock expenditure	Staffing (extra hours)	Total cost of project
£195 200	£195 200	£195 300	£25 200	£20 00	11.5 hpw	£220 500
		May 2002 – February 2003		May 2004 – February 2005		% change
Total book issues		43 941		56 111		+28%
Total income generated		£5.410		£7 237		+34%
Total number of AV issues		2 392		4 488		+98%
Total number of new members		379		1 330		+251%
Total number of computer sessions		613		6 143		+902%
Total number of visitors		N/A		33 880		N/A

Library		Date closed		Date opened		Closure period
Crosshills		29 May 2004		22 July 2004		54 days
Gross capital budget	Net capital budget	Total capital spend	Total revenue spend	Stock expenditure	Staffing (extra hours)	Total cost of project
£35 250	£25 000	25 000	£10 250	£8 000	5 hpw	£35 250
		August 2003 – February 2004		August 2004 – February 2005		% change
Total book issues		12 354		15 414		+25%
Total income generated		£815		£1 443		+77%
Total number of AV issues		359		1 049		+192%
Total number of new members		140		448		+220%
Total number of computer sessions		1 101		1 474		+34%
Total number of visitors		6 786		8 294		+22%

Library		Date closed		Date opened		Closure period
Whitby		27 February 2006		7 December 2006		282 days
Gross capital budget	Net capital budget	Total capital spend	Total revenue spend	Stock expenditure	Staffing (extra hours)	Total cost of project
£475 000	£450 000	£450 000	£25 000	£60 000	0	£500 000
		January 2005 – September 2005		January 2007 – September 2007		% change
Total book issues		65 504		86 462		+32%
Total income generated		£6 236		£13 352		+114%
Total number of AV issues		5 773		7 181		+24%
Total number of new members		700		2 306		+229%
Total number of computer sessions		9 613		14 150		+47%
Total number of visitors		N/A		88 649		n/a

Library		Date closed		Date opened		Closure period
Knaresborough		19 November 2005		29 June 2006		230 days
Gross capital budget	Net capital budget	Total capital spend	Total revenue spend	Stock expenditure	Staffing (extra hours)	Total cost of project
£485 000	£450 000	£450 000	£35 000	£60 000	0	£520
		July 2004 – June 2005		June 2006 – June 2007		% change
Total book issues		125 000		159 549		+28%
Total income generated		£14 232		£19 683		+38%
Total number of AV issues		8 952		11 065		+23%
Total number of new members		830		1 758		+111%
Total number of computer sessions		12 163		18 228		+49%
Total number of visitors		164 726		208 634		+26%

Lowestoft, Stowmarket, Lakenheath and Felixstowe Libraries, Suffolk: Refurbishments that are Prize-winners

Mike Ellwood

Lowestoft – the sunrise library

Lowestoft is the most easterly point in Britain, on the north Suffolk coast. It has a population of about 58,000. In common with other seaside towns it has been suffering from economic decline with the run-down of traditional industries like fishing, low wages, unemployment and low inward investment. Fifty-two per cent of the population lived in wards listed amongst the 2000 most deprived in the country. It is relatively isolated from the rest of the country because of poor transport links.

The current library, replacing the 1905 Carnegie Library destroyed during the Second World War, opened in 1975 after many delays, but was very much a Sixties landmark building designed for a county borough. It even included a meeting room for the library committee! It is on three floors plus a basement, with the top floor as a staff area. There was lots of wood panelling and open staircases and a foyer paved with blue slate. It had a mezzanine floor above the lending library, a large traditional reference library upstairs, a record library and a separate children's library but included real innovations, such as a darkroom in the basement for hire, a coffee bar and a large meeting room with stage and projection facilities. It is in a good location next to the bus station and car parks, and just behind the main shopping street.

Why was a refurbishment needed?

The building was proving very inflexible as service ambitions changed. Services had been put into the building, such as the Schools Library Service, which took a lot of the staff floor, and in 1986 a branch of the Suffolk Record Office, which occupied half the reference library and half the basement. The introduction of ICT caused even more pressure on space.

Various piecemeal changes had been made over the years to alleviate the pressures. The doors from the mezzanine to the reference library were removed to improve access, the traditional in/out counter was removed to ease flow, and eventually the reference library was moved out onto the mezzanine to make room for lending stock.

A new shopping precinct and market square were built between the library and the main shopping street so another entrance was created. This required a corridor and entrance lobby to be carved out of the children's library taking away about a third of the space and most of the windows, making it very stuffy and awkwardly shaped.

Mechanical and electrical services were getting to the end of their designed life, especially the lifts which were very unreliable. The shelving was failing and had only been partially replaced with a different system. The 'new' carpet on the ground floor had been patched but was threadbare. So the whole building was looking very shabby and run-down. It suffered from overheating when the sun shone, but was cold in winter. The heating system was a complicated mixture of radiators, convectors and underfloor with inadequate controls, which baffled everyone who tried to deal with it.

The record office search room had proved to be very successful and needed more space and investment to meet its rigorous inspection requirements but looked very temporary and didn't afford suitable levels of security or acceptable environmental conditions. The coffee shop was hidden away upstairs with only borrowed natural light and looked dated. The building urgently needed a radical rethink to bring it up to standard and present services appropriately.

The scheme

It soon became apparent that Suffolk Libraries would not be able to access sufficient funds to cover everything that needed to be done. However, being in a designated Objective 2 area the project was eligible for European funding. The New Opportunities Fund (NOF) was also running its Community Access to Lifelong Learning programme at that time. A complicated funding package was put together by an external funding officer, who wrote bids for funding from NOF CALL (New Opportunities Fund, Community Access to Lifelong Learning) and the European Regional Development Fund (ERDF). Suffolk Libraries could provide the match funding from their accumulated capital allocations.

The project, known as ASK Lowestoft, obtained the NOF CALL money but then there were long delays in getting the ERDF funding decision. It got to the stage where NOF was going to take the money back because the programme was finishing and nothing had started, before the final decision was given on the ERDF application. Meeting the NOF deadline drove the project on, so the pressure was not entirely unhelpful but was very worrying at the time. Reconciling the timetables and deadlines of different bodies seems to be a major problem for projects reliant on funds from more than one source, as they never match but are interdependent as far as the project is concerned. In addition, as the scheme developed it became apparent that the library capital was insufficient; fortunately Suffolk Libraries were able to access the newly created County Council Single Capital Pot to cover the shortfall.

Given the time it had taken to develop the project it was hardly surprising that some of the basic ideas and assumptions began to change. It began to experience 'project creep'. The council was looking to introduce a local service centre with Waveney District Council and the library was an ideal location. This brought its own contribution to the funding. Then to create more space it was agreed to relocate the Schools Library Service to more suitable premises, which needed to be done during the works. The North Lowestoft Sure Start was beginning as the project got under way and they contributed funding for a toy library, which also needed to be accommodated.

The brief

The final brief was to fill in the mezzanine floor and maximize space. This would then accommodate a learning centre on the first floor, a public access service centre on the ground floor, and a properly designed record office search room. In addition heating, lighting, data cabling and power were to be updated and the lifts replaced. Energy efficiency and solar gain were to be reviewed. It was going to stretch the budget to the limit so the basement and the top, staff only, floor were excluded from the project. The interior was to be updated with colour, new carpets, shelving and furniture. Extra public computers had to be accommodated with spare capacity for future growth. The design contract was awarded to Charter Partnership and construction to Barnes Construction.

The final scheme

The existing meeting room was far too big for most groups and had an unpleasant echo because of the parquet floor and wood panelling. The stage area was rarely used at all. As most use of the room was made in the evenings, a large area was empty most of the day, so it was decided that this space, together with the adjoining coffee shop, would be used to create a search room and office, and a 50-seater meeting room, while the projection room and store became a further office and sorting room.

The mezzanine floor was filled in to create one large first floor space. The ground floor was more problematical. The building has a central service core making it impossible to open out the floor space. One of the aims was to remove the need to have the children's library staffed all the time, so it had to link into the adult library. The only way this could be done was by moving the workroom to the top floor where the Schools Library Service was, incorporating the loading bay into the building and moving the children's library away from the market. The resulting space has attractive features like a wet play area, floor lighting, spelling wall and a mural. It also has child-friendly toilets. It is separated from the main library by a glazed corridor that forms the fire exit for the upper floors, but with double fire doors across which can be kept open. Not ideal but it meets requirements and is easily supervised.

The area nearest the shopping precinct entrance (former children's library) became the Service Centre or Navigator and the new coffee shop, Pages. A kitchen was created under the stairs with seating along the windows to the door. This compromise has created some difficulties because the space is narrow, it can be draughty when there is an easterly wind, and it can get very hot because of the large non-opening windows, despite film and blinds. It is a walk through to the rest of the building, which can be a problem. With hindsight the attractive curved wall should have been further into the Navigator.

A lot of effort went into upgrading fire protection. The open Sixties feel meant that stairs needed to be enclosed in fire wells. The windows on the front and rear elevations were replaced with double glazed units and aluminium-coated panels substituted for some of the glass. This has reduced solar gain and heat loss, and, together with solar film on the skylights, has made the building more comfortable. Proper heating controls were fitted to ensure an even temperature throughout. Generally the ventilation and airflow has improved. Air-conditioning has been installed in some places, because experience has shown that even the improvements made did not deal with all of the ventilation issues. Convector heating units fitted into the ceilings of the main spaces also help by being used like fans in the summer.

Figure 17.1 Suffolk County Libraries, Lowestoft Library, exterior

The exterior was redecorated outside the project by the maintenance team, who painted the render a stark white to contrast with the bright panels in the gunmetal window frames. The aim was to make the library stand out as an interesting contribution to the streetscape, instead of looking staid and dull. With the building being so severely rectangular, the effect is of a Mondrian painting. The corner was crying out for something, and the vertical 'the Library' sign was devised, with a quirky 'the' set at an angle, which has since been used in other places.

Interior design

This was led by the in-house team, but working closely with the architect and Point Eight, the shelving suppliers. It had to be simple, bold, bright but inexpensive. The walls were painted magnolia with colour coming from the fabric covered notice boards and the red feature walls. The carpet was blue with grey inserts around counters and self-service machines. Counters were red with beech tops along with the furniture for the 3M self-service machines.

Figure 17.2 Suffolk County Libraries, Lowestoft Library, interior

The feature wall on the ground floor just lists all the services in the building in different typefaces, colours and directions, while on the first floor it has quotations about libraries. The record office has a timeline showing key events in the history of Lowestoft, while the meeting room has what can only be described as a coloured barcode. The architect designed these, along with the logo for the coffee shop and the hanging guiding. The children's library mural represents the sun rising over the sea, the emblem of Lowestoft.

A single style of chair was chosen for the whole building, except the coffee shop, upholstered in red, as were the sofas and armchairs. A key feature on the first floor is a large cross-shaped arrangement of computer benching with beech tops and red up stands.

All the shelving is Point Eight Libratec in beech with silver shelves, except in the children's library where it is all red with blue end panels and the teenage area where it is their silver Rotar range. Study tables with cable management were positioned so that cabling in the ceiling void could be brought down to convert them into computer workstations if needed in the future.

The project

The project was starting at a time of change in Suffolk Libraries, with a restructure and the people who were involved in writing bids and getting backing, leaving. When it finally got the go-ahead, no one had been involved in it from the start and all bar one were novices, with no experience of anything on this scale. It was extremely complex and unlike anything else Suffolk Libraries had done. The budget was limited and the library could not move off site, so there were issues around maintaining services. Stock had to be stored at minimal cost. Staff needed to be redeployed as well as being involved in the project. The record office search room had to be relocated and the Schools Library Service moved out. In addition, all the external funding had to be looked after and budgets monitored; ongoing work with partners like Sure Start and Lowestoft College had to be done, and communication and consultation with users and stakeholders were necessary.

A member of library staff was seconded to the project full time to deal with external funding and liaise with the architect and contractors and coordinate activity around delivering the project. There was a team of staff consisting of the county manager, locality manager, library and deputy library manager, stock manager, ICT project manager, and public service manager from the record office. These formed their own teams to work on various work streams.

A lot of work went into communicating the changes to the public, and users of different services, especially as the record office search room moved out to Oulton Broad Library. The entire library had to be shrunk to fit into the original children's library so a lot of thought went into spreading the demand. Interestingly the number of visits fell by 45 per cent but the number of readers with items on loan only fell by 21 per cent. Nearby Kessingland and Oulton Broad libraries had extra opening hours and a mobile library had extra stops added in Lowestoft (this was later removed through lack of use). Sunday opening was started and readers encouraged to borrow more books at a time. To compensate for reduced choice Lowestoft readers were given free reservations for Suffolk stock. This also acted as a pilot for the countywide abolition of reservation charges.

The works

For a year before the project started a lot of work was done on weeding the stock and clearing out junk. Work started on 13th May 2002 with the first phase of a 3-phase programme – closure of the children's library to allow for all the internal partitions to be removed and the carpet to be patched up.

The entire building closed on 28th May to move approximately 40,000 stock items into the children's library, reopening on the 5th June, while staff had 3 days to clear virtually the same amount and send it into storage, and move the record office search room out. The second phase began on 10th June. This was completed on 25th October and the library closed again from 28th October to 3rd November so everything could be moved back to the ground floor. The stock was set up in a screened off area in the centre, so the public wouldn't see the final effect. The final phase started on the 4th November on the old children's library area. Point 8 started installing the furniture on the first floor and record office on 11th November so staff could start unpacking stored non-fiction there and setting up computers.

On 27th January 2003 the service was reduced to an enquiry desk and a self-service machine just inside the shopping precinct entrance where readers could drop off books, request and collect items. This was to give time to re-shelve the ground floor. The library reopened on Monday 24th February 2003 with the official ceremony on Wednesday 26th.

The results

In some ways this project went far beyond the traditional refurbishment and even 5 years later the effects are still being felt. There are the statistics like 65 public computers, a new record office, a learning centre, a public access point for council services and so on which tell their own story, but the refurbishment has changed what the library offers the community and how it is delivered. Once staff realized that it wasn't just new paint and carpet, they embraced the challenge of change and looked at how they worked and were empowered to make changes to suit the new situation. The library started to work with Lowestoft College and Sure Start to bring new users in to experience the new facilities. It started the move towards outreach work that has since spread round the county. It has raised the profile of the library in the town.

Interestingly its effects have gone way beyond the town, with readers and councillors from other parts of the county liking what they see and asking for the same for their communities. The library has become the flagship for Suffolk Libraries and a model for service delivery in other big libraries, as well as a standard setter for style.

The team who cut their teeth on the project have gone on to apply what they learnt to other projects round the county, but still use Lowestoft as a benchmark. A lot was achieved with a modest budget. There are areas that could have been better but they are still better than they were. If more money had been available it might have helped but the project was constrained by the site and the only option was to maximize interior space.

The finishing touch – Lowestoft won the Public Library Building Award in 2003 for a large library refurbishment.

Stowmarket – and there was light!

Stowmarket is a market town of around 14,000 people between Bury St Edmunds and Ipswich on the A14 and the Norwich-to-London railway line. It attracts people from the surrounding villages for shops and services. It developed, with the arrival of the canal and then the railway, into an industrial town and is still home to large companies like ICI not least because of good transport links.

The library is situated behind the main shopping street in the conservation area facing the parish church. It is a low, brick building blending in with the surroundings. Although signposted from the main street, it is not easy to identify as a library from a distance. A large aluminium sign was designed for the front to improve visibility and make a statement about the purpose of the building.

It was opened in 1985 and highlights how libraries and their building needs have changed in the last 20 years. Stowmarket was a divisional library, carrying out back-room work for a group of smaller branches, and the base for a mobile library. As result, the building incorporated a mobile garage, a large workroom and staff room, and a librarian's office. There were also two smallish meeting rooms and toilet with a separate entrance, which were to be hired out to community groups. One room was let as an office to an outside body for a time but generally take up of this type of accommodation was much less than expected. The other room became the training suite for Suffolk Library staff because of the availability of parking and the fairly central position in the county.

New mobile libraries outgrew the garage which became a store and collection point for recycling. Back-room functions were either centralized, like stock processing, or computerized, like requests, so that the staff areas were far larger than required. The growth of IT put pressure on the public space and the computers were often sited to suit the cabling rather than the customers. As a result, equipment was scattered wherever there was a space rather than following a logical layout.

Why a refurbishment was needed

Light levels both natural and artificial have always been a problem. The ceiling is relatively low so the narrow floor-to-ceiling windows cannot bring light far into the building. The main frontage faces north, with tall trees in the churchyard taking the light. The library is wrapped round a south-facing courtyard but the blinds were usually drawn to prevent glare and heat gain. The poor light level was further compounded by the exposed dark brickwork, a cream-textured ceiling which didn't reflect light, dark wooden ceiling panels in places and the dark brown carpet and olive green shelving. The artificial lighting was insufficient and despite modifications was barely up to standard.

Ventilation was similarly poor but got worse with warmer summers and increasing numbers of computers. The window openings are quite small so it was difficult to get a cross-draught and create a movement of air. There is considerable heat gain from the south-facing courtyard and the sun is on the building all day.

Although the floor plan was interesting, a U-shaped building round a courtyard, with the meeting rooms and staff areas on the left, there were a lot of small irregular shaped areas near the entrance and a lot was wasted, as access was needed for the doors. The public area was L-shaped requiring two staffed points. The courtyard, which could have been an asset, but looked abandoned with a few overgrown shrubs surrounded by concrete.

The furniture and fittings were coming to the end of their lifespan and were looking very tired and tatty. New things had been bought, like IT furniture, which didn't match the rest, so the whole place was looking messy and dated.

The brief

The Suffolk County Council architect was basically asked to deal with the problems within a tight budget and planning restraints. The priority order was light levels, natural ventilation and rationalization of the floor space, along with replacing the furniture and fittings. Other requirements included removing barriers to access and providing an accessible public toilet with baby changing facilities. The brief evolved as solutions were worked through and options were costed.

The final scheme

To overcome the low light levels and poor ventilation in the western side of the building two large opening roof lanterns were built. The library resembles some of the 19th-century industrial buildings in Stowmarket, which sometimes have roof lanterns, so this is an appropriate and attractive solution. Seven new, high-level opening windows were installed on the western wall primarily to help create a through draught, but also to bring in natural light.

In the north-eastern corner the meeting rooms, staff room and kitchen were removed, increasing the natural light and ventilation, as well as removing the awkward spaces.

The ceilings were given a smooth finish and the wooden area plastered. They were painted white, along with the walls, to reflect the light. A new lighting layout using low energy fittings was installed.

The garage was converted into a training suite with appropriate lighting and air-conditioning, while leaving a small area as a loading bay. The workroom was divided up into working, rest and kitchen areas. The courtyard was given a ramp so it is accessible to everyone, and has been replanted, and garden furniture installed.

The dark and unwelcoming entrance with exposed dark bricks and a dark wooden ceiling is all on one level but access was difficult, even after the outer doors had been automated, because of a large display case with single manually operated doors on either side, and a collection of leaflet racks. The entrance wasn't wheelchair and pushchair friendly or particularly welcoming – more of an obstacle course. The entrance was redesigned to improve access, the barriers cleared away, the walls whitened and a single automatic sliding door fitted. After some discussion it was decided to dispense with inner doors and partially screen the lobby. So the benefits of a draught lobby are retained without the problems caused by inner doors. It was a step towards a retail look while keeping an eye on heating and cleaning costs. Given the design of the existing building, this solution seems to have worked well with no complaints about draughts; the screen is used for library guiding.

The counter was near the door, very convenient but a cause of congestion. Suffolk Libraries place an emphasis on self-service, so in line with current Suffolk thinking it was decided to move the counter to the western wall maintaining sight lines removing the bottleneck and making self-service options the first rather than the last choice for borrowers. The self-service terminals are now prominently located between the door and the counter encouraging use.

The construction contract was awarded to DC Construction, Ipswich, furniture and shelving to Demco Interiors and signage to Sign Dynamics, Ipswich.

Interior design

Given the problems of light levels, care was taken over the choice of colours and finishes. The library team retained control of the design. The bare brick was plastered and painted. Although exposed brick was in keeping with the original design it did not help the light levels or the impression that we hoped to make on users. The same applied to the area of wooden ceiling which felt oppressive. The textured ceiling was given a smooth skim and painted white to reflect the light. For a public building the ceiling heights are quite low so it was decided to paint the walls white to obscure the distinction between wall and ceiling. This has successfully created the impression that the ceilings are higher.

Colour has been added to some walls to draw the eye further into the building. There is a deep yellow area on a dark north wall, dark red behind the counter and lime green in the children's area. A mid-blue carpet was chosen as a compromise between practicality and lightness, and red fabric-covered notice boards fitted.

Demco Interior's Xolys range of shelving was chosen throughout, because of its light and airy look, but with a different colour for the children's area. Shelving along the walls is 1.8m high while the island units are 1.5m to help open the space.

There is little space for decoration on the walls above the shelving but library related quotations in black lettering were used to attract the eye and provide a sense of interest and humour. A welcome sign in white vinyl lettering went on the wall behind the counter, while the names of current children's authors in different fonts and colours made a simple but effective display in the children's area.

Figure 17.3 Suffolk County Libraries, Stowmarket Library, children's area

Layout

The U-shaped floor plan has been used to help create separate zones for different activities in an informal way. The children's library is in the eastern wing near the toilet but away from the entrance. The computers are concentrated near the entrance, as they tend to generate noise but are within sight of the counter. We know from consultation that teenagers don't like their area to be with the children's area, so they have a quiet corner in the western wing near the sound and vision collection. The rest of that wing is used for fiction and quiet reading with comfy chairs.

User involvement

There had been continuing discussions with the Stowmarket Library User Group about the building defects for many years. Once the scheme had been worked up there was a week of consultation in October 2004 with plans displayed and questionnaires distributed, and senior managers and councillors on hand to engage with users. Feedback was then fed into the final plans. Throughout the project there was a special notice board with plans and updates to keep readers informed.

Project management

A small team from the library service was formed to sign-off designs and provide information for the architect and the shelving company, and also to deal with all the service aspects of the project. The building and electrical works were run by Property Services in their established way but with the attendance of the asset manager and ICT project manager from Suffolk Libraries. The asset manager acted as the link between the two teams and had power to make decisions and authorize expenditure.

The library team consisted of the county manager, the stock manager, library manager and asset manager. They were able to work on particular work streams, with the asset manager in the project manager role, and able to call on others for publicity and engaging with stakeholders. This approach has worked well in Suffolk for other library projects, though Stowmarket had a smaller team. The trick is getting the balance right between being small enough to make quick decisions and having enough people to do the work. Here the size of team was right. The local staff were given the opportunity to comment on proposals and make suggestions on both the scheme and the programme.

The work programme

The programme was governed by the need to keep a staff training facility available and keeping the library open as much as possible, with staff access to facilities. The work was divided into three phases, starting with the garage and staff room. Once the training room had been created, the next phase was the rest of the east wing up to the entrance, and the final phase was the west wing and entrance. There was a week's closure between Phases 1 and 2 and another between Phases 2 and 3. It added to the length of time needed but reduced the disruption to the service to a minimum and reduced the need for off site storage of stock. The phasing also caused problems with maintaining a network within the building. The electrical mains ran through the roof space where the roof lanterns were going and had to be moved in Phase 3, which meant a total power switch-off. This had to be carefully programmed in because other sites in Stowmarket were connected to the library and they also lost their network.

The works

A lot of preparatory work was done before the work proper started. Stock was weeded, staff areas and cupboards cleared out and rubbish removed. One of the meeting rooms was taken over for staff use.

Contractors arrived on site on 10 January 2005 and started work in the staff areas and garage leaving the public areas unaffected. On the 14 February they moved into Phase 2. This was done without closing the library more than its usual closed day because, apart from the counter and some computers, there was little to move, as most of the stock was in the Phase 3 area.

During Phase 2 some stock was sent to storage and new stock, apart from popular titles stockpiled. Staff were able to access the new staff area across the courtyard, and, apart from the noise, readers were almost getting a normal service.

The transfer to Phase 3 was the most difficult as the library was only closed for five days (4–8 April), and all the stock and shelving had to be moved out of Phase 3 into Phase 2. This was done by the staff with a few reinforcements. Staff worked to a temporary layout, designed to hold as much stock as possible to avoid using storage. A new temporary counter was created from old desks and limited number of public computers set up. Public access was through a fire escape door at the side of the building. There were very few grumbles, and people were finding new areas of stock they didn't normally read! It also gave the public a taste of what the new-look library was going to be like.

Work on Phase 3 finished on 21 May 2005: shelving delivered and installed from 23 May. The library closed from 25 May until 10 June to move back into the whole building. The staff found this a bit tight, as there was a bank holiday. They also needed time to recover from the heavy physical work before the reopening.

The result

The project took 21 weeks in total. The total cost was £320,000, with £300,000 coming from Suffolk County Council capital funds and the rest from the libraries' budget. The public space has been increased by 35 per cent from 332m² to 450m², an increase of 118m². A small meeting room for councillor surgeries and advice sessions, and an accessible toilet with baby-changing facilities have been provided. A fully equipped training suite was built. The project fully met the brief in that light levels have increased significantly, both natural and artificial, and ventilation improved. The bright colours and new furniture have transformed the building.

The refurbishment has gone down well with users. As one reader said in the PLUS survey: 'The new layout and revamp makes a lighter and brighter atmosphere.' And another said: 'Since its refurbishment it is a pleasure to visit.'

Lakenheath – a refurbishment by stealth

Lakenheath is a village of around 4500 inhabitants situated in the far north-west of Suffolk on the edge of the Breckland, a thinly populated area of sandy soils and pine forests. Like many villages it has lost shops and services in recent years. It is famous as the home of RAF Lakenheath, one of the main USAF bases in the UK. This means that a fair proportion of the community is connected to the airbase and has access to facilities, like libraries, there; thus library use is lower than would be expected for a community of this size. As a result, the library did not have a high priority for investment when compared to busier places. It attracts about 25,000 visits per year and has about 21,000 issues. It has a stock of 6500 items and has one self-service machine and three computers for public use.

The building

The library is housed in the former Co-operative Society haberdashery, next to a general store, on the main road through the village. There is ample on-street parking. The total floor space is 72m². It opened in the 1970s and there was minimal conversion work done and little investment thereafter. The exterior was covered in unpainted brown pebbledash, and it retained the original shop windows. These were covered to half height by hessian-covered boards, which displayed a collection of dead flies, so it wasn't clear to the passer-by what the building was or if it were open. It certainly did not look attractive or appealing. There were steps up to the door.

The interior was the standard magnolia walls and brown carpet, with non-adjustable wooden shelving. Odd bits of furniture had been bought over the years and IT equipment squeezed in where possible, so the public computers were on the staff counter. The building was reasonably sound, just a few cracks from settlement. However, the shop windows could not be opened, causing overheating; there were trailing cables; visually it looked a mess with mismatched furniture and books on their edges, as they didn't fit the shelves.

Background

The refurbishment arose from a number of circumstances, which although not related to Lakenheath, had a big impact. Following a restructuring in 2001, the library service had for the first time an asset manager, responsible for the buildings, in regular contact with the maintenance department and other fund holders. About the same time the county council changed the way capital funding was allocated to departments allowing competitive bids to be made. The Disability Discrimination Act (DDA) was on the way, and, following the success of the Lowestoft Library refurbishment, there was a determination to improve libraries throughout Suffolk.

The catalyst was the DDA. The disability officer had funding to bring access up to standard and Lakenheath received a new wheelchair-width door and impressive ramp, which led to a shoddy library. This work was carried out in 2003, with the public using the side fire exit.

In the meantime following on from criticism of children's libraries in Suffolk by the Best Value inspectors, Suffolk Libraries were successful in getting a three-year programme funded from the Single Capital Pot to revamp all the children's libraries, including Lakenheath.

The scheme

Having decided revamping just the children's area would make things look worse, a shopping list of what was required to improve matters was drawn up. It ranged from the obvious like new shelving and carpet to replacing the windows so they could open. It never started out as a full refurbishment but evolved into one as it became apparent what was needed to be done.

The biggest problem was siting the IT without taking up valuable wall space or cluttering up the centre with all the cabling problems that causes. In the end it was decided to create a small IT area out of part of the staff area, which was basically a corridor. The extra 10m² though small allowed enough flexibility to make full use of the existing public area.

The interior was painted white with a blue carpet and green fabric-covered notice boards fitted. The new space was signed up as the e-zone and attractive guiding put round the walls. Basic white metal shelving and new furniture completed the fresh but restful interior.

The other main priority was improving the frontage to promote the service and attract passers-by. The windows were to be treated as an asset rather than a hindrance, so the boards were removed, windows replaced and the children's library positioned in one of them. People could see in. The pebbledash was painted white to make the library stand out in the streetscape and a large black 'The Library' sign put up.

Funding

Modest amounts of money came from various sources; children's library capital, DDA funds, maintenance mini-pot 2004 (a sum of money devolved to departments to spend as they think fit on their buildings), library funds and the maintenance budget. Traditionally the maintenance budget had been strictly spent on the basis of need and to a timetable, but having one person in the library service looking after buildings meant that he could negotiate with the maintenance team to modify their timetable and bring work forward and influence the specification of the work so it would fit in with the vision of the service.

The structural work including new windows, lighting upgrade, creating the new space, decorating and carpets came to £15,000 and a further £10,000 was spent on furniture and equipment.

The work

The library closed on 21 March 2005 for four weeks. The main priority for Suffolk Libraries was to maintain some form of service to the public, however reduced, to make sure they retain their library habit. Readers were encouraged to take out more books to see them through the closure, but a spare mobile was parked on the road opposite the library for those who had forgotten or needed to pick up requests. In common with most building projects the issue of what to do with the stock was a problem, given the remoteness of Lakenheath. However, the village hall helped out by agreeing to store the boxed-up stock in a spare room. This cut down transport and storage costs. Extra staff were drafted in to help with the stock. The library reopened on time on 19 April.

The result

The finished library reflects the current Suffolk Libraries thinking on library design. It proudly proclaims what it is to the outside. It has a fully accessible entrance with sufficient space inside for wheelchairs and buggies to move round. There is a bright and lively children's area with modern child-friendly furniture. Light levels and ventilation have been improved. The public area has been increased by $10m^2$ to $58m^2$. Modern shelving, clear signage and furniture, comfortable seating, along with the e-zone for IT, emphasize the message that this is a modern library service, offering the same quality of service to everyone regardless of where they live or which service point they visit.

The statistics show a 42 per cent increase in new borrowers after the refurbishment and a 24 per cent increase in visitors. User satisfaction measured by the PLUS survey show 90.1 per cent of users scoring it good or very good compared with 81.8 per cent before.

Small service points often have problems attracting large amounts of capital because the money usually ends up where it will have the biggest impact on the largest number of people. Lakenheath was fortunate in that the building was sound and big enough for service needs, so only a relatively small amount was needed. It never started out as a complete refurbishment, but just grew into one, as each element was funded. It shows the value of having someone with an overview of funding sources and good contacts with the budget holders.

The piecemeal approach can be risky, as there is a danger that a scheme will be left half finished, but if, as in this case, each element is relatively self-contained, the risks are minimal. Eventually a tipping point is reached, where it becomes easier to get money, because stakeholders can see results and can see how much better it could be if everything were done.

Felixstowe – the gulls come to town

Felixstowe is an Edwardian seaside resort, which is now home to the largest container port in Britain. Despite excellent transport links the town and neighbouring villages, surrounded on three sides by water, are relatively isolated. The population is around 30,500, drawn by employment at the port or by its attraction as a commuter base for Ipswich and beyond.

The present building, opened 1966, was the first post-war purpose-built library in the old county of East Suffolk. It was designed, like many East Suffolk libraries, to cope with an expanding population and service growth. They took the 1981 projected population figure of 26,000 as a starting point and designed for that. The result was a spacious 410m^2 public space. It had shelving for 20,800 books and gramophone records and was built by local builders for £36,398, including the oak shelving. This proved very farsighted as the population grew and services changed. The building was still just coping 20 years beyond its designed life.

It was a very typical design of its time, mainly single storey but with a mezzanine floor, parquet floor, open stairs, pendant lighting, wood panels and fixed wooden shelving. It was light and airy with lots of windows. It had a distinctive wing-shaped roof but a rather dull exterior with rendered panels.

The library occupies a good position on the edge of the main shopping area beside bus stops and opposite a large car park.

Why a refurbishment was needed

The library was well used but showing signs of wear. It had been given a carpet but there had been little investment in fixtures and fittings. The shelving made it very hard to change the layout as services changed. The installation of computers had been particularly insensitive with trunking criss-crossing most of the walls to reach corners where a computer would fit. Odd bits of shelving had been bought, along with non-matching display equipment, so over time the interior looked a mess.

The library was performing badly environmentally, with low levels of insulation and single-glazed, ill-fitting metal windows. It was expensive to run, but cold in winter and too hot in summer.

The arrival of the DDA had emphasized the problem of the mezzanine. There was no lift so it was hard to find a satisfactory use for a space that was in any case hard to supervise. The rest of the library was on one level but the ramp wasn't up to standard.

The decoration was mainly magnolia with mushroom woodwork, a brown carpet and exposed wood – so very dull and old fashioned.

The brief

The brief was to update the interior, improve its environmental performance, install a lift to any first floor areas, upgrade lighting and electrics, create more space and meeting rooms, and liven up the outside. One of the conditions attached to the funding was to provide a work or training opportunity for adults with learning difficulties, so a café was added to the brief. There was also a concern to future-proof the building, by giving it maximum flexibility.

Developing the brief

The first decision was to retain and update, rather than disguise, the original Sixties feel. This was influenced by the swing in taste towards that period as much as anything. There was a piece of land behind the library and some car parking in council ownership which could be used to extend the public spaces.

The library service was clear that the stock would not be split over more than one floor, because experience shows it is hard to attract people upstairs. The decision as to what goes upstairs is always difficult to explain to readers, and the stock and space tend to be underused. It takes away the flexibility to rearrange the stock in a logical way as sections shrink and expand. There can also be problems around supervision.

It was evident that it was impossible to fit everything onto the ground floor. The mezzanine itself was a problem. Being only 75m² it did not justify a lift, but couldn't be used without one. During a survey it was discovered that the mezzanine did not have sufficient load-bearing capacity for library or meeting-room use. To create the extra space required, a second floor would have to go into the extension. This would accommodate the lift and make the mezzanine accessible to all. After a long discussion it was agreed that all the stock and the café had priority for the ground floor and anything else would have to go upstairs. The solution for the mezzanine was to turn it into the staff area, with a small delivery room left beside the lift on the ground floor, near the delivery door.

The design of the entrance caused a lot of discussion. There was an oversized draught lobby, which reduced the width of the library and was a dominant feature when seen from the mezzanine. It was full of leaflets and clutter. It was decided it should, at the very least be reduced to a minimum. The architect looked at other options such as a screen outside, as part of the redesigned ramp, to deflect the wind, then an internal glazed screen, but they were discounted as giving opportunities for vandalism and creating barriers. In the end, it was agreed to remove the lobby and just have a powerful heat curtain. In the end this has been a sensible choice as there have been few problems with draughts and the curtain is rarely needed.

As part of the development process, most of the staff, together with a local councillor and the architect, went on a trip to London to look at some new libraries. It was partly to update everyone on current thinking but also to get staff to think beyond just a fresh coat of paint and new shelves. It helped generate discussion, queries and suggestions. It was important that local staff took ownership of the project and get involved.

Engagement with the community

Felixstowe Library has received a high level of support from local county councillors over the years, who, following on from the success of Lowestoft, encouraged the library service to bid for funding. The town council is also very supportive and has a joint library committee with the county council.

An intensive programme of public consultation started in November 2004 with two events with plans displayed and staff on hand to discuss them and hand-out questionnaires. This was followed by staff visits to primary and high schools, and youth groups, including one for those with learning difficulties, and session for Home Library Service volunteers. The results were mainly around provision of public toilets, furniture and stock. There was also the chance for staff and public to try out some sample bays of shelving. Throughout the project there were items in the local papers, councillor visits, and plans and updates on display in the library.

One of the strengths of this project is the successful way expectations have been managed, especially with so many stakeholders. If this goes wrong, the final outcome, however successful to the outsider, is unsatisfactory. Realism was introduced from the beginning with the strong message that not everything could be achieved for various reasons and compromises would have to be made.

This was accompanied by a 'Be careful what you ask for, you might get it!' approach to make sure that everything going into the scheme was well considered and sustainable. Then once the project kicked off there could be no surprises. Everyone knew what the project was going to deliver, had signed up to it and were working towards it. The surprise would be in how well it was delivered.

The final scheme

The final plans were for a two-storey extension at the rear, keeping close to the original roofline, to house the lift, staff and public toilets, meeting rooms and fire escape. The rest of the building was to be refurbished. A fully accessible raised floor was fitted for the wiring throughout the ground floor, which then meant the doors and stairs needed to be modified. All the windows were to be replaced with sealed double glazed units and the upper and lower panes on the front replaced with panels to introduce colour to the frontage and reduce solar gain.

The mezzanine was to be divided into workroom, office and staff room with an open walkway linking round from the stairs to the lift in front of the new rooms on the first floor. As the balustrading is mainly glass it is clear to readers there is more upstairs. The workroom is glazed so staff can see the counter and most of the library.

Figure 17.4 Suffolk County Libraries, Felixstowe Library, interior

The old roof was to be insulated and all the old convector heaters replaced with modern units above shelf height to increase flexibility. This, together with the double-glazing, meant that the existing boiler had enough capacity to heat the extension. All the existing cabling was to be removed and hidden.

The final challenge was to convert the single storey wing housing the staff areas into an attractive coffee shop.

Café Libra

Although there are coffee shops in two other Suffolk libraries, this one is unique in that it is run as a social enterprise. It reflects the merging of libraries and social care into one new directorate: Adult and Community Services. It is an excellent example of how the different services can work together. It provides five part-time jobs for young adults with learning difficulties to help them into the world of work. It gives them the initial training and then lets them get on with a real job, but with support. It gives them the chance to be wage earners, interact with the public and develop their confidence and skills. The aim is that they will be able to move on to other jobs with the skills they have gained and an employment history.

There is an Internet café area, as well as tables and chairs and armchairs. Newspapers and magazines are displayed there. There is also a large TV screen showing news programmes that can be used for advertising. It has a lively friendly atmosphere, created as much by the staff, who enjoy their work, as by the customers, and attracts all ages. It is a meeting point for parents bringing toddlers to pre-school activities and the focus of the first baby café in a library in the country, where mothers get advice on breastfeeding from midwives and the babies get checked.

Building contract

The council's Property Department was beginning to develop partnership tenders for large projects and decided to use this approach for Felixstowe. Under this method, the contract doesn't go to necessarily the cheapest contractor but the one deemed best able to work with the council to deliver the best scheme and best value. The asset manager was closely involved with the contractor selection process as the client. The contractor works with the design team contributing their experience and knowledge, especially on buildability and products. Once the scheme is agreed the target price is set. If any savings are made they are shared between the client and contractor and likewise any overspends. Any changes or extras are compensation events charged for by the contractor. This approach produced a saving of at least £52,000 for the client.

Interior design

This was kept in house, but working closely with FG Library Products and Malcolm Andrews, the shelving and furniture suppliers, and Sign Dynamics, a local signage specialist. It was decided to emphasize the light, spacious feel of the library by painting the walls and ceiling white and get away from the dull colours previously there. This helped lighten the ground floor of the extension that has little natural light. The colour comes from the mid-blue carpet with grey inserts.

On the walls, at high level, are large colour photographs of local scenes and views of the port. They have proved popular with residents and visitors alike. The main feature on the wall facing the entrance is a steel sculpture by Suffolk artist, Paul Richardson, of seagulls on rigging. It is quirky and fun, is loved by everyone and has been a great talking point.

Working with FG Library Products, attractive furniture was designed for the DS self-service terminals in a cluster by the entrance, and another unit at child height in the children's library.

Suffolk Libraries have been trying to get away from the large monolithic counters that act as a barrier between staff and public, and which are often the most noticeable object in a library. As the public increasingly use self-service there is less need for large counters with several computers, and it is more important for the staff to move easily out into the library to assist readers.

Felixstowe was the first place to test these ideas fully. A single counter was replaced by two pods in the form of two curved desks, one at standing height, the other seated, with space for the CPU and cash drawer underneath. There was also a mobile drawer unit for each. The printer, DVD storage and stationery were put into an alcove behind. Visually they were not intrusive in light wood and perforated grey metal panels, but operationally they caused problems. They had to be repositioned to discourage the public from going round behind them, making the staff feel uncomfortable and raising concerns about personal information being on show. It was also found that the worktops weren't large enough and they had to be replaced. However, they now seem to be functioning as intended.

The shelving, chosen in consultation with the public and staff, was Schulzspeyer Rondea, and Felixstowe was the first UK public library to have it. It was chosen because it is the exact opposite of the solid oak shelving that was there before. It looks light and delicate but is easy to adjust, and has nice touches like the flag-like guiding above the bays. The uprights are gunmetal and the shelves light wood with chrome fixings, and together with other items from the Schulzspeyer range it all looks stylish and sophisticated.

The children's library has the same shelving system but in red and yellow. It has a large bespoke reading boat, incorporating kinder boxes and seating, as its centrepiece. It has its own small-sized self-service machine and smaller versions of the AMA Fabrications 'rocket' audiovisual display stands, plus the usual assortment of children's furniture. It is located under the mezzanine with floor lights and has its own distinct feel.

Layout

The intention was to go for zones rather than discrete spaces for different activities or users. This was to keep the space as open and flexible as possible and because functions overlap, and readers like to sit where they feel comfortable regardless of the designed purpose of the area. Fiction and large print were arranged in the existing building, with the children's library under the mezzanine, while the non-fiction and the teenage area with Playstation and listening posts went into the ground floor extension, near the staffed point for supervision. Internet computers and study tables were placed throughout. Newspapers and magazines were placed just inside the café to create the commercial coffee-shop feel.

One of the early surprises is that the Teen Zone is very popular with older readers when the teenagers are at school. It is probably because it is fairly enclosed and out of the way.

The runs of shelving are fairly long but curve to break up the formality. The longer runs help readers find their way through the sequence, and are broken up with tabletop display units. The quick choice collection and requested items are in front of the main door near the self-service machines.

Project management

This followed standard Suffolk Libraries practice with a small team of staff consisting of the county manager, asset manager, stock manager and the library manager and her assistant, with others when needed, looking at the design and dealing with all the service related issues (like communication and service continuity), while property services had their own project team dealing with the construction work. The asset manager was part of property's team, attending site meetings and linking back to the library team, and acting as the channel of communication between client and contractor. Occasionally both teams met together but usually separately, as they worked in different ways and it was more time efficient.

The works

A two-phase programme was agreed to allow the library to stay open as much as possible. Enabling works commenced on 9 May 2005 to create a new staff door and fire escape through a window, make changes to alarms and get the contractors set up. The first phase proper started on 31 May working on the extension but with the mezzanine, staircase and rear wall screened off, and the library operating as normal, though staff had to vacate their area for three days in August while steel and heavy loads were craned over it.

Good progress was made and the handover of Phase 1 was brought forward to 12 December. The library closed for a week and the stock was crammed into the ground floor extension and the staff areas emptied into the new staff areas upstairs. A fire exit at the side was turned into the new public entrance. It was a trying time for the staff with lots of noise and days without heating.

Following some design changes the second phase was completed a month early on 31 March. The shelving arrived on 5 May and once most of it was installed the service to the public was reduced to just returning or collecting requested items. The library closed completely on 15 May and reopened on 23 May.

The results

The project came in just under the budget of £1,008,000 and was on time. Total floor space has increased from 515m^2 to 782m^2. There is space for a varied programme of activities and events for all ages. There has been a 31 per cent increase in new borrowers, visits up 10 per cent and issues up 7 per cent. It has proved popular with readers and stakeholders, and there are plans to copy Café Libra in other places.

Felixstowe won a delegates' choice award from the Public Library Building Awards 2007.

Further sources

Designing libraries – the gateway to better library buildings: www. designinglibraries.org.uk/. Accessed 16 October 2007.

Jenkins, G. (2004), 'Winning by design', *Public Library Journal*, Spring 2004, 10–12.

Public Library Building Awards – delegates' choice 2007: www.cilip.org.uk/ specialinterestgroups/bysubject/public/awards/awards2007/delegates/default. htm. Accessed 16 October 2007.

Public Library Building Awards – winners 2003: www.cilip.org.uk/ specialinterestgroups/bysubject/public/awards/awards2003/default.htm. Accessed 16 October 2007.

PART 6
(1) Snapshots: Some Refurbishment Case Studies in Brief

An interactive, community hub for reading with social activities for readers.
– Newquay Library, Cornwall

(2) Case Studies Reviewed

Designed to support the student learning experience from the moment of entry.
– Learning Resource Centre, Northumbria University

Once the preserve of the few.
– British Museum Round Reading Room

Chapter 18

Snapshots:
Some Refurbishment Case Studies in Brief[1]

Michael Dewe and Alan Clark

As the first chapter illustrated, renewal of our library buildings has been a continuing process but has been brought into sharper focus in recent years as a feature of library service modernization. The preceding chapters have shown in detail how individual libraries have responded to this modernizing challenge through the refurbishment, remodelling and sometimes extension of their existing premises. This chapter offers in briefer form, further examples from various library sectors both within and outside the UK, to illustrate the nature and range of library refurbishment in recent years.[2]

In the case of heritage buildings the reasons for choosing refurbishment rather than new build will include some of the following:

- the architectural worth of the building
- the quality of construction
- location
- relationship to neighbouring buildings and facilities
- funding available for renovation
- the cost of renovation in comparison with new build.

Academic libraries

Heritage buildings

The British Library of Political and Economic Science, London School of Economics, moved into the former headquarters and warehouse of W.H. Smith in 1978 and totally remodelled it again in the 1990s.

This represents one extreme of building renovation. The historic shell of the building was retained – cleaned and with appropriate windows provided – and the interior was gutted and wholly recreated. The BLPES collections had to be outhoused during the three years of the rebuilding scheme.

Not surprisingly this was a hugely expensive scheme. An important factor in fundraising was undoubtedly the status of the library as a research collection of national and international importance. The fundraising programme from 1993 to

1998 is described in an article by Wilkinson which also compares the British and American context of such fundraising initiatives.[3] The redevelopment of what is now known as the Lionel Robbins Building followed a 1994 feasibility study from Foster and Partners, who were subsequently appointed as architects in 1998. With funds in place in 1999, the redevelopment of the Grade II listed 1916 building could go ahead.

The new building occupies 20,000m², of which the library occupies 16,000m²; it provides 1686 reader places and in addition to library and computing facilities, has an archive reading room and store, group study rooms and training suites. The fourth floor and the newly built fifth floor are occupied by the LSE Research Lab.[4]

A major feature is the light-filled atrium and spiral stepped ramp ending in a partially glazed dome, angled to maximize daylight and minimize glare. Other design features of the new Lionel Robbins Building are:

- the creation of a double-height ground floor from a dingy basement
- windows that automatically respond to building temperature, giving natural ventilation
- energy-efficient lighting operating on a presence detection system including strip lighting above book shelves and study place spotlights
- book shelves placed to absorb noise and separate quiet study areas at the perimeter of the building
- nearly silent glass lifts
- replication of facilities on each floor to offer a user-friendly layout.

The building was commended in the 2002 Civic Trust Awards. Further building took place in 2007 to expand areas such as the course collection.[5]

John Rylands, a successful Manchester industrialist, died in 1888. His wife, Enriqueta Rylands, commissioned a memorial library, designed by Basil Champneys (1842–1935), who had carried out much other architectural work in Oxford and Cambridge. The resulting John Rylands Library (1890–1905) – 15 years in its creation and for which it would seem no money was spared – was extravagantly and richly designed and decorated. The main area consisted of a vaulted central space with books in alcoves and a gallery. But the John Rylands Library is more than just a magnificent period piece, because it houses one of the UK's major collections of books, manuscripts and archives. By the 1990s structural deterioration was endangering the building and its collections. The 'Unlocking the Rylands Project' was launched to conserve the Grade 1 listed building and to improve its physical access and facilities.

In Spring 2007, the library reopened after a £17 million refurbishment. The 1890s Victorian Gothic sandstone building has gained a new entrance wing housing a reception area, café and gift shop. The upper floors of the building have also been restored with new reading rooms, storage areas and a conservation studio.

Schemes of this magnitude are perhaps only possible with libraries like the John Rylands and BLPES whose research importance is widely acknowledged. The renovation attracted funding from the Heritage Lottery Fund, the European Regional Development Fund, the University of Manchester itself and many trusts, businesses and individuals.

Such schemes are expensive not just in money but also in their temporary effect on use of the collections. During the three-year closure many of the library's collections of four million books and manuscripts were stored in a Cheshire salt mine, where the stable dry atmosphere provided ideal conditions for preservation. 'The project has enabled the University of Manchester to keep the collections in the building created for them over a century ago and to make these treasures accessible to all' stated Bill Simpson, University Librarian and Director of the Library.[6]

Designed by Sir James Pennethorne, King's College London, Maughan Library is a Grade 2* listed nineteenth-century building. The former home of the Public Record Office it is claimed to be the first purpose-built fire-proof building in England. The closed access record office was transformed into the open access Maughan Library and Information Services Centre at a cost of £35 million.[7] Evans notes the high cost of purchase and remodelling of the building and sees this as a reassuring assertion of 'the value of a good library service to a leading academic institution'.[8] Even with this level of cost some proposed work had to be shelved or postponed until further funding was available.

A major restoration of the structure and fabric of the original building including the domed octagonal Round Room was undertaken. The library also occupies the former Rolls Chapel (now renamed the Weston Room after a donor) with its stained-glass windows, mosaic floor and monuments. Internally, major remodelling of the building has provided better access; 1300 study spaces with a high level of ICT provision, media facilities, a wide range of access facilities and a café.[9]

In addition to its restoration of the Maughan Library, King's College, with its library facilities spread across a number of campuses, has embarked on a three-year programme, Connected Campus, to create a virtual campus. This is part of the college's ten-year strategic plan (2006–16) and emphasizes the joint importance of physical buildings and electronic access to collections and resources.

The 1829 Wilkins Library, University College London, is a Grade 1 listed building designed by William Wilkins, the architect of the National Gallery, which had undergone some previous restoration in the 1950s. Wilkins' original vision was for a large open-plan library room on the first and second floors of the south side of the building approached by stairs from the octagon. As in many schemes involving landmark buildings, the renovation raised concerns as to whether alterations would complement the existing architecture, leading UCL to respond, 'UCL wishes to reveal the hidden glory of Wilkins' original architectural concept with a sensitive series of refurbishments in the existing library spaces and to make the best possible use of those later additions and alterations to the fabric which are architecturally significant'.[10] It is instructive to note that Wilkins' original concept was never built due to shortage of funds and as a result 'the library's entrance and service rooms at the top were much smaller than originally intended, cramped and dark – grossly inadequate for a student community of UCL's current size'.[11]

The first phase involved replacing the main staircase with a stone-clad helical staircase with glass sides and a bronze banister giving an impression of lightness, enhanced by light from an existing large window.

Other changes include improving access with a new lift and changes to the siting of staff space. A cramped 1950s issue desk became a photocopying and workstation area and a spacious new issue desk area was created from the space formerly occupied by the card catalogue. Existing small rooms were given new functions, for example as a multimedia viewing area.

Wherever possible, original furniture was re-used. However, re-use of some shelving was ruled out by safety concerns about its height. Some existing doors were refurbished and shelving and bookcases restored.

Further phases of restoration will include the remodelling of reading rooms to provide improved study facilities and enhanced network capabilities.

This gradualist approach to the renewal of the library is part of the university's strategic plan for the renovation and rebuilding of its premises.[12]

One of Harvard University's prestigious libraries, the Widener Memorial Library founded in 1915, underwent extensive renovation between 1999 and 2004 to safeguard the future of the collections and to increase user space. As in many buildings of this age all major infrastructure systems from HVAC to lighting, fire suppression and security required upgrading. Additionally two new reading rooms and staff workspace were constructed in the building's two interior light courts.[13] This renovation won an AIA/ALA Library Building Award in 2005.

Imagine the challenge of remodelling a 1930s theatre, a listed building by the architect and critic, H. Goodhart-Rendell, to encompass multimedia and IT library needs. The Victoria Centre Campus Library, Westminster Kingsway College, was 'listed for its quirky and challenging design. This included polychromatic brickwork and freely interpreted classical details'. The theatre had already been converted to a book-centred library in the 1950s but the planners could not have predicted the changes that IT would bring. The architect involved in the remodelling noted that 'the previous design provided a clear lesson that things in the world of education can change beyond anticipation'. Given the building's listed status the aim was to:

- 'Create a contemporary structure which would improve the environment and meld with the original design concept'.
- 'Maintain the sense of space, light and levity'.
- Create a mezzanine level to increase floor space.

The resultant design, a sensitive modernization which still reflects the history of the space, featured:

- a semi-glazed mezzanine with a chequer board floor of glazed and other floor panels
- a mezzanine sitting on a lightweight steel column grid, demountable to ensure future flexibility
- increased natural light throughout the space
- glazed partitioning installed on the ground floor and mezzanine
- the preservation of original features – the theatre's proscenium arch was restored and protected.[14]

Girton College Cambridge opened its new Duke Building in 2005.[15] This 1042m² extension to the existing Grade 2 listed building houses an environmentally controlled repository for archives and special collections; IT resources area, meeting room, staff offices and cloakroom facilities. The care taken in integrating the new extension with the existing building included the use of similar materials – hand-made brick terracotta, lead and oak in the new building – and close attention to the views of the new building from the old. Because of this the roof of one wing of the new building was planted with sedum.[16] Similar attention to the functional relations between the two parts of the library with glass walls and uninterrupted sight lines triumphantly demonstrated that extensions need not be random additions to an existing building. The Duke Building won a number of design awards; from RIBA in 2006, the Civic Trust in 2007 and the SCONUL Library Building Award for smaller buildings, also in 2007.

London, Manchester, Cambridge (both England and Massachusetts, USA) have outstanding academic library buildings of architectural and historic worth that are of continuing value to the communities they serve. These snapshots demonstrate that through renewal – often expensive and time-consuming – heritage buildings from the nineteenth and twentieth century can remain of enduring usefulness and merit into the twenty-first century.

Other academic library refurbishments

It is not only heritage buildings that are the subject of large-scale extension and refurbishment. The David Bishop Skillman Library Lafayette College, Easton, Pennsylvania was an award-winner in the 2007 American Institute of Architects/ American Library Association Library Building Awards. Here, an existing 7153m² building was extended by 2601m² and the whole layout of the library reconceived to turn it from a late 20th-century library focused on the printed media and individual study, into a 21st-century library with casual reading areas, meeting rooms, group study and teaching rooms, digital project rooms and of course a café. It also has 25 per cent more reader places; collection growth space for 20 years and improved staff workspaces. Externally the new extension wraps around the older core.[17]

The renovation of the 1932 Doheny Memorial Library at the University of Southern California involved its closure in 1999.[18] This enabled a seismic retrofit to ensure future safety and the remodelled library received a Los Angeles Conservancy Preservation award.

The building was originally designed in the style of the times 'with grand reading rooms, cavernous stacks and ornate entrance hall'. The renovation, which reopened in 2001 after two years' work, had to respond to:

- building wear and tear
- greater use
- stricter building codes
- providing an IT environment.[19]

Designed by Nicholas Burwell Architects, the £7 million extension to the 1970s Plymouth campus library, University of Plymouth, opened in September 2004. The extension design concept of January 2003 was to provide a resource-rich, high-quality study environment to foster scholarship. Work started on site in July of that year. The original 4500m^2 building gained an extra 3000m^2. The resulting building attracted a Concrete Society Award in 2005 for excellence in the use of concrete.

The design solution organized the old and new parts of the building around an atrium, with noisy and quiet areas graded away from the space both vertically and horizontally. Attention was paid to techniques which would aid acoustic deadening. The flexible interior consists of a linked series of reading rooms, rather than one open plan area.

Other features of the renovations, which resulted in a 25 per cent student increase in student use after reopening, included:

- the relocation of the main entrance to the double-storey height entrance area with a lift enabling improved disabled access between levels
- individual workspaces around the library perimeter
- lowered ceilings, angled windows and clerestory lights. The extensive use of natural light also provided easy navigation and security
- a new café
- 24/7 access to computers
- new self issue and self-return machines.[20]

Even before the completion of Northumbria University City Campus Library's £6 million refurbishment in 2007, the basement and first-floor areas were the subject of a JISC/HEFCE case study into best practice as a building 'designed to support the student learning experience from the moment of entry'.

The refurbishment provided:

- A welcome desk staffed by customer support staff, expanding its role from the security function previously provided by caretaking staff.

Figure 18.1 Plymouth Campus Library, University of Plymouth, atrium

- A first-floor student support hub – face-to-face enquiries and telephone links from six floors, augmented by learner support team visits to all six floors, throughout the day.
- A spacious self-service area on the ground floor including an open access Key Text Collection controlled with the help of RFID tags.
- A variety of study environments – from the informal Learning Café, including a shop, to flexible learning spaces where students are encouraged to reconfigure furniture and IT to suit their requirements, and bookable research hubs and study rooms, offering spaces for quiet study and meetings.[21]

The £1 million makeover of the Main Library, University of Reading ground floor is designed so that visitors come in to the building via a contemporary, uncluttered entrance floor offering key services. Refurbishment of the first floor includes new group and quiet study rooms and the IT and wiring infrastructure have been upgraded, with wireless network access available on all floors.

Other changes to the library include:

- a bigger short loan collection (renamed the course collection) with additional study space
- an integrated reception and information desk
- an enlarged café
- a ground-floor Knowledge Exchange space for informal academic interaction, where a variety of furniture can be arranged to suit group needs
- on the first floor a joint IT help desk and multimedia loans service
- new enclosed balustrades to enhance staircase safety.[22]

The Keele University Library refurbishment, carried out in two phases in 2006–2007, improved the entrance area, the main service points, the library floors, and created a group study area. The project led to:

- an up-to-date, comfortable environment with an inviting ambience
- a choice of study spaces
- group study rooms with networked PCs and data projectors to facilitate project work
- a refurbished music library
- individual study carrels for both students and researchers
- a building-wide wireless network
- improved disabled user facilities
- a better refreshment area that recognizes the library's role as a social space
- refurbished toilet facilities.[23]

The refurbishment of the Headingley Library, Leeds Metropolitan University completed in 2007 featured:

- a new ground floor group study area
- an improved layout with all books in one sequence
- extended wireless network with laptops available for loan
- a doubling of the silent study area seating
- a new comfortable area as an informal space for eating, drinking and study
- three IT labs with new presentation equipment
- a purpose-built disability resource room
- modern storage systems for journal back-runs
- a one-to-one support room for confidential discussions.[24]

Benefaction, York University itself and the HEFCE Poor Estates Fund provided finance to enable the building of the Raymond Burton Library for Humanities Research at the University of York. The funding permitted the relocation of Blackwell's University Bookshop to the Market Square, the redevelopment of the ground floor of the J.B. Morrell Library and an extension to accommodate the Humanities Research Library.

Following work on the Morrell Library ground floor, the new wing of c. 2300m^2 (opened in 2003) houses:

- existing special collections in environmentally controlled storage
- collections of primary sources in microform
- multimedia facilities
- academic conference and study space.[25]

These brief case studies, mainly of late twentieth-century buildings, illustrate how university libraries have adapted to the varied effects of the IT revolution through changes in their methods of processing and delivery of learning and research materials and by the provision of a wide and varied range of formal and informal environments for group and individual study and research.

National, state and special libraries: heritage buildings

The Main Library of the Canadian Parliament was the only part of the original parliament buildings to survive a devastating fire in 1916.

Planning for the conservation, rehabilitation and upgrade of the building began in 1995, although building didn't start until 2002. The inadequacy of the original building for housing the parliamentary collections had been recognized from its opening. In 1952 an electrical fault caused a fire in the dome which resulted in large scale damage to both fabric and collections. The library building was closed for almost four years whilst repairs were carried out. Since then the building has continued to be affected by age, weather and air pollution. Due to the scale of work involved and fears for the safety of the collections, two renovated locations were made ready for the closure of the main library in early 2002.[26]

As well as preserving a building opened in 1876 and with the aim of extending its working life by 50 years, there was a need to:

- bring the building up to modern standards
- preserve historic collections
- create a physical environment in line with contemporary library standards.

Three inter-related objectives of the scheme were conservation of the library's existing features; repairs to the damaged fabric and upgrading the building to meet both current building standards and anticipated demands. Sound environmental thinking was also central to the scheme. This included close control of temperature, humidity and air circulation, thermal windows and energy efficient lighting to provide a better environment for staff, readers and collections. Eighty-two per cent of construction waste was also diverted from landfill disposal.

The move back to the main library, completed in 2006 allowed a 'fresh start':

- Collections had been repaired, cleaned, conserved and reorganized more efficiently.
- The main library now only housed part of the collection with some services and storage located elsewhere.
- The primary electronic reference collection was available to all those with access to the parliamentary library network.
- The library's ceremonial role was given increased prominence and increased space was allocated for guided tours.[27]

When the staff and collections moved to the British Library's new St Pancras building in 1998, the opportunity arose to redevelop the 'hidden' courtyard housing the famous British Museum Round Reading Room surrounded by its book stacks and associated library accommodation. The outcome of the redevelopment was the creation of the glazed Great Court by Foster and Partners, using part of the space vacated by the library, at the centre of which is the restored Round Reading Room.

Originally built with brick, as the exterior of the reading room was not able to be seen, the circular building is now clad with limestone to match the now visible and renovated courtyard walls. Inside the library, the original 19th-century colour scheme of azure, cream and gold has been restored. The north side of the building has an elliptical extension, with shop, restaurant and two galleries; the upper floor is reached by two grand stone staircases.

The renovated library as the centrepiece of this awe-inspiring Great Court, provides exhibition and social spaces, and is both a tourist attraction and a public reference library. As such, it houses the Walter and Leonore Annenberg Centre, a database of objects in the museum's collections, and the Paul Hamlyn Library for adults and children of books which complement the database content.[28]

Figure 18.2 British Museum, Great Court and Round Reading Room

The Reading Room collections have recently been moved whilst the building hosts the First Emperor of China's Terracotta Army exhibition from September 2007 – April 2008.[29] Facilities usually available in the Reading Room are available in the Paul Hamlyn Library during that period. The Reading Room will revert to its normal use in early 2009.

The State Library of Victoria, Melbourne originated with buildings started in the 1850s and its spectacular domed reading room was opened in 1913. By the 1980s the library had difficulty in housing its expanding collection in satisfactory conditions and the building showed clear signs of overcrowding and neglect. No construction or renovation work had been carried out for nearly 30 years.

A State Library redevelopment project was started in 1990 with the aim of reconfiguring '22 buildings on a two-hectare site to create a world-wide facility in the heart of Melbourne'. Where in the past the State Library has shared its location with the Museum and National Gallery of Victoria, it now occupies its entire city block site.

The redevelopment project, completed in 2005, lasted 15 years and cost an estimated A\$200 million. It involved both renovation and new build, 'to provide expanded onsite and online facilities and services to library users':

- new reading rooms, galleries and exhibition spaces
- increased public access to information technology
- greater availability of books and other printed materials on open shelving
- related facilities such as a café, shop and conference centre.[30]

Situated by a lake, the National Library of Australia in Canberra is Australia's largest library and is heritage-listed. It houses a main reading room, a number of specialist reading rooms, an exhibition gallery, stacks, a preservation section, the *bookplate* restaurant and a shop. Opened in 1968, the library has of late undergone a refurbishment and reorganization of some of its reading rooms, and the construction of off-site warehouses and other works. Behind such changes lies the need to meet:

- the changing needs of users, staff and technology
- the storage needs of an ever-expanding collection.

The off-site store, the National Library Annexe, completed in 1998, helped to solve storage problems and funds were also allocated for an additional warehouse which will house hardcopy serial and newspaper collections.

In 2002 the library refurbished its third-floor Asian Collections Reading Room, unchanged since the buildings opening in 1968, and also the lower ground floor Newspaper and Microform Reading Room 'to take advantage of new technologies and to provide a more attractive and welcoming environment for readers'.[31] The refurbishment of the Asian Collections Room permitted the creation of a long-term readers' room and further consultation and e-resource provision, while the refurbished Newspaper and Microform Reading Room provided a new browsing area, more workspace and enhanced IT facilities.

The National Library is considering reducing the number of separate reading rooms to make the best use of staff and to save visitors from having to consult different formats in different rooms. The progressive implementation of electronic call slips to request material, wireless internet in the main reading room and a large number of fixed PCs are also part of the library's planned IT provision.

A building project to refurbish the podium, the platform surrounding the building, is expected to be completed by October 2008. The refurbishment includes an upgrade of external handrails, stairways, the perimeter podium balustrade and the café's outdoor area which will provide additional lakeside seating. There are also plans for a new Treasure Gallery to give improved facilities for the display of iconic items from the library's collections.[32]

Smaller specialist subject collections also provide examples of refurbishment.

Following an earlier 1980s extension and refurbishment, which included 3.75 miles of extra library shelving, the Royal Society of Medicine's Wimpole Street London premises, experienced further extensive refurbishment in 2003–2004. This resulted in a new lecture theatre and improved facilities for members and refurbishment of the Royal Society of Medicine Library. Important in this case, as in many renovations of historic buildings, were the simultaneous needs to modernize and to harmonize.[33] The renovation featured:

- New lighting and decoration of reading rooms and staff offices.
- The strengthening of all library floors.
- A new staircase to link the first and second floors.
- A new rare books reading room with conservation studio attached.
- Additional shelving. This was given a continuity of style with existing shelving, by the addition of coloured back panels to both.
- IT network access in all study spaces.[34]

Not surprisingly, these brief descriptions of a small sample of national, regional and special libraries illustrate similar refurbishment needs related to the age of buildings as their academic library counterparts. In addition, despite some differences in patterns of use, these libraries have had to respond to many of the same changes in the nature of their users' needs as have university libraries.

Public libraries

Heritage buildings

Built in stages over 21 years from 1907–28, Hamilton Townhouse, South Lanarkshire, contained a public library, offices and town hall. In 2002 the A-listed building was closed to allow for a £9 million regeneration that restored the exterior and brought internal facilities up to current standards.[35] This was part of a £20 million programme of developing resources for the arts in South Lanarkshire. The refurbished building by architects Coltart Earley, also includes a 900-seater auditorium and acts as a base for the council's community learning and arts development teams.[36]

The redevelopment provided improved access, including lift access to the upper floor; an IT training suite and an IT suite for children and young people.

Hamilton Townhouse Library won the Architect Meets Practicality Award and the Mary Finch Award for Accessibility, in the Public Library Building Awards in 2005.[37]

Forest Hill Library in the London Borough Lewisham, is a Grade 2 listed building. Opened in 1901, the library was recently closed for an extensive £1 million upgrade, reopening in December 2007. During closure a mobile library service was provided.

Working with English Heritage, this major refurbishment included:

- repairs to the roof, ceiling, plaster and paintwork
- an overhaul of the heating, lighting and power supply systems with attention paid to energy saving measures
- DDA compliance – improved access to the front and rear of the building, accessible toilets and library signage.[38]

Public consultation, both before construction and after completion, is now a common feature of library building schemes and Lewisham's consultation threw up a number of requirements, such as a buggy park, which were included in the final design. Other features of the restored building include a lounge area with informal seating, and improved IT facilities, including three large plasma screens, X box and Playstation.

As at Lewisham, the Vale of Glamorgan's Barry County Library renovation was preceded by a consultation process; this involved library staff and groups of users. A group of young people helped with the design of a chill-out space within the youth area of the library. Pupils from a local school also created an Arts Wall.

Throughout the building care has been taken to provide a wide range of reading, relaxing and learning spaces for individuals and groups.

The new library was opened in 2007 as part of a town centre redevelopment including the town hall, town square and park. The public area of the library occupies two floors of a new extension to the town hall, which is a listed building. One of the successes of the renovation has been the functional and aesthetic linking between the old and new parts of the building. The integration of the library into the overall civic development extends to the library's WiFi computer network, access to which is managed through the library's computer booking system and whose coverage includes the adjacent town square and park.

Access facilities include automatic entrance doors, lift, disabled toilets and induction loops at issue counters.[39]

While Brighton and Hove City Council's flagship Jubilee Library was attracting media attention, the same council was undertaking a very different library building scheme, restoring the 1908 Carnegie building of Hove Library. Opened in May 2006 after a scheme lasting only eight months and costing £350,000, the work combined restoration of the original fabric and a significant programme of improvements.

Original oak floors and plaster mouldings were restored and a domed glass ceiling, original doors, stained-glass and oak bookcases were retained.

Improvements to accessibility include a public glass-walled lift, a staff lift, toilets with disabled access and baby changing facilities. Lighting was improved and CCTV added to improve security.[40]

As with other libraries described above, the Carnegie-funded Walsall Central Library of 1906 is just over one hundred years old. Like other libraries of the period, the building had a large newsroom and lending department on the ground floor and a reference library, magazine and ladies room on the first floor – but no children's library. Subsequently space was found for a children's library, an art gallery and museum. In the 1960s the building underwent a major modernization and in 1964 it was decided to build an extension to accommodate a children's library, teenage area, record library, art gallery, museum, and space for exhibitions and meetings.

Figure 18.3 Walsall Central Library, exterior

Source: Rita Mills

Over the years the central library has housed many services, some of which, such as local history, have now been moved elsewhere. The Walsall Library and Museum now houses a ground floor lending library and children's library with a reference library and IT learning suite on the first floor. The museum occupies two galleries on the first and second floors. In 2002–2003 a modern entrance foyer was constructed to link the two buildings, creating a new main entrance with lift access to all floors.[41]

Swiss Cottage Library in the London Borough of Camden is an acclaimed Basil Spence building opened in 1964. Originally intended as part of a civic centre, only the library and adjoining swimming pool were built. Restoration of this style icon of the 1960s in 2003 included cleaning the exterior to reveal the original black-and-white geometric forms, plus substantial internal renovation to provide facilities suitable for current needs, including enhanced IT provision, study spaces and a café. This involved some internal alterations and the loss of furnishings which Spence had designed for the building. The library renewal was part of a wider development of the Swiss Cottage site.[42] The library won the Interior Design Award in the Public Library Building Awards, 2005.[43]

The public library buildings featured above date mainly from the first 60 years of the 20th century. Some such as Barry County Library are part of larger schemes; others are free-standing buildings and, like Hove, show that the Carnegie legacy is still important 100 years later. Features common to these refurbishments are a respect for original fabric and decoration, improved physical access and provision of a wide range of materials, IT facilities and physical spaces to attract diverse groups of users.

Other public library refurbishments

Opened in 1974 as Scunthorpe Central Library, this was a controversial building. It is an almost windowless brick structure. Office landscaping was employed in creating its layout and an integrated environmental design was applied to produce an energy-efficient structure. The entrance to this rather unusual building was through a large glazed pyramid.[44]

The library was refurbished during 2005, and given a new name – North Lincolnshire Central Library. This reflected a wish for it to be seen as a facility for all local people, rather than just those living in the town. The refurbishment made changes to both the exterior and interior of the library.

On the outside:

- It did away with the dark glass pyramid, creating a lighter and airier new entrance with wider automatic doors.
- Windows were inserted either side of the ground floor entrance to provide more natural light.
- Shrubbery and half-height ornamental walls close to the entrance were removed because of litter and vermin problems.

- A new handrail was provided on the approach to the library.
- Better parking for cycles was put in place.

On the inside:

- Fiction, with separate shelving for some genres and a quick pick section, large print collections, the People's Network and other computers, and the children's library were accommodated on the ground floor. Previously there was a large back-room office on the ground floor and users had to use the stairs or lift to reach all the library stock.
- The first floor now houses an integrated reference and non-fiction collection, local studies materials, musical scores and daily newspapers.[45]

Although sited in a good location, the 1950s 'box' Brookline Branch Library (1154m^2) – remodelled at the beginning of the 1990s – was thought less than ideal by the Carnegie Library of Pittsburgh. The concept for its renovation was to make the library 'more street-front', transforming an anonymous hemmed-in structure with few windows into a modern space filled with natural light. This idea was achieved by:

- Having a glass store front – putting the community living room on display.
- The removal of a mezzanine floor to create a two-storey high space with clerestory windows.
- Replacing the rear wall of the library with a glass wall, protected by an aluminium trellis with horizontal slats.

This was a prize-winning renovation and attracted an award from the US Library Building Award Program in 2005.

In the UK the Love Libraries campaign aimed to show what could be achieved with comparatively small resources.

Reopened in early June 2006 as an 'I Love Libraries' project, following a 12-week refurbishment costing £70,000, Newquay Library, Cornwall, a 1960s building, now has a new internal design and layout. It now boasts:

- Colourful visuals with a local sea theme.
- A quick choice section plus a comfortable reading area with coffee, newspapers and magazines.
- A TeenZone with sofas.
- A family corner.
- Investment in new stock included:
  - graphic novels and manga
  - a quick dip Cornish collection
  - thematic arrangement of stock
  - face-on displays

  – displays of audio and recommended books
- A 24/7 online catalogue that permits booking computers and ordering and renewing books online.
- Eight computers installed in a double-seated bar stool style area.
- Coloured rubber flooring and better lighting.

In creating this new environment the emphasis was on the library as 'An interactive, community hub for reading, with social activities for readers'. A big effort was made to attract new users to the library through professional marketing, making use of a uniform house style and using better-quality marketing materials.

As part of the 'Love Libraries' campaign,[46] Newquay Library benefited from a range of external expertise in marketing, publicity, events organization, interior design and furnishing, customer care, retail display, reading and staff training.

Newquay and the other Love Libraries campaign libraries – Coldharbour in Kent and Richmond on Thames – showed that building improvements and service developments can feed off and influence each other, and that shared expertise can produce striking results in a short time and for comparatively small sums of money.[47]

The extreme 'makeover' approach to library renovation is perhaps shown by the example of the Court Square branch of the Queens Borough Public Libraries New York. Here MDA Design Group formulated a makeover which from conception to completion took five months and which was executed in three weeks.

The library, on the first floor of the 49-storey Citibank Building, was 167m² in size and had remained substantially unchanged since its opening in 1986.

The design approach was to re-imagine the space, making it inviting to enter, attractive to use and easy to navigate, and with layout, furniture and clear signage-stimulating movement. Zones were arranged so that heavily use materials were prominently displayed. In this small library, space was at a premium and self-service terminals freed up space for other uses and freed up staff time for other forms of service to the users.[48]

The demand for intensive makeovers was confirmed in the USA in 2007 when Demco Library Interiors ran its second $10,000 Room Makeover Contest. This attracted entries from 122 libraries and media centres in public, school and university libraries.[49]

Also in the USA, the Robin Hood Foundation has targeted school libraries in high-poverty neighbourhoods and, as in the Love Libraries campaign, provided professional expertise as well as financial support. One renovation, the library of Public School 192, New York City won an American Library Association/ American Institute of Architect's award in 2007. Keynotes of the renovation of the 223m² library were high design standards and low capital and recurrent costs. 'Major materials including bamboo, formaldehyde free wheat-straw board and recycled plastic were used for their low environmental impact and low cost.'[50]

Although many library refurbishments are one-offs there are considerable advantages for library authorities in a series of refurbishment projects running serially or in tandem. Sometimes success with one scheme can make it easier to get approval and funding for subsequent ones. Other advantages include:

- capitalizing on staff expertise and experience
- achieving a uniform brand.

UK local authorities which have implemented such rolling refurbishment programmes include Nottinghamshire Libraries – Ladybrook, Toton (2004); Balderton, Beeston, Bircotes (2006)[51] – and North Yorkshire.

North Yorkshire saw investment in the libraries and re-branding as key factors.[52] The initiative (see also Chapter 16) was sparked off by a new library building at Ripon and the subsequent large increase in its use, which showed that investment in buildings, stock and services produced significant results. Subsequently £6.2 million was invested by the local authority in a programme of refurbishments ranging from cosmetic quick fixes to major rebuilds, all coordinated by the same project manager.

This last group of public library refurbishments illustrate two important points.

Firstly, refurbishment need not be solely about expensive remodelling of heritage buildings, but as at Newquay and the Court Square Branch Queens, New York, can achieve significant results in short timescales and with limited funding.

Secondly, that an overlong cycle of building refurbishment (at intervals of 20-40 years) is unsatisfactory to provide a library service in tune with user needs and expectations within a satisfactory physical environment. A discussion of potential scenarios for ongoing library renewal, rather than an irregular cycle, is provided towards the end of the next chapter.

Summary

The buildings featured in this chapter, like those in the case studies in the rest of the book, exemplify the reasons why libraries are refurbished and a range of approaches to refurbishment.

They illustrate the design objectives of refurbishment and the challenges and design factors faced by the planners, librarians, architects, designers and contractors involved in such projects.

The final chapter will summarize and comment on the issues raised by the library building projects featured in this book.

Notes

1   For lists and details of refurbished public and academic libraries of 2001–2005, *see* Dewe, M. and Clark, A.J. (2007), 'Library buildings' in *British Librarianship and Information Work 2001–2005,* edited by J.H. Bowman (Aldershot: Ashgate), 372–89.

2   For a further discussion of the public library context, *see* Dewe, M. (2006), *Planning Public Library Buildings: concepts and issues for the librarian* (Aldershot: Ashgate), Chapter 5, 'Alternatives to new library buildings'.

3   Wilkinson, J. (1998), 'Fundraising for university library development: the case of the London School of Economics', *New Review of Academic Librarianship* **4,** 133–46.

4   *SCONUL Library Buildings Database. London School of Economics*, available at: www.sconul.ac.uk/library_buildings/buildings/lse. 29 February 2008.

5   *LSE Library, the Library Building*, available: www.lse.ac.uk/library/abthli/arch.htm. 29 February 2008.

6   'John Rylands Library reopens after £17m transformation', available at: www.24hourmuseum.org.uk/nwh_gfx_en/ART50788.html. 11 March 2008.

7   *SCONUL library buildings database. Kings College London*, available: www.sconul. ac.uk/library_buildings/buildings/kcl. 29 February 2008.

8   Evans, C. (2003), 'Library buildings visit: LSE Lionel Robbins Library and King's College Maughan Library, November 2003'. *SCONUL Newsletter* 30, 7–8.

9   King's College London, available at: www.kcl.ac.uk/library/maughan.html. 29 February 2008.

10 *University College London. The Wilkins Library*, available: www.ucl.ac.uk/campaign/ priority-projects/projects/wilkins. 16 January 2008.

11 Hyams, E. (2006), 'A classic renewal: UCL's building programme', *Library and Information Update* **5** (7–8), 31–2.

12 Hyams, E. (2006), 32; *UCL Library Services – Wilkins building refurbishment*, available at: www.ucl.ac.uk/Library/wilkins. 29 March 2008.

13 *Hcl.harvard.edu Widener Library History*, available at: http://hcl.harvard.edu/libraries/ widener/history.html. 17 February 2008.

14 Jamieson, I. (2006), 'Remodelling a listed library building', *Multimedia Information and Technology* **32** (2), 36–7.

15 *SCONUL Library Buildings Database – Girton College, University of Cambridge*, available at: www.sconul.ac.uk/library_buildings/buildings/cambridge7. 18 March 2008.

16 *About Girton College Library,* available at: www-lib.girton.cam.ac.uk/about/index. html. 18 March 2008.

17 *Lafayette College Library Skillman Library Expansion and Renovation*, available at: http://ww2.lafayette.edu/~library/renovation/index.html. 18 March 2008.

18 Gleason, M. (2002), 'University of Southern California's Doheny Memorial Library reopens', *College and Research Libraries News* **63** (1), 8.

19 *University of Southern California. Doheny Memorial Library*, available at: www.usc. edu/libraries/locations/doheny/. 29 March 2008.

20 *SCONUL Library Buildings Database. Plymouth University Library*, available at: www.sconul.ac.uk/library_buildings/buildings/plymouth3. 4 March 2008.

21 Hordon, K. (2007), 'Northumbria University: milestone 1 completion of £6m library refurbishment', *Sconul focus* **40**, 122–3.

22 *University of Reading Library, Main Library Makeover*, available: www.reading.ac.uk/library/about-us/news/lib-2007-news-makeover.asp. 4 March 2008.

23 'Keele University: building refurbishment', (2007), *Sconul focus* **40**, 115–16.

24 'Finlay, H. (2006), 'Leeds Metropolitan University: Headingley Library refurbishment' *SCONUL focus* **38**, 134; 'Leeds Metropolitan University: Headingley Library refurbishment', (2007), *SCONUL focus* **40**, 117.

25 *University of York. University Library and Archives*, available at: www.york.ac.uk/services/library/libraries/campuslibs.htm. 30 March 2008.

26 Dorsay, J. (2004), 'Renewal of the library of Parliament', *Feliciter* **50** (6), 248–51.

27 *Government of Canada. Library of Parliament*, available at: www.parliamenthill.gc.ca/text/cmplbr/lbrprl-e.html. 9 March 2008.

28 *The British Museum Review 2001* available at: www.thebritishmuseum.ac.uk/pdf/annualreview0001.pdf. 5 November 2007; Davidson-Arnott, F. (2006), 'Reborn to new glory: the British Museum Reading Room', *Feliciter* **52** (2), 79–81.

29 *British Museum Reading Room*, available at: www.britishmuseum.org/the_museum/history_and_the_building/reading_room.aspx. 8 March 2008.

30 *State Library of Victoria Building Redevelopment Project*, available at: www.slv.vic.gov.au/about/pastfuture/building/redevelopment.html. 9 March 2008; Van de Velde, J. (2003), 'The State Library of Victoria foundation: a perspective', *Australian Academic and Research Libraries* **34** (4), 243–50.

31 *National Library of Australia Gateways* No. 57, June 2002, available: www.nla.gov.au/pub/gateways/archive/57/p18a01.html. 9 March 2008.

32 *National Library of Australia Annual Report 2006–7* available at: www.nla.gov.au/policy/annrep07/NLA-introduction.pdf, p.3..9 March 2008.

33 *Serota Library Furniture. Case study: The Royal Society of Medicine,* available at: www.serota.co.uk/cases/rsm.htm. 9 March 2008.

34 Snowley, I. (2005), 'Building for the future', *Library and Information Update* **4** (3), 28–31; *Royal Society of Medicine History of the RSM. RSM buildings*, available at: www.rsm.ac.uk/welcom/buildings.php. 8 March 2008.

35 Harper, P. (2005), 'Building better libraries', *Public Library Journal* **20** (4), 4–7.

36 Barr, J. (2004), 'Vision and integration', *Information Scotland* **2** (5), 13–4.

37 *CILIP Public Libraries Group. Public Library Building Awards 2005*, available at: www.cilip.org.uk/specialinterestgroups/bysubject/public/awards/awards2005/winners2005.htm. 7 March 2008.

38 *Lewisham Council Forest Hill Library Project*, available at: www.lewisham.gov.uk/LeisureAndCulture/Libraries/ForestHillProject.htm. 7 March 2008; *Lewisham Council Forest Hill Project Public Consultation Meeting 26th October 2006,* available: www.lewisham.gov.uk/NR/rdonlyres/AEA7998D-FF71-4773-AA9B-BE06025AC01C/0/ForestHillConsultationMtg261006.pdf. 7 March 2008.

39 Jones, S. (2007), 'New library – new opportunities', *Y Ddolen* 46, 18–9; *Vale of Glamorgan Barry Library*, available at: www.valeofglamorgan.gov.uk/working/libraries/full_time_libraries/county_library_at_barry.aspx. 18 March 2008.

40 Stone, A. (2006), 'A Carnegie restoration.' *Library and Information Update* 5 (7/8), 59.

41 *Walsall Council, Leisure and Culture: central library story*, available at: www.walsall.gov.uk/index/leisure_culture/libraries/central_library_centenary/central_library_story.htm. 4 January 2008.

42 Harper, P. (2005), 5.

43 *Camden Council Swiss Cottage Library*, available at: www.camden.gov.uk/ccm/navigation/leisure/libraries-and-online-learning-centres/swiss-cottage-library/. 7 March 2008; Stungo, N. (2003), 'Tome capsule' *RIBA Journal* 110 (8), 24–30, 32.

44 Ward, H. (ed.) (1976), *New Library Buildings 1976 Issue: Years 1973–1974* (London: Library Association), 24–7.

45 *North Lincolnshire Council – Central Library Improvements*, available at: www.northlincs.gov.uk/NorthLincs/Leisure/libraries/yourlocallibrary/centrallibrary/CentralLibraryImprovements.htm. 7 March 2008.

46 McKearney, M. (2006), 'Love Libraries: creating a fresh image', *Library and Information Update* 5 (11), 36–40.

47 Howard, C. et al., (2006), 'Transformed by love', *Public Library Journal* 21 (3), 2–6.

48 Martin, E. and Kenney, B. (2005), 'Express makeover', *Library by Design* (supplement to *Library Journal*) Fall, 1-.

49 'A room makeover contest draws a herd' (2007), *Library by Design* (supplement to *Library Journal*) Fall, 28.

50 *American Library Association News April 17 2007*, available at: www.ala.org/Template.cfm?Section=pressreleases&template=/contentmanagement/contentdisplay.cfm&ContentID=155669. 18 March 2008.

51 *Designing Libraries Database. Entries for Balderton, Beeston, Bircotes, Ladybrook and Toton*, available at: www.designinglibraries.org.uk. 7 March 2008.

52 Blaisdale, J., Fay, D. and Garbacz, S. (2006), 'Introducing a new branded look', *Library and Information Update* 5 (7/8), 43–7.

Chapter 19
Case Studies Reviewed

Michael Dewe

The preceding chapters have described in greater or lesser detail a number of case studies of library building renewal in various library sectors both in the UK and abroad. This chapter endeavours to outline some themes, issues, practices, problems and outcomes that appear common to many of these accounts, as well as bringing out the distinctive aspects of some individual case studies. It also draws upon some additional library refurbishment experiences in the UK, USA and Hong Kong. This case study review follows the general sequence of a project from initiation to an evaluation of the refurbished library.

Chapter 1 outlined the major forces for change emanating from government bodies and agencies and the funds they are able to make available for library renewal. The case studies have mentioned these and other drivers for change, such as Best Value reviews and the Comprehensive Performance Assessment in the public library sector, as well as the significance of local pressures and reviews. All point to the need for a radical rethink of library services in order to bring them up to standard and modernize the buildings that house them. A major concern is to 'Alter perceptions and challenge the stereotype' – marketed in North Yorkshire as a 'New look, no shush' – and to change the image of libraries that are thought of as dull, dingy, unappealing, old-fashioned, quiet, boring, uninviting and outdated. However, the challenge is not just about changing the image but, for example, dealing with other issues, such as a larger student body in universities, the social role of libraries, whatever the sector, and a wish to increase library loans, ICT use and visits.

Assessing the library building

The need for an improved physical environment in libraries derives from a number of common drawbacks to existing service points that show up in the case studies, such as neglect, building defects and worn-out building services. Neglect occurs when there has been little or no building investment in library premises, except perhaps an earlier but superficial renovation, and small service points may well be overlooked. Thus libraries may be essentially unchanged since opening, as in at Suffolk or at Scarborough– the latter's building had been largely untouched since its opening in 1934. In Australia, the State Library of Victoria had not experienced construction work or renovation for nearly 30 years. Building defects, and resultant costly repairs, stem from poor maintenance over a long period of time: in Dublin's case a building condition that required major intervention. And mechanical and electrical services may also be coming to the end of their designed life. Other drawbacks might be due to:

- *Lack of space* – for service development, collections and for staff and users, although new library elements may still be added later, such as the People's Network and, at Lowestoft, accommodation was later provided for a schools library service and record office that put pressure on space.
- *Unopened areas* – some areas not open to the public due to health and safety issues, as in Leek Library.
- *Piecemeal change* – to attempt to alleviate particular problems.
- *Furniture and fittings* – these may now be at the end of their lifespan and with new additions not matching the originals.
- *Disability Discrimination Act (DDA) compliance* – for instance, there was no lift to the mezzanine at the 1966 Felixstowe Library.
- *Unsatisfactory environmental conditions* – for users and for collection preservation at, for example, the London Library and the record office at Lowestoft.

A building in need of renewal, however, also presents opportunities for change and development precisely because of the passage of time:

- *Changing role* – of an individual service point.
- *Changing nature of the library's operations* – at Stowmarket the staff areas are now larger than required and many libraries have gone over to self-service for the issue and return of library materials.
- *Release of space* – because other occupants move out of the library, as was the case at Dublin.
- *Dispersed services* – the wish to bring services together, as at Winchester.

It may also be the time to resolve the drawbacks of a library's earlier building history – the long history of library extensions between 1935 and 1978 at the Hartley Library, Southampton, for example.

The librarian's task in bringing about change in the building to be refurbished is much helped if there is support from various groups, such as students, library staff and elected members or trustees for example. The task is also made easier where opportunities for partnership exist that enable satisfactory funding to be acquired or the possibility of a shared buildings with access to other local authority or institutional services.

Studies and surveys

Many refurbishment projects start with a review or report on the library building or buildings. Market research that includes public consultation may also be employed, as a way of understanding what needs to be done and preparing for forwarding the renewal process. The challenge can be quite complex, as in Dublin, where it was the tripartite one of building conservation, refurbishment and new build.

For public libraries various publications influence developments such as *Framework for the Future, Better Public Libraries* and *21ˢᵗ Century Libraries: changing forms, changing futures*, as well as others like the adult Public Library User Survey (PLUS) of 2004–2004 utilized at Barnsley.

A market plan with a 'product concept', such as that at the National Library of Wales and North Yorkshire can stem from market research that includes a range of methods:

- user and non-users surveys, including for instance visits to local schools
- focus groups – in North Yorkshire they considered reasons for not using libraries
- household surveys
- telephone polls
- library users groups – at the National Library of Wales and at Stowmarket Library, for example.

For the library building (or buildings) itself, other more specialized studies may be called for, such as:

- an architect's report
- a physical feasibility study (National Library of Wales)
- the creation of a building conservation strategy (Dublin)
- asset management assessment – that at Barnsley in 2003 rated many structural and other building features as 'poor'.

Consultation and communication

Although market research involves a structured assessment of users and their needs through a range of consultation methods, further consultation and communication will be needed at other stages in the project. For example:

- input from academic staff, students and library staff to the library brief, as at the Kenrick Library
- the display of plans and proposals, as at Torquay, together with items in the local newspapers
- validation of the design by disabled people

- user studies carried out at Malmö in connection with the design of information desks
- involving young people in library refurbishment design, discussed in more detail below.

Communicating with users and potential users during planning for change is important, but it is wise to indicate that not everything wished for can be promised or achieved and compromise may sometimes be necessary.

Young people and library design

Getting young people involved in library makeovers is being encouraged by library related organizations and individual library authorities in the UK: for example, the DfES-funded pack published by the Reading Agency and the education charity ContinYou (previously Education Extra), *Enjoying Reading: public library partnership with schools*. This aimed at helping public libraries and schools to work together for young readers; it gives library staff ideas for creating partnerships with schools, including running book awards, and putting young people in charge of library makeovers. They have ideas and opinions about design and want a library space that is for themselves and their friends.[1]

This approach is endorsed by the Isle of Wight libraries officer, who, as part of the development of the library service to children and young people that has taken place, writes that managers now include young people in decisions affecting all functions, including website design, library refurbishments and reader development'.[2]

At Norfolk Public Library, Virginia, US, a library volunteer, who is also an architectural designer, worked with a teen advisory group to create a Teen Zone and renovate the children's room. The Teen Zone was created from an empty hallway, with half the funds provided by Friends of the Library. It resulted in a comfortable place to 'hang out' with:

- a bright colour scheme
- black furniture
- a special collection of young adult literature
- a work of art – an abstract six-sided painting.

The success of the Teen Zone convinced the city to provide dedicated funding to redecorate the children's library – 'lipstick and rouge' was what was needed. New carpet, and the replacement of pastel walls with 'kaleidoscopes of wild and attractive colors and forms', transformed the children's library. As a result of the makeover, use of the library by teenagers has doubled and the youngsters like the spaces that they had help design.[3]

Strategic thinking and planning

A number of public library authorities have embarked on a programme of refurbishment as part of a corporate or other strategy, such as:

- Staffordshire, where a 2000 Best Value review resulted in a five-year plan to improve the library service – the 'Library Vision'.
- Torbay, where, following *Framework for the Future*'s publication, a working party produced a ten-year development blueprint which recognized the inadequacies of Torquay Library.
- Leicestershire was provided with a capital budget of £5 million to rebuild or renovate 40 libraries during 2002–2008 as part of a corporate strategy to improve its libraries. A capital programme project board manages the overall programme and by August 2007, 32 libraries had been completed.
- As part of a public access strategy, a programme of refurbishment to transform the overall look and feel of North Yorkshire libraries was undertaken and 18 libraries refurbished from 2003–2006.

At the National Library of Wales, the completion of the 1992 storage facility at the rear of the building enabled strategic thinking about the use of the older parts to create the Visitor Experience, although there was a lack of emphasis placed on upgrading reading room facilities. This has subsequently been remedied. The London Library's strategic plan for 2002–2007 was drawn upon in the preparation of the architect's brief, while the upgrading of the Wilkins Library at UCL is part of the strategic plan for University College London.

In the United States, the Better Jacksonville Plan is a library development strategy that involves a new main library (opened in 2005), six new branches and the renovation of 12 existing branches.[4] Also in the US, Queen's New York Library plans to renovate or build anew all of its 63 libraries. Twelve renovations were carried out in seven months on a rolling schedule with buildings closed on average for 14 weeks during which time limited service was provided by a mobile library. It was commented that: 'Merely changing light bulbs in a system of that size created shock waves.'[5]

Location assessment

Determining factors in the decision to refurbish a library building must be that it still occupies a suitable location and is of sufficient size (or capable of extension) to accommodate all that is wished for in the renewed library. At Winchester, rather than a refurbishment, a new building was originally mooted next to the much admired Hampshire Record Office but there was no support for this proposed site. Glasgow University Library underwent an options appraisal to evaluate whether new build or a refurbishment was best and the latter option was chosen, as the library was in the optimal location for campus development. In Dublin, the Pearse Street library building is on a major access route into the city but its landlocked site posed construction difficulties and similar construction problems were posed at the Waterford Library site.

As remarked elsewhere, the difference in planning a new library to re-planning an existing building is that in the latter case it requires people to work within the limitations of what exists (the building and its site), rather than create something new to fit stated needs. This, as will be seen, is not without its difficulties, one of which may be that the older building may be in a conservation area, like Stowmarket Library, Suffolk, or a listed building, or perhaps both. Local planning authorities, the local civic society and the appropriate national heritage body, like English Heritage, will need to be consulted as to what building developments and changes are acceptable. Experience seems to show that the earlier this involvement takes place the better it is for the project's progress. The London Library involved Westminster City Council at an early stage, carried out an historic building impact assessment and obtained planning consent in late 2005: its scheme was specially commended.

The case studies exemplify the benefits of informed negotiation and occasions when compromise is called for, over colour schemes, for example, and when meeting conservation requirements can cause delay.

Acquiring the funding

Sources of external government funding, including the National Lottery, were noted in Chapter 1 and the case studies demonstrate the diversity of financial arrangements and sources that have made refurbishment projects possible. Library refurbishment funds may rely on one or a mix of sources – the library service's budget and local authority or institutional resources – the Single Capital Pot as at Lakenheath Library, Suffolk, for example – and contributions from other local authorities. In some instances matched funding by the local authority or institution is required. Other sources tapped for funding could include:

- VAT refund and Access Centre bid money
- European funding, as at Lowestoft
- partnership with developers – as in North Yorkshire
- Disability Discrimination Act funding utilized at Lakenheath
- fundraising – at the London Library
- sale of surplus buildings – the old library HQ at Winchester
- benefaction – Wolfson Foundation funding at the Hartley Library, Southampton University and for further work at the British Library of Political and Economic Science (LSE)
- Higher Education Funding Council for England – capital 3 funding.

In Ireland, central government contributes financially to approved library building projects, as is the case in some other countries, Finland for example.

In Chapter 17 on Suffolk it is noted that 'Reconciling the timetables and deadlines of different bodies seems to be a major problem for projects reliant on funds from more than one source'. The value of having someone with an overview of funding sources and good contacts with budget holders is also emphasized.

Sometimes phased projects require the acquisition of additional monies to proceed to the next stage, and a tight or reduced budget means that priorities are reaffirmed and compromises accepted as at the Kenrick Library. Glasgow University Library found that phasing was better than a single operation and made for better financial streaming and planning. The Hartley Library, Southampton, wanted a total renewal of its environment and embarked upon three linked projects.

The brief

There is much evidence in the case studies of the key importance of the architect's brief and a library supplier's specification in bringing about successful change. As has been seen, the brief, whose compilation is often an evolving process, and may proceed from a primary or outline brief to a secondary brief, as at the London Library, is used, for amongst other things, to spell out the aims of the refurbishment project and to offer guidance on the design principles to be followed.

The architect and other specialists

In some instances the choice of architect for a library refurbishment is governed by the availability of an architectural service within the local authority, as for the Dublin project. In other instances, such as the London Library, outside architects are chosen, perhaps after interviewing a number of practices and asking for conceptual responses to an outline brief. Or the architect may be chosen as the result of an architectural competition, which was the case in Malmö. North Yorkshire used a variety of architects and contractors for its library projects.

Where necessary other specialists – structural and electrical engineers, a cost consultant, for example – are employed in connection with renewing the building's structure and services as well as a building contractor. Winchester used a contractor selection procedure whereby the county council's Major Framework Contract process invited two already approved contractors to submit bids, the successful contractor working closely with the design team. A similar arrangement is found in Suffolk for large projects, such as at Felixstowe Library, under the council's property department's partnership tenders scheme.

A project might also make use of particular consultants for marketing and display and employ an interior designer, as well as contracting for library furniture and equipment. Hampshire's renowned local authority architectural service available to the Winchester Discovery Centre provided a complete package – interior design, consulting engineers and other specialists, helping to simplify the whole design process.

Design for refurbishment

Design objectives

The overall aim at Barnsley was to 'create a modern public library, fit for the 21st century, which would be attractive and encourage more people to visit'. More precise design objectives included:

- clarity, coherence and integration (Hartley Library)
- flexibility, accessibility, security and ambience (priorities at Waterford)
- a different atmosphere to that of older-style library buildings with a more open spacious feeling
- to create a template for other projects
- branding – the Discovery Centre concept pioneered in Kent and in Hampshire adding to the modern library mix 'whatever is appropriate locally from a range of activities and functions'
- a refurbishment that respects the building but with a corporate image established through, for example, signage and colour, as in North Yorkshire for example
- recognition of the library's ceremonial role for official visitors and guided tour by increased space provision, as at the Main Library of the Canadian Parliament
- the library's role in providing a social and informal space – Keele University Library and Leeds Metropolitan University, Headingley Library
- provision for special collections of local history, rare books and manuscripts, for example, Glasgow University Library
- creating a learning environment with different study settings for groups and individuals, which reflect current and developing learning patterns.

Learning centre concept

As noted elsewhere, there has been a tendency for some academic institutions to rename their libraries as learning centres or learning resource centres and both Leeds Metropolitan (LMU) and Sheffield Hallam (SHU) have erected new buildings, and refurbished and extended older libraries, re-launching them as learning centres.[6] The underlying principle behind the learning centre concept is the concern for learning activities not just supporting resources.

The renovation of LMU's Beckett Park Campus Library posed problems, as it was a listed building and certain features, such as stained-glass windows and decorative plasterwork had to be retained and incorporated. As library service continued, there was a greater need for day-to-day contact between building workers and staff.

In both their new and refurbished buildings, LMU and SHU felt that the interior design must be attractive to students and comfortable to support and encourage lengthy periods of study. Particular design challenges include those associated with large numbers of computers and the management of noise. Some characteristics of real and virtual learning that are complementary are:

- activity and movement rather than quiet and serenity
- learning centre design shows the influence of department stores and business centres
- group work and conversation allied with drinks, snacks and mobile phone calls.

Activities which develop and support virtual learning will take up the space released by smaller print collections.

Design challenges and ideas

A major design challenge for those refurbishing an older library building is that of blending old and new. The general approach to the integration of old and new building fabric seems to be that of retaining and restoring the older architectural features, e.g. ceiling height, glazing and timber floors as at Dublin, with new space designed in a contemporary style with perhaps some reference to the past through the choice of materials. At Felixstowe the idea was to retain and update the 1960s feel, while at the John Rylands Library the refurbishment resulted in a mix of 1890s architecture and modern construction and facilities.

Design challenges will also relate to the library façade, the satisfactory joining of old and new elements, as well as form and function clashes. Changes to the exterior of Lowestoft gave it a Mondrian look, enhanced by the quirky 'the Library' sign, while the improvement of Lakenheath's frontage helps to promote the service to passers-by. In Dublin there is a distinct contrast between the old and new façades but improvements to the library exterior, may, as at Torquay Library, be too costly to be carried out. At the National Library of Australia, the opportunity was taken to refurbish the podium around the building.

In joining old and new – as at Malmö – a common design challenge is adding to and then linking an old building with a new one. Some case study solutions included a two-storey library extension at Felixstowe linked by a mezzanine; a link–bridge between buildings at Leek Library and between the old and new extension at Long Eaton. In Ireland there is a first- and second-floor glass bridge at Waterford and a new internal street – a continuous corridor – in Dublin.

In the beauty versus function battle it was thought at Malmö that beauty had triumphed – staff were in cold conditions in the entrance; there was hardly any wall space to put shelving against because of the amount of glass and beautiful signs had won out over readability. The placing of function before aesthetics at the London Library made difficulties for the fundraising team who needed visual images to sell the project.

Other ideas and challenges will be a response to creating better access, in every sense of the word, whether retail principles will be utilized in library design and to what extent self-service will be employed.

- *Better access* (by lifts and stairs) and facilities, especially for the disabled; two new DDA compliant user lifts were provided at Barnsley, a lift and toilets in the extension at Felixstowe and improved disabled facilities are now offered at Keele University Library.
- *Utilizing retail principles.* For example, Staffordshire's use of consultants to improve the user experience, establish appropriate traffic flows and ensure that the library lived up to retail levels of presentation and cleanliness.
- *Use of self-service* – the implementation of RFID at Barnsley, for example.

As with all refurbishments, decisions will need to be made about, for example, the use of floor space, the role and organization of staff and collections and the integration of ICT.

- *Floor space use* – deciding how the building would be utilized and organized. Some examples are:
  - a rationalization of the floor space as at Stowmarket leading to an increase in public space
  - the incorporation into the existing building of departments previously located elsewhere or relocation of some elements of the library service to another building – in Dublin the library HQ was incorporated into the Pearse Street building but bibliographical services were moved to Cabra, a new library (2001)
  - deciding how different floors would be used – three of the four floors are for public use at Waterford, where the library is seen as a journey of discovery with each area allowing glimpses into others: 'one book leads to another'
  - at the London Library decisions were needed as to how the library was to be organized after its link on five levels to the newly acquired Duchess House (now T.S. Eliot House)
  - the creation of reading rooms from an interior light court, as at Harvard
  - there is the rather special case of the British Museum Round Reading Room, which now has a new role, as it is no longer part of the British Library, and stands within the new setting of the Great Court.

- *The role and of organization library staff*
    - reconfigured from subject to type of material at the Hartley Library, Southampton, with staff facing the entrance for an effective welcome and orientation service
    - staff working in new ways at Malmö
    - customer care training given at North Yorkshire.
- *The organization of the collection or collections* – for example:
    - the categorization library stock as in the Torquay experience
    - a reconfiguration of stock from subject to type of material at the Hartley Library, Southampton
    - at Malmö, the Castle building represented fantasy and history, the Cylinder of Light building the future and knowledge
    - an improved layout at Headingley (LMU) by having one sequence of books
    - reference and non-fiction material integrated at North Lincolnshire Central Library.
- *Integration of ICT* – its configuration to suit groups and individuals in various locations. This can involve:
    - creating a complimentary mix of print and electronic resources
    - upgrading ICT equipment and installing new furniture, as at Barnsley
    - wireless network provided at Keele and extended at Headingley (LMU)
    - multimedia facilities offered at the University of York Library
    - Kings College London, of which the Maughan Library is part, envisages a virtual college campus
    - accessible raised floor for wiring at Felixstowe.

Other design issues might concern the reuse of refurbished, existing furniture and shelving; the employment of a standard fit-out method, where more than one library is to be upgraded – as in Leicestershire – which 'non-library' elements are to be included like a museum, exhibition spaces, catering facilities and shop. Finally there is often a desire for a surprise element in the building, on entering the library, for example – the elusive 'wow' factor. The light-filled atrium at LSE's library creates a stunning effect.

Design features

Design features in refurbished libraries will often be concerned with, for example, the entrance area, the use of new building materials, the renaming of library areas, the library layout and the better use of colour and lighting.

- Entrances
    - a new entrance created at Leek Library through the District Office
    - Glasgow University Library remodelled its entrance area
    - a new members' entrance formed at the London Library

- – a new entrance created at the Sunderland University Library
- – a new main entrance created at Walsall Library
- – the redesign of entrance hall at the Hartley Lbrary, University of Southampton.

- Use of glass – in external walls and for interior partitions.
- Zones – different zones for different library activities and groups of users, often denoted with new names like 'Hub', Teen Zone, and Inter@ct.
- Colour – the use of signature and accent colours and of white to give a lighter feel to the interior; also colour from carpet, and improvements to ceiling and floor finishes.
- Graphics and decoration
  - – graphics on walls above shelving at Stowmarket
  - – a feature wall, children's mural and coffee shop logo at Lowestoft
  - – a large colour photographs of local scenes and views of the port at Felixstowe, as well as a quirky steel sculpture
  - – although not mentioned in the case studies, there is the refurbishment featuring distinctive artwork to complement the library setting at Thatcham Library, Berkshire.
- Lighting – this is not just a question of levels, design and effectiveness but also of energy conservation and better fittings. Natural light is an important feature of the three buildings making up the Malmö Library.
- Layout improvements
  - – library stock – 'the spine' concept at Leek Library
  - – quick choice – books and browser area leading to adult fiction beyond (Leicestershire), and at Felixstowe where the area is next to self-service machines
  - – a linked series of reading rooms at the University of Plymouth Library, rather than a large open plan area
  - – counters – generally moved away from the entrance; at Felixstowe replaced by pods. There is an integrated reception and information desk at Reading University Library
  - – self-service and robotic sorting – in use at Malmö
  - – study and research facilities – group study and research rooms at Glasgow University Library – and increased seating.
- Other improvements
  - – the provision of better designed areas for children and young people
  - – multi-purpose rooms – reading rooms convertible to reception or lecture space
  - – museum provision – at Leek and Winchester
  - – facilities and amenities – casual seating, refurbished toilets, water coolers, and lockers. A library café is *de rigeur*. At the Hartley Library Internet café type computers are provided
  - – off-site facilities – the Library Research Annexe at Glasgow University.

Building constraints and opportunities

It will have been observed that design solutions proposed in the case studies were sometimes hampered by the characteristics of the building to be refurbished. The shopping centre library at Birstall, Leicestershire is a good example of design ideas defeated by building constraints and costs. Unlike new buildings, refurbished building will pose known constraints, as well as opportunities to correct building faults and other problems, some of which may be longstanding.

- Building orientation – the refurbishment of Stowmarket needed to combat lighting and ventilation problems caused by the library' orientation.
- Building repairs to roof at Barnsley; roof insulated at Felixstowe.
- Mechanical and electrical systems that improve the physical environment – automatic solar blinds at Glasgow University; air conditioning at Barnsley.
- New technology improvements – an Internet café area created at Felixstowe.
- Structural change – central balcony enclosed with glazed screen at Barnsley; two large opening roof lanterns to improve light and ventilation installed at Stowmarket.
- Windows – replaced at front and rear of Lowestoft some by aluminium-coated panels; new opening windows installed at Stowmarket.
- Shape of building – the U-shaped building at Stowmarket requiring two staffed parts but useful in creating separate zones of refurbishment.
- Mezzanines – the mezzanine floor filled in at Lowestoft.
- Health and safety – stairs enclosed in fire wells at Lowestoft; poor ventilation at Stowmarket improved.

Structural and other problems

Any building project can run into problems caused by inadequate specification, damaged equipment, contractor delays and changes to regulations. However, in dealing with a refurbishment that involves proposed demolition and new construction, particularly in veteran and vintage buildings, then unexpected problems may arise, possibly delaying progress and incurring additional costs. Some case study examples are:

- Restrictive physical limitations at Dublin which originally had no lift, almost vertical stairs and a frontage making ramped access difficult.
- Roof and floor problems at Long Eaton Library.
- Untied brick walls in an 1838 building at Winchester.
- Wet rot, erosion of façade stone and structural design faults in the limestone entrance portico of Dublin Library.

- Archaeological finds – the finding of archaeological remains, or even the threat of finding such remains, as at Winchester, can have an impact on a project. In Waterford, the design outcome of the brief was influenced by the discovery of a medieval wall in the basement area.
- Health and safety issues – the discovery of asbestos at the National Library of Wales and Barnsley.
- More work on lift shafts needed than anticipated at Barnsley.

Dealing with the problems whether large or small scale, which may entail site meetings and crisis management – working through and dealing with problems as they arise – is a necessary skill. In Chapter 13 on Waterford, Jane Cantwell lists six points to help deal with such crises, of which three are: 'Don't be intimidated by jargon'; 'Be specific as possible in the initial brief', and 'Small details *do* matter!'

A structural problems case study

Renovating old libraries can pose technical problems as regards their structure and building services and this is exemplified well by a case study of the renovation and expansion of the Li Ping Medical Library of the Chinese University of Hong Kong, completed in early 2003.[7]

A shortage of library space had been recognized in 1987 but was not really remedied to meet user needs by a small 1995 expansion. Space was not the only problem, as the accommodation was considered old and shabby with a poor furniture layout and dated building infrastructure.

The upgrading involved the integration of two libraries and acquiring adjacent space and the renovation was carried out in two phases. The experience highlighted many general issues, such as funding problems, rushed planning and the differences between librarians and architects, as well as those related to a hospital environment, like construction noise.

The structural and other problems identified in this project were:

- the floor loading could not take high-density compact shelving
- a new furniture layout was hampered by numerous load-bearing structural columns of differing sizes and at varying distances
- the ceilings of three different heights
- the location of building services.

The case study shows the efforts made to mitigate the impact of these problems on the design of the library, some exacerbated by the absence of updated structural and mechanical drawings.

The librarian identified a number of lessons learned from the project and suggests that with old buildings it is wise to have a thorough examination 'to discover any possible obstacles to construction such as hidden pipes and wires. The earlier these problems are known, the better they are addressed' and a readiness to accept compromise when appropriate is necessary.

Not the whole building

As we have seen in some university libraries, for example, renewal may not be concerned with a complete building but with one inadequate element, a particular floor or an unsatisfactory entrance area. The latter was the case in the USA at White Plains Public Library, where, concerned with the kind of impression its large entrance made (just under 560m^2), and what should be located there, two models were suggested:

- the concierge model – librarians greet patrons and provide assistance
- the kiosk model – basic information is supplied and staff floor walk and assist patrons in the stacks.[8]

The case studies provide examples of the models adopted in UK libraries.

At Lakenheath, Suffolk, the improvement of one aspect of the building led to the realization that more needed to be done and resulted in a more complete refurbishment.

Project management team

A common practice for libraries is the formation of a project team to oversee and manage the refurbishment. Membership of the team could be quite varied depending upon the scale and nature of the project: at North Yorkshire refurbishment was led by service head, support services manager and local area manager. For the Suffolk refurbishments an asset manager was involved with the project team, while in Leicestershire use was made of the county council's property section. As regards team size, it is suggested that it should be 'small enough to make decisions and big enough to do all the work'. For some schemes two teams would be formed: a team carrying out the work of design and construction and a library team with various managerial levels in membership. Where the two-team approach was necessary, then the project manager, preferably full-time, would be the link between the two.

For library staff involved in the project management team, there could be a lack of experience of larger-scale refurbishment projects, which could be quite complex – in Dublin it involved three buildings – and work could be handicapped by staff changes. Nevertheless, some additional arrangements may be necessary to forward the project, such as:

- operational subgroups (Dublin)
- a client review group meeting weekly to enable progress between the monthly meetings of the building project steering committee (London Library)
- fortnightly site meetings facilitated by the architect (Barnsley)
- a house team, working closely with the architect and the library supplier, like the one which handled the design of the interior at Lowestoft.

In assessing library suppliers' quotes, Barnsley used a scoring matrix, whereby three major library furnishing companies were invited to tender, a scoring matrix compiled and each submission evaluated against its criteria. By contrast, Leicestershire made use of a local shop fitter, who had built up a reputation over its work for the library service.

The project team or some of its members may make visits to the newest and best comparable library schemes in other parts of the UK. Both Leicestershire and Barnsley undertook such visits, the latter to see new designs and layouts and how they worked in practice, in particular the use of RFID. The Designing Libraries website can be of help here in identifying appropriate libraries to be visited.

During refurbishment

When library refurbishment is to take place three major challenges will probably have to be confronted and planned for because work is being carried out on the building:

- library closure
- maintaining the library service
- managing the site.

Additionally, structural or other problems that may occur, as described earlier, will have to be dealt with by the project team as they arise.

Library closure

If the scale of construction and other work is considerable, or the library is a small one of limited space, it may be necessary to close the building for an agreed period. Closure may be avoided where circumstances permit the phasing of the work to be done (as at the Wilkins Library), although this will involve some moving around in the building until project completion and which will usually require some brief periods of closure. The completion of Phase 1 at the London Library meant some interim fitting out (rather than final design solution) while fundraising went ahead for the next stage. Sometimes, the funding may not be available to move off the site and the library has to function around the changes to the building, as at Lowestoft.

If the building is to be closed for a significant period of time, then thought will have to be given to planning for the redeployment of library staff, the storage of books and other library materials, as well as furniture and equipment. The logistics of returning all these elements to the refurbished library must also be planned for and, as the Barnsley experience shows, it is no small task.

Maintaining the library service

If library closure is to take place, then some form of alternative, temporary service is usually put in hand, as users should not be completely deprived of their local library service during building works. Sometimes there may be problems in finding alternative accommodation and a number of solutions may be used:

- Borrowers may be referred to other service points in the vicinity, perhaps with additional opening hours.
- Temporary accommodation may be found in a nearby vacant building or a school to house a probably restricted service.
- Loan and reservation benefits may be offered during closure.
- A temporary location for staff to work on stock and other tasks in connection with the coming reopening of the refurbished library will also be essential.
- A mobile library service with extra stops will be provided.

During this temporary service, librarians can expect a decline in library visits and use.

Site management

Where the library is to be kept open during refurbishment, which may for example involve the demolition of part of the existing structure, then thought must be given to managing safe access to, into and around, the building. This could involve:

- the redirection of pedestrian and vehicular traffic
- temporary signage
- a temporary entrance
- ensuring that staff and visitors are not exposed to threats to their health and safety, such as dust and noise and periods without heating or utilities
- dealing with the concerns of residents affected by the renovation work, as at the London Library and in Dublin and Waterford.

Whether the library is to be closed or not, the public and staff should be kept fully informed about the refurbishment and its progress, with milestone dates and events being identified. The ideal is a continuation of service with the minimum of inconvenience, for example, making arrangements for retrieving material that is temporarily inaccessible, and seeing that there is no threat to the well-being of the library visitor. Readers are generally very appreciative of what is being done to overcome the service difficulties posed by refurbishment.

Reopening the library

There will undoubtedly be considerable interest and curiosity about the refurbished library when its reopening is announced and thought should be given to:

- an opening ceremony
- a programme of events
- increased opening hours
- publicity – in the temporary library and media, for example, leading up to the reopening.

Post-refurbishment review

A post-refurbishment review in Leicestershire is carried out after six to eight weeks and then there is a review after 18 months. Such reviews will seek to:

- remedy building snags (Barnsley)
- see to adjustments and repairs (Waterford)
- resolve problems like acoustic difficulties (Kenrick Library),
- respond to the need for more study rooms, a breakdown in zoning and lift problems (Hartley Library).

As a result of the review at Malmö, the north-facing problem entrance was closed, providing more space for the café.

Along with an evaluation of the physical structure, librarians will want to know whether the building was delivered on time and to (or even under) budget and is value for money. An assessment will also be made of the building's impact, achievements and benefits, both locally and more widely.

Impact and reaction

As well as accepting praise for what has been achieved by way of refurbishment, staff may have to deal with reaction – criticism and negative comments. Such reaction may occur at any point in the project. For example, due to protest, the public's wish to retain the old entrance at Leek Library (previously a designated fire exit) was agreed to. There was controversy over the X box 360 proposal at Torquay as well as a negative response to fiction categorization. Protest occurred over the removal of a couple of trees at Malmö and the replacement of the story-telling cave – until visitors saw the new one!

The impact of the refurbishment may be gauged from:

- user satisfaction – positive customer comments and the tendency to stay longer, and information gained from PLUS surveys
- levels of use – shown by rises in visitor and book issue figures and in the use of the People's Network
- a tour of building by disabled users, as at Barnsley
- ongoing consultation
- the role of staff – customer response to new ways of deploying staff.

Re-planning and refurbishing a library always involve change and while there will be those who welcome such developments other may find change unsettling after reopening. Blackburn Central Library, but not one of the case study libraries, which reopened after refurbishment in 2003, decided to anticipate likely negative comments through staff training. Questions and comments that might arise, to which staff were trained to respond positively, included:

- I liked the library just the way it was.
- The library is for your generation, not ours.
- The self-service machine never works …
- Where have all the books gone?

Achievements and benefits

A number of achievements and benefits stem from a successful refurbishment, for example:

- At Lowestoft it 'Changed what the library offers the community and how it is delivered'.
- The experience can be applied to other projects or to later phases of an ongoing project. At Leicestershire a de-briefing meeting identifies best practice and this is used to update the design brief.
- Features can be copied to other places, the Café Libra in Felixstowe, for instance.
- The status of refurbished libraries may rise – within the library service Lowestoft was seen as a flagship for Suffolk Libraries; in Sweden, Malmö has received many visitors, including architects and librarians because of its innovative new elements and refurbishment of the old.

- Innovative design and layout can form the template for other libraries in the refurbishment programme and in North Yorkshire libraries are now felt to express a more professional look.
- There is an increase in floor space following a library extension as well as operational benefits.
- Excellent refurbishments and extensions attract awards;
  - the British Library of Political and Economic Science received a Civic Trust Commendation (2002)
  - Brookline Branch Library gained a AAI/ALA award in the US Library Building Award programme (2005)
  - the University of Plymouth Library was given a Concrete Society Award (2005)
  - Swiss Cottage Library, Camden, received a Public Library Building Award (2005)
  - a British Building Maintenance Award (2006) was given to Glasgow University Library from the Institute of Maintenance and Building Management
  - Waterford's awards were, amongst others, from the Royal Institute of Architects in Ireland and shortlisting for the Best Public Building Category LAMA award (2007)
  - Public Library Building Awards were given to Lowestoft (2003) and Felixstowe (2007).
- The library service is seen as good partner and is attractive to external agencies and partners – Lowestoft is a public access point for council services.

Time and effort

The time and effort invested during a project may be considerable – 13 years at the National Library of Wales and 15 years at the State Library of Victoria – and can dominate the work of those most directly involved who need good project management and negotiation skills. A high degree of cooperation is also required from all those concerned. Time delay at Waterford meant compromise on aspects of the project and, as at Torquay or at the Hartley Library, not all targets or goals might be met. As noted earlier, library staff and users live through a great deal of disruption that may last for a significant period of time.

Renewal – a continuous process

In considering how libraries can renew themselves in the future, three scenarios are suggested:

- A local initiative, also using inspiration from best practice design models.
- Cooperation – libraries sharing design costs or making use of library sector branding offers.
- A national library service with a range of standard designs.

Local initiative and best practice

By its nature refurbishment, as instanced in this book, is not a continuous process but a cyclical event with varying time intervals. Refurbishment becomes necessary when the library service and its building get left behind by changes in fashion, service developments, operational methods and neglect. While satisfactory maintenance helps keep some criticism at bay, only starting again – which in a sense is what refurbishment is about – ensures the necessary radical change that is needed after a substantial time lapse.

Some things might done, however, to stave off the need for refurbishment out of desperation and replace it with planned refurbishment or other options such as new build. This could be seen as a more continuous (if never-ending) process, especially if facilities management is seen as a necessary skill for all those with day-to-day responsibility for a library and its building. Some helpful actions could therefore be:

- acknowledging the need for and planning for shorter periods between refurbishment, as part of a development strategy
- always making the best use of existing space, some of which may now be excessive for some areas, may be underused or no longer used at all
- if new library service features are added and require more space than is really available in the library, librarians should be prepared to review other provision with a view to its reduction or elimination
- ensuring that new furniture and furnishings complement existing items
- considering whether current refurbishment proposals contain elements or features that will quickly date, as keeping up with what is fashionable and trendy may only ensure short-term satisfaction.

And finally it is useful to look to best practice models that can be adapted locally or even nationally, as found on the Designing Libraries website, with its increasing library sector coverage, and, for example, in the American Trading Space project described below.

Trading spaces: reinventing the library environment

Rather like the three libraries chosen for the Love Libraries campaign to renew their libraries (see page 11), Mount Laurel Library, New Jersey was selected as a demonstration site for the Trading Spaces Project.[9]

The aim behind the demonstration site 'was to redesign Mount Laurel's layout and to encourage and coach staff to merchandize library collections and develop new ways of doing business'. It was hoped that Mount Laurel Library would act as a model for libraries not only in New Jersey but nationwide. The refurbishment, which did not involve a large sum of money and was not just about renewing the interior of the library building, had a number of elements:

- meeting and greeting library visitors
- constant assessment of library practice and displays
- an internet café
- a wireless network
- themed environments for families, teens and quiet study
- popular collections with an emphasis on face-on display.

Those involved in the project offer plenty of published and online advice to make such a 'reinvention' work. One comment was that: 'Librarians love to "ooh and ah" over $80 million buildings, but 99.9 per cent of us will never have one. Start where you are. You could end up with approachability, flexibility and style that the big boys lack'.[10]

Our case studies seem to demonstrate that all three qualities are indeed possible in the UK's many refurbished libraries.

Cooperation – sharing design costs

A 2006 report suggests that cost effectiveness and rapid refurbishment of the public libraries in the UK could be achieved if councils cooperated on the design of new and refurbished buildings because current practice is uneven and there needs to be at least a doubling of capital expenditure. The £80 million lottery money (see page 9) would have given better financial benefits for English local authorities had they discontinued reinventing the wheel and utilized a number of design templates. This approach characterizes the retail and leisure industries, producing unique stores often in old buildings. Design templates would allow library authorities to:

- erect functional libraries using standard design elements
- construct buildings that are quick to put up and cheap to maintain
- apply this method economically to build many high-quality library premises permitting ample variation.

Local authorities, notably Lancashire, have in the past used this standard design approach to new library construction but it would have to be used in a somewhat different way for the refurbishment of existing buildings. The case studies demonstrate how this is being done through, for example, standard fit-outs and branding. Some branding, such as Gloustershire's 'Library Brand', developed at the county's Bishop's Cleeve Library, together with James Ford Design, created the design template, which is now offered more widely and is available to other libraries services to adopt at a fraction of the cost.[11] This is in competition with other commercially available consultants and suppliers.

A national library service and standard designs

A national library service, particularly for public libraries, is an unlikely development in the immediate future but, if taken up, could suggest in the long-term national standard library designs and branding applicable throughout the UK. While such a high street retail approach might be welcomed by some, it could end up by destroying the remarkable diversity of the UK's library building estate.

However, the idea of a national centre for library design has been floated a number of times, particularly in the boom building years of the 1960s. Some 40 years ago, the present author suggested the setting up of a Library Design and Research Department in the context of the establishment of a UK Library Centre that could have the following (somewhat updated) tasks as part of its activities:

- the design of library buildings – advising on all aspects of library planning, design and construction; creating a range of standard library designs
- the design of library furniture, fittings and equipment – providing information on these topics, with a special emphasis on information and communications technology
- library methodology – advising on those library routines, procedures and methods affecting library layout and design; advising also on library start-ups.[12]

Part of the future plans of the Designing Libraries Project (see pages 6-7), funds permitting, is the creation of 'The Centre for Library Design'. This would promote the better planning and design of libraries, their buildings and equipment in the UK and beyond through its education, information and consultancy services aimed at librarians, architects, designers, planners, suppliers and community groups. At present the project is located in Hugh Owen Library, University of Wales Aberystwyth, and its electronic interface is the Designing Libraries website (www.designinglibraries.org.uk). Such a centre would need its partners – a professional organization or library school – and appropriate funding. It would provide a marvellous support system for the continuing work of library renewal, as well as library conversions, extensions and new build.

Notes

1 'DfES backs school-public links' (2005), *Library + Information Update* **4** (1/2) 9; *Enjoying Reading: public library partnership with schools*, Reading Agency, available at: www.readingagency.org.uk. 8 March 2008.

2 Jones, R. (2005), 'We all work with children…', *Library + Information Update* **4** (5), 39.

3 Reed, S.G. (2002), 'Norfolk architect becomes volunteer extraordinaire', *American Libraries* **33** (4), 74–5.

4 Oder, N. (2004), 'Huston's Gubbin heads for Jacksonville', *Library Journal* **129** (20), 24.

5 Magnani, P. and Romeo, A. (2007), '6 tips to surviving library construction', *Library Journal* **132** 15 May, 'Library by design' supplement, 14–15.

6 Hines, R. (ed.) (2003), 'Building new environments: the physical space' in *Centred on Learning: academic case studies on learning centre development*, edited by E. Oyston (Aldershot: Gower), 153–79.

7 Lam, L.M.C. (2006), 'Meeting the challenges of expansion and renovation in an academic medical library: a case study of the Li Ping Medical Library of the Chinese University of Hong Kong', *New Library World* **107** (5–6), 238–46.

8 Rogers, M. (2007), 'Remaking the entry', *Library Journal* **132** 15 May, 'Library by design' supplement, 9.

9 *Trading Spaces: reinventing the library environment*, available at: www.sjrlc.org/tradingspaces/. 19 March 2008.

10 Bernstein, J.E. and Schalk-Greene, K. (2006), 'Extreme library makeover one year later', *American Libraries* **37** (4), 66–9.

11 *The Library Brand*, available at: www.thelibrarybrand.co.uk. 19 March 2008.

12 Dewe, M. (1968), *Library Supply Agencies in Europe* (London: Library Association), 184–6.

Bibliography

Atkinson, J. and Morgan, S. (2007), 'University libraries', *British Librarianship and Information Work 2001–2005*, edited by J.H. Bowman, Aldershot: Ashgate, 57– 81.

Building Better Library Services (2002), London: Audit Commission.

Better Public Buildings: A Proud Legacy for the Future (2006), London: CABE.

Better Public Libraries (2003), London: CABE and Resource.

Bryson, J., Usherwood, B. and Proctor, R. (2003), *Libraries Must be Buildings? New Impact Study*, London: Resource.

Creating Excellent Buildings: A Guide for Clients (2003), London: CABE.

Framework for the Future (2003), London: Department Culture, Media and Sport.

Coates, T. (2004), *Who's in Charge? Responsibility for the Public Library Service*, London: Libri Trust & Laser Foundation.

Designing Spaces for Effective Learning: A Guide to 21st Century Learning Space Design (2006), Bristol: JISC.

Dewe, M. (ed.) (1987), *Adaptation of Buildings for Library Use*, Munich: Saur.

Dewe, M. (ed.) (1989), *Library Buildings: Preparations for Planning*, Munich: Saur.

Dewe, M. (1995), *Planning and Designing Libraries for Children and Young People*, London: Library Association.

Dewe, M. (2006), *Planning Public Library Buildings: Concepts and Issues for the Librarian*, Aldershot: Ashgate.

Dewe, M. (2007), *Ideas and Designs: Creating the Environment for the Primary School Library*, Swindon: School Library Association.

Dewe, M. and A.J. Clark (2007), 'Library buildings', *British Librarianship and Information Work 2001–2005*, edited by J.H. Bowman, Aldershot: Ashgate, 372–89.

Dubber, G. and Lemaire, K. (2007), *Visionary Spaces: Designing and Planning a Secondary School Library*, Swindon: School Library Association.

Fraley, R.A. and Anderson, C.L. (1990), *Library Space Planning: A How-to-do-it Manual For Assessing, Allocating and Reorganizing Collections, Resources and Facilities*, 2nd edition. New York: Neal-Schuman.

Hines, R. (ed.) (2003), 'Building new environments: the physical space', *Centred on Learning: Academic Case Studies on Learning Centre Development*, edited by E. Oyston. Aldershot: Gower.

House of Commons, Culture, Media and Sport Committee (2005), *Public Libraries: Third Report of Session 2004–05*, London: HMSO.

Joint Funding Councils' Libraries Review Group (1993), *Report* (The Follett Report), Bristol: HEFCE

Jones, W.G. (2006), 'Library buildings at the threshold of change', in *Advances in Librarianship*, vol. 30, edited by D.A. Nitecki and E.G. Abels, London: Academic Press, 201–30.

Leadbeater, C. (2003), *Overdue: How to Create a Modern Public Library Service*, London: Demos.

Martin, E. (2003), 'Historic libraries and their enduring value', *Planning the Modern Public Library Building*, edited by G.B. McCabe and J.R. Kennedy, Westport, CT: Libraries Unlimited, 229–45.

Nilsson, S. (ed.) (1997), *A Library for all Times*, Stockholm: Swedish Arts Council. (An account of the Malmö Library refurbishment and extension.)

Public Library Service: IFLA/UNESCO Guidelines for Development (2001), Munich: Saur.

Sannwald, W.W. (1997), *Checklist of Library Building Design Considerations*, 3rd edition. Chicago, IL: American Library Association.

Scottish Funding Council (2006), *Spaces for Learning*, [London]: AMA Alexi Marmot Associates.

Scottish Further Education Funding Council (2003), *Resources and Services Supporting Learning: A Service Development Quality Toolkit*, Glasgow: Scottish Library and Information Council.

Serota, M. (2007), *Principles of Library Design*, Also available at www.serota. co.uk.

Services Supporting Learning in Wales: *A Quality Toolkit for Evaluating Learning Resource Services in Further Education Colleges* (2005), Cardiff: fforum.

Tomorrow's Library: Views of the Public Library Sector (2003), Belfast: Department of Culture, Arts and Leisure.

Ward, R. (2007), 'Public libraries', *British Librarianship and Information Work 2001–2005*, edited by J.H. Bowman, Aldershot: Ashgate, 14-28.

Williamsburg Regional Library (2001), *Library Construction from a Staff Perspective*, Jefferson, NC: McFarland.

Woodward, J. (2000), *Countdown to a New Library: Managing the Building Project*, Chicago, IL: American Library Association.

Worpole, K. (2004), *21st Century Libraries: Changing Forms, Changing Futures*, London: CABE and RIBA.

Websites

CILIP, Public Libraries Group, Public Library Building Awards, available at: www.cilip.org.uk/specialinterestgroups/by subject/public/awards. 20 February 2008.

Designing Libraries: The Gateway to Better Library Buildings, Statistics, available at: www.designinglibraries.org.uk/stats/data/?=catproj.

Enjoying Reading: public library partnership with schools, Reading Agency, available at: www.readingagency.org.uk. 8 March 2008.

Higher Education Funding Council Wales, widening access, available at: www.hecfw.ac.uk. 25 February 2008.

JISC, infokits, available at: www.jiscinfonet.ac.uk/infokits/learning-space-design. 25 February 2008.

Leading Learning and Skills (lsc), Design Guidance, available at: http://designguidance.lsc.gov.uk. 29 March 2008.

The Library Brand, available at: www.thelibrarybrand.co.uk. 19 March 2008.

MLA Programmes, Audit of Library Buildings, available at: www.mla.gov.uk/resources/assets//L/librarybuildings_10218.pdf. 20 February 2008.

MLA Programmes, Library Design Workshops, available at: www.mla.gov.uk/programmes/framework/framework_programmes/Library_design_workshops. 20 February 2008.

Northern Ireland, Department of Culture, Arts and Leisure, Library Buildings, available at: www.dcalni.gov.uk/index/libraries/library_buildings.htm. 20 February 2008.

PLUS surveys, available at: www.ipmarketresearch.net. 16 March 2008.

IPF is the commercial arm of CIPFA and carries out tailor-made market research to establish levels of demand for services, reasons for non-use, for example.

Reading Agency [Headspace], available at: www.readingagency.org.uk/youngpeople/headspace. 25 February 2008.

SCONUL, space planning, available at: www.sconul.ac.uk/hottopics/space planning. 25 February 2008.

Trading Spaces: Reinventing the Library Environment, available at: www.sjrlc.org/tradingspaces/. 19 March 2008.

Index

Illustrations and plans are listed in bold type

academic library buildings 12-14, 79-109,
    221-9
access centres 177, 178, 180
accessibility 37, 117, 119, 129, 150, 167,
    208, 210, 223, 226, 234, 235
    disabled people 75, 94, 226
    see also wheelchair access
acoustics 83, 86, 226
adaptive technology 38, 140
Adsetts Learning Centre, Sheffield Hallam
    University 82
air-conditioning 84, 94, 95, 96, 127-8, 150,
    161, 162, 169, 198, 204
ambience
    after refurbishment 38, 53, 75, 83, 87,
        90, 106, 108, 150, 151, 175, 176,
        228, 232
    prior to refurbishment 31-3, 59, 79-80,
        87, 92, 101, 179, 195-6, 203, 208,
        211
    see also exteriors; interiors; noise;
        'wow' factor
archaeological finds 64, 146, 148
architects 24, 70, 71, 86, 116, 142, 146,
    168, 175, 186, 199, 249
    architectural services 58, 60-1
    observing library use 82
    relations with librarians 63, 120, 126
    selection of 81, 125-6
    see also project management team
architectural competitions 133
architectural drawings 36
archive services 58, 165
    buildings 117
    collections 101, 104, 114, 225
    search rooms 197, 222
    see also local studies provision
art deco design 43, 44, 45, 53
art galleries 24, 58, 60, 61, 64
art nouveau design 31, 33

art works 65, 215
asbestos 70, 71, 74, 95, 96, 169
Ashby de la Zouche Library, Leicestershire
    174
asset managers 160, 206, 208, 215, 217
atriums 73, 92, 95, 98, 134, 145, 147, 148,
    222, 226
audio-visual facilities 46, 71, 74, 148, 149,
    151, 162
audio-visual stock 29, 33, 61
auditoriums 73, 134, 135, 162, 234
awards 3, 6, 238
    academic libraries 14, 90, 222, 224,
        225, 226
    public libraries 10-11, 39, 154, 171,
        237

baby-changing facilities 33, 151, 187, 203,
    235
balconies 46, 48, 84, 134, 162
banners 167
Barnet, London Borough of
    see Hendon Library
Barnsley Central Library 159-71, **161**, **163**,
    167, 245, 252, 253, 255, 256, 258,
    259, 260
Barry County Library 3, 234
Beckett Park Campus Library, Leeds
    Metropolitan University 250-1
benching 46, 83, 84, 200
benefaction 130
    buildings 71, 101, 126, 146, 229
    funding 129
best practice models
    see design templates; Designing
        Libraries (website); Love Libraries
        campaign; Trading Spaces project
Best Value reviews 21, 32, 58, 115-116,
    159, 173, 209
Better public libraries (CABE) 5, 174, 245

bibliographical services 115-116
Big Lottery 9, 11
Birmingham City University
   see Kenrick Library
Birstall Library, Leicestershire 178-9, **180**, 255
Bishop's Cleeve Library, Gloucestershire 265
black and minority groups
   extended provision for 37
Blackburn Central Library 261
blinds 90, 95
book bars
   see Headspaces
book storage 117, 127-8, 165-6
   see also storage space
books 61, 105
   range of provision 61, 232
booths (seating) 90
borrowers
   see users
Braille signs 150, 162
branch libraries 5, 6, 115, 116, 118, 159, 164, 165
branding 22, 46, 47, 185-7, 239
   see also Library Brand template (Gloucestershire)
briefs 33, 80-1, 82, 94-5, 104, 114-115, 179, 186, 197, 203, 249
   catalyst for change 121
   development of 212-213
   outline 61, 70, 125, 146, 175
Brighton and Hove Libraries
   see Jubilee Library; Hove Library
British Building Maintenance Award 90
British Library xv, 15
British Library of Political and Economic Science, London School of Economics 221-2, 248, 253, 262
British Museum Round Reading Room xv, 230-2, **231**
Brookline Branch Library, Carnegie Library of Pittsburgh, USA 237, 262
browsing areas 123, 136, 174
budgets 217
   effects of cuts 41, 135
   value for money 151-2
   see also capital programme budgets; funding
building conservation 70, 113, 116-117, 126, 147, 230
building contracts
   see contracts
building management systems 71
building services 71, 164
   renewal of 95, 197, 224, 234
   see also heating; lighting, etc
buildings
   see library buildings
business libraries 150

CCTV 35, 71, 150, 235
Café Libra 217
   as social enterprise 214-5
cafés 58, 61, 65, 106, 108, 115, 118, 142, 160, 187, 198, 216, 222, 223, 225, 226, 229, 232, 236
   as social space 228
   baby café 215
   learning café 228
   location of 162
   outdoor area 233
   see also restaurants
Camden, London Borough of
   see Swiss Cottage Library
Canadian Parliament
   Main Library 229-30, 250
capital programme budgets 9, 13, 21, 60, 80, 82, 98, 159, 173-4, 208
   and phased buildings 103, 207
   controlling costs 74, 152
   use of cost consultant 125, 126
   see also budgets; funding
Carnegie libraries 4, 11, 31, 113, 195, 235
Carnegie Library of Pittsburgh, USA
   see Brookline Branch Library
carpets 44, 84, 167, 169, 199, 209, 215
carrels 83, 84, 86, 90, 97, 228
ceilings 90, 95, 234
   glass feature 49-50, 235
   height of 116, 203
   painting of 83, 204, 215
Centre for Library Design
   proposal for 265
chairs 44, 139, 148, 200

change
 drivers for 12, 21, 89, 98, 101, 103,
  105
 resistance to 27
children's libraries 28-9, 34-5, 139, 153,
  162, 180
 bespoke furniture 167
 better designed areas 179, 197, 216
 criticism of 141, 209
 see also young people
Chinese University of Hong Kong
 see Li Fing Medical Library
circulation space 37, 115, 147, 148
 see also traffic flow
Citizen's Advice Bureau 58
cloakrooms 115, 129, 225
Coalville Library, Leicestershire 176-8,
  177
coffee bars
 see cafés
Colburn Library, North Yorkshire Libraries
  192
collections 84, 98, 103, 107, 123, 22-3, 229
 conservation of 94, 124, 230
 development of 153
 growth of 67-9, 225, 232
 integration 104
 lack of space for 124
 off-site warehouses for 232
 print and electronic sources mix 101
 storage during renovation 230
 see also special collections; stock
colour 92, 151, 169
 after refurbishment 83, 167, 199, 204-
  5, 209, 215
 choice of 44
 corporate schemes 175, 185
 in heritage buildings 25, 27, 44, 230
communication 37, 130, 245-6
 with public 65, 200
 with suppliers 36
 see also consultation
community libraries 173, 180
computers 46, 137, 139, 151, 160, 161, 205
 cable management 200
 configuration 46, 149
 provision of 29, 197, 226, 237
 seating for 46, 168

 see also information and
  communications technology (ICT)
conference facilities 71, 115, 232
conservation (of buildings)
 see building conservation
conservation (of library materials)
 facilities for 98, 108, 124, 128, 129,
  222, 232
console games 33
construction 36, 117, 126-7
 additional costs 36, 152
 best time for 95
 logistics of 96
 management of 127, 130
 new materials 119, 147, 148, 238
consultants 22, 43, 60, 69, 71, 74, 125,
  126, 127, 174, 238
consultation 47-8, 120, 154, 187, 213
 comments on plans invited 47, 165,
  206, 213, 245-6
 methods 64, 187
 with academics 80, 94
 with children 37
 with civic societies 33
 with others 37, 94, 126
 with planning and heritage officers 126
 with public 24, 47, 64, 70, 161, 185,
  234
 with staff 33, 80-1, 82, 94, 161, 174,
  234
 with students 80
 with user groups 70, 234
contractors 33, 70, 74, 81, 164, 168, 180,
  186-7, 207
 co-operation with staff 86
 cost effectiveness 127
 selection 64, 96, 215
corporate identity 176
counters 187, 199
 redesign of existing 43, 44, 46
 relocation 174, 204
 replaced by pods 215-6
Court Square Branch, Queens Borough
  Public Libraries, USA 238
courtyards 34, 71, 73, 133-4, 203-4, 234
crisis management 152
Crosshills Library, North Yorkshire
  Libraries 193

customers
see users
Cymal
see Museums Archives and Libraries
Wales

DVDs 37, 59, 61, 174
David Bishop Skillman Library, Layayette
College, Eastern
Pennsylvania 225
daylight
see natural light
decorative features 215
see also mosaics
Derbyshire Libraries, Archives and
Information
see Long Eaton Library
design 117-120, 126, 160, 185
challenges and ideas 116-117, 251-3
changes 74, 169
concepts 34, 58-9, 69, 116, 125, 237
constraints 125
cooperation by councils in 264
costs 82
features 253-4
form follows function 63, 82, 113, 120
lack of clutter 175
objectives 43, 81-4, 90, 103-4, 108,
114-115, 174, 230, 250
outcomes 28-9, 97-8, 127-9, 153-4, 175
see also retail principles
design principles 61, 104-5, 117-119, 176
design process 23-5, 43-4, 69-71, 81-2,
125-7, 147, 161-2, 174-5, 185-7
involvement of teenagers in 146, 180,
205, 234, 246
revision of initial design 82
stages of 126
design solutions 33-4, 44-6, 71-3, 126, 127-9
internal street 118
the 'spine' 25
design team
see project management team
design templates 9, 185, 264, 265
Designing Libraries (website) 6-7, 8, 265
Designing spaces for effective learning
(JISC) 14
desking 90, 97, 149, 168

Disability Discrimination Act (1995) 8, 10,
13, 61, 104, 159, 187, 208, 211,
234
disabled people 79, 228, 229
building tours for 171
designing for 140, 167
input from 70, 140
compliments from 37-8
see also accessibility; signs
discovery centres 5, 58-9, 250
display areas 29, 35, 35, 162, 188, 216, 233
Doheny Memorial Library, University of
Southern California 225-6
donors
see benefaction
doors 141, 213, 235
automatic 35, 150, 204, 234
Drwm (Drum), The 68, 72, 73, 75
Dublin City Library and Archive 113-121,
114, 118, 119, 244, 245, 248, 249,
251, 252, 255, 257, 258, 259
Duchess House 125, 127, 129, 130

Eastfield Library, North Yorkshire 189
education facilities 59, 71, 75
electronic information services 81, 98
electronic materials 101, 104, 105, 230
electrical systems 84, 95, 115
see also lighting
Enderby Library, Leicestershire 180-1, 181
energy efficiency 91, 96, 160, 197, 222,
230
English Heritage 24, 64, 234
approval process 27, 33-4
see also listed buildings
enquiry desks 61, 84, 94, 108, 228
rationalization 33
reconfiguration 105
see also information desks
entrances 129, 142, 148, 153, 212
new 94, 98, 134, 135, 217, 222, 236
redesign of 27, 74, 106, 108, 204
relocation 69, 71, 75, 226
environmental conditions 94, 96, 230
for collections 94, 124, 127
monitoring systems 91
surveys of 80, 82

exhibition spaces 59, 60, 71, 73, 75, 109, 115, 118, 153, 232
extensions
    academic libraries 79, 92, 101, 103, 104, 225, 226, 229, 234
    national libraries 67-9, 70
    public libraries 33, 35, 60, 117-120, 133-4, 146-8, 213, 217
    special libraries 125
exteriors 33, 148
    improvements to 44, 119, 130, 199, 209, 213, 233, 236
    prior to refurbishment 79, 117, 208

feasibility studies 69, 89, 103, 114-115, 126, 222
Felixstowe Library, Suffolk 11, 211-17, **214**, 244
fiction 46, 138, 174, 206, 216, 237
    categorization of 50-1
fire protection 128, 198
    alarms 97, 162, 169, 217
    doors 97
    exits 27, 197, 213
    lifts 108
    smoke detection 97
flexibility 13, 61, 81, 104, 105, 108, 139, 141, 150, 151
flooding 32, 117, 128
flooring 90, 95, 129, 233
    glass 146
    poor condition of 32, 36
    raised 139, 213
    rubber 238
    slate 73
    stone 139
    timber 116, 235
focus groups 21, 183
Follett Report (1993) 13, 94, 101
Forest Hill Library, Lewisham, London Borough of 234
Framework for the future (DCMS) 5, 6, 41, 159, 245
funding 9-10, 13, 43, 60, 71, 80, 82, 95, 101, 103, 106, 116, 159, 173-4, 196-7, 207, 209, 223, 248-9
    and increase use targets 41-3, 51
    case for refurbishment 8

fundraising 129-30, 221-2
furniture 35, 43, 45, 90, 139, 148, 149, 151
    integrated with building design 147
    reconfiguration by students 228
    reuse of 24, 235
    standard designs for 175
    storage during refurbishment 166
    see also library suppliers; shelving
further education libraries 14

galleries 134, 135
Girton College Library, Cambridge 235
Glasgow University Library 89-99, **89**, **93**, **99**, 247, 249, 250, 253, 254, 255, 262
    history 91
    1968 building 91-2
glass
    use in library buildings 116, 118, 134, 225, 237
    as partitions 34, 83
Gloucestershire Libraries
    see Bishop's Cleeve Library; Library Brand template
Gosport Discovery Centre 63
graphics 167, 200, 205
group study rooms 83, 84, 86, 87, 90, 104, 108, 225, 228, 239
guiding
    see signs

Hamilton Town House Library, South Lanarkshire 11, 233-4
Hampshire Library and Information Service
    see Gosport Discovery Centre; Winchester Discovery Centre
Hampshire Record Office 59, 247
Hare, Thomas Henry (architect) 4
Harrison Learning Centre, University of Wolverhampton 82
Hartley Library, University of Southampton 14, 101-109, **102**, **107**, **109**, 244, 248, 249, 250, 253, 254, 260, 262
Harvard University, USA
    see Widener Memorial Library

Headingley Library, Leeds Metropolitan
    University 229, 250, 253
headquarters buildings 59, 115-116, 119
Headspaces (book bars) 11
health and safety issues 8, 24, 33, 43, 64,
    97, 104, 160
heating 34, 70, 71, 108, 160, 198, 212, 214
help desk
    see enquiry desks
Hendon Library, Barnet, London Borough
    of 4
heritage buildings
    academic libraries 221-5
    national libraries 67-75, 232-3
    public libraries 21-53, 59- 66, 113-121,
        233-6
    special libraries 124-131, 229-232
Heritage Lottery Fund 69-70, 71, 103, 223
high demand collections
    see short loan collections
Higher Education Funding Council for
    England 13, 79, 80, 103
Higher Education Funding Council Wales
    13
Hong Kong
    see Li Fing Medical Library, Chinese
        University of Hong Kong
Hove Library 235
humidity 95, 96, 230

Idea Stores 5, 57, 160
image 183, 185
impact assessments 9, 75, 87, 90, 141-2,
    154, 210, 217
    increased use 29, 38, 170, 188-94
    see also Public Library User Surveys
        (PLUS)
information desks 136, 139, 140, 148, 150
    see also enquiry desks
information and communications
    technology (ICT) 94, 233
    academic libraries 13, 83, 84, 90, 94,
        95, 97, 101, 104, 225
    digital project room 225
    IT laboratories 229
    reconfiguration by students 228
    virtual campus 223
    impact on space 14

public libraries 136, 142, 152, 154,
    214, 216
    centralized management of 151
    provision of 33, 35, 223, 234, 236
    sections for 29, 160
    siting of 209
state libraries 232
see also computers; Internet
information technology (IT)
    see information and communications
        technology (ICT)
interior design 97-8, 130, 139, 148, 160,
    185, 199-200, 204-5, 209, 215-216,
    237
    see also ambience; layouts
interior designers 60, 106
Internet 35
    access to 150, 151, 214, 216, 233
    café provision 106
Ireland
    library buildings 12, 113-121, 145-55
Isle of Wight Libraries
    involvement of young people in library
        design 146

J.B. Morrell Library, University of York
    14, 229, 253
JISC
    see Joint Information Systems
        Committee
Jacksonville Libraries, Florida, USA 247
John Rylands University Library,
    Manchester xv, 12, 222-3, 251
Joint Information Systems Committee
    (JISC) 14
Jubilee Library, Brighton 3, 160

Keele University Library 228, 250, 252
Kennel Club Library 15
Kenrick Library, Birmingham City
    University 79-87, **83**, **85**, 245, 249,
    260
King's College London
    see Maughan Library
Knaresborough Library, North Yorkshire
    Libraries **186**, **188**, 194

Lakenheath Library, Suffolk 208-210, 248, 251, 257
Lancashire Libraries 9
laptops 90, 229
Layayette, College, Easton, Pennsylvania
    see David Bishop Skillman Library
layouts 92, 105, 146, 151, 152, 175, 178, 179, 180, 184-5, 197-9, 205-6, 216, 219, 237
    internal views 147, 148
    floor replication 222
    see also interior design
learning 95, 120-1
    changing patterns of 101
    environment 94, 98, 103
learning resource centres 12, 14, 82, 250-1
    entrance hall as 106
lecture theatres
    see auditoriums
Leeds Metropolitan University 250, 251
    see also Beckett Park Campus Library; Headingley Library
Leek Library, Staffordshire 21-30, **23**, **26**, **28**, 244, 251, 253, 254, 260
Leicestershire Libraries 247, 253, 257, 258, 261
    see also Birstall, Coalville and Enderby libraries
Lewisham, London Borough of
    see Forest Hill Library
Li Fing Medical Library, Chinese University of Hong Kong 256-7
LibQUAL+ surveys 90
librarians 121, 136, 142
    academic liaison 104
    relations with architects 63, 120, 126
libraries
    roles of 5, 57-75, 98, 104, 228
Libraries for Life (Cymal) 9
Library Brand template (Gloucestershire) 265
library buildings
    aesthetics vs. function 129, 135, 139-40
    assessment for renewal 343-4
    constraints and opportunities 95
    employment of specialists 126, 249-50
    guided tours of 141-2
    integration of old and new fabric xv, 22, 119, 130, 223, 233, 234
    negative reaction to design proposals 103, 141, 260-1
    retaining period feel and features 29, 116-117, 130, 147, 212
    sale of surplus premises 60
    shape of 134, 160, 174, 178, 203, 205
    studies and surveys 69, 82, 245
    support for building projects 103, 115, 116, 121, 189, 213
    temporary accommodation 163-4
    see also heritage buildings; link buildings; types of library, e.g. public library buildings
library campaigns 11
library closure 36-7, 163-6, 201, 206-7, 223, 225, 229-30, 258-9
    maintaining library service during 36, 50, 73, 106-7, 164-5, 200, 201, 210, 217, 234, 259
Library Design Centre
    proposal for 265
library design workshops 7
library members
    see users
library moves 86, 107
    logistics 163-6, 169, 200, 210
Library Research Annexe, Glasgow University 94, 254
library service 98, 104, 105, 113
    after refurbishment 153
    improvement plans 21
    integration 104
        by material type 105
    student centred 103
    transformation of 57, 65, 188
    see also change; library closure
library suppliers 36, 106, 164, 167, 199, 215
    assessing tenders of 44, 167
lifts 84, 92, 98, 104, 117, 129, 135, 150, 161, 162, 169, 178, 211, 212, 224, 234
    glazed 118, 222, 235
light
    see lighting; natural light

lighting 43, 46, 84, 90, 91, 95, 96, 139,
    146-7, 148, 151, 175, 203-4, 233,
    235
    in listed buildings 27, 118
    over shelves 159
    see also energy efficiency
link buildings 27-8, 34, 117, 124, 133-4,
    234, 236
listed buildings xv, 11, 25, 31, 59, 115,
    116-117, 123, 221-5, 232, 233-4,
    236
    planning consent for 24, 27, 33-4, 64
lobbies 179, 212
local authorities
    reorganization 59 (UK), 113-114
    (Ireland)
Local Public Service Agreements (LPSA)
    41
local studies provision 29, 148, 154, 160,
    174, 237
    research facilities 59
    see also archive services
locations
    see sites
London Library 123-131, **128**, 244, 248,
    249, 252, 253, 258, 259
Long Eaton Library, Derbyshire 31-9, **32,
    34, 35,** 251, 255
Love Libraries campaign 11, 237-8
Lowestoft Library, Suffolk 195-202, **198,
    199,** 244, 248, 251, 254, 255, 258,
    259, 261, 262

MLA
    see Museums, Libraries and Archive
    Commission (MLA)
maintenance 32, 50, 90, 91, 97, 159
    lack of 21, 78-80, 173, 211, 232
Malmö City Library, Sweden 133-46, **134,
    137, 138,** 246, 249, 251-2, 253,
    254, 260, 261
Manchester University
    see John Rylands University Library
market research 183
    methods 183
    product concept 70
marketing 70, 141-2, 188, 189, 238
    altering perceptions 189

Maughan Library, King's College London
    223, 253
mechanical and electrical systems 70, 115,
    197, 198
meeting rooms 58, 115, 129, 150, 151, 160,
    213, 225
    creation of 197
    for consultation 189
    presentation technology for 162
mezzanines 92, 148, 153, 197, 211, 212,
    213, 224-5, 237
mobile libraries 116
    as temporary service 36, 165, 187, 201
mosaics 31, 34, 145, 223
Mount Laurel Library, New Jersey, USA
    264
multimedia facilities 223, 224, 228, 229
multipurpose rooms 60, 61, 64, 115, 128-9
museums 24, 25, 58, 236
Museums Archives and Libraries Wales
    (Cymal) 9-10, 14
Museums, Libraries and Archive
    Commission (MLA) 5, 6, 7, 9
music and drama services 228

national libraries 15, 67-75, 232-3
National Library of Australia, Canberra
    232-3
National Library of Wales, Aberystwyth
    15, 67-75, **63, 72, 73,** 245, 247,
    256, 262
National Lottery
    see Big Lottery; Heritage Lottery
National Screen and Sound Archive,
    National Library of Wales 69, 71,
    75
natural light 34, 97, 98, 118, 135, 147, 160,
    203-4, 225, 226, 237
Newquay Library, Cornwall 11, 237-8
newspaper areas 135, 148, 154, 174, 214,
    216, 237
noise 79, 80, 86, 87, 140-1, 162, 226
non-fiction 137, 150, 174, 176, 216
    integrated with reference stock 237
Norfolk Public Library, USA
    young people and library design 246
North Lincolnshire Central Library 236-7,
    253

North Yorkshire Libraries 239, 245, 247,
    248, 250, 253, 257
  see also Colburn, Crosshills, Eastfield,
    Knaresborough, Northallerton,
    Scarborough, Sherburn, and
    Whitby libraries
Northallerton Library, North Yorkshire
    Libraries 191
Northern Ireland refurbishment funding 10
Northumbria University City, Campus
    Library 226, 228
notice boards 175, 205, 209
Nottinghamshire Libraries 239

offices 36, 115, 129, 134, 160, 225, 233
one-stop shops 24, 29, 30, 58
opening hours 63, 98, 159, 160, 185, 188,
    189, 201
options appraisals 92, 126, 127
Overdue: how to create a modern public
    library service (Leadbeater) 5
Oystermouth Library, Swansea 9

parking 75, 208
  for disabled people 150
partnerships 22, 173-4, 176, 185, 189
  with local authorities 24, 185
People's Network 24, 61, 159, 168, 237
  suites for 162
periodicals 61, 128, 229
  electronic access 98, 104, 108
  shelved together 105
phased refurbishment 84, 95-6, 104, 106,
    129, 131, 206-7, 217, 224, 228
photocopying facilities 124, 224
planning process 23-5, 33, 43-4, 59, 60-4,
    69-71, 81, 104, 105-6, 120, 136,
    147, 163-6, 174-5, 185-7
  as continuous process 133
plans
  see architectural drawings
plasma screens 75
Plymouth Campus Library, University of
    Plymouth 226, **227**, 254
post-project reviews 39, 131, 176, 260
printed material 97, 98, 101, 104, 105, 107
program(me)s
  see briefs

project management 43, 120, 121, 152
  time and effort invested 232
  use of consultant 125, 126, 127
project management teams 33, 47, 63, 70,
    81, 136, 147, 152, 175, 257-8
  library team 43, 80-3, 147, 161, 163,
    186-7, 200, 204, 206, 215, 217
  meetings 86, 126, 165
  responsibilities of individuals 120
  sub-groups 120
  working relationships 126, 130, 217
public libraries 4-11
  and regeneration 121
  as meeting places 59, 142, 149, 150, 215
  increased use aim 41
  need for radical change debate 5-6, 57
  negative image of 5, 15
  roles of 150
  under investment in 21, 41, 208
  see also impact assessments
Public Library Building Awards 10-11,
    154, 202, 217, 234, 236
public library buildings
  adapted from other uses 174, 208
  as access point for council services 197
  audit of English buildings 7-8
  better environment needed 5
  building priorities 173
  decline of 41
  fit for purpose 8
  gross library space 8
  influential publications 174
  value of 8
  see also shared buildings
Public Library Service Standards 51
Public Library User Surveys (PLUS) 37,
    47, 154, 160, 174, 176, 178, 207,
    210
  see also impact assessments
Public School 192, New York, USA 238
publicity 165

Queens Borough Public Libraries, USA
  see Court Square Branch
Queen's New York Library, USA 247
quick choice areas 22, 174, 216, 237
quiet areas 108, 150, 161, 162, 174, 206,
    222, 226, 228, 229

radio frequency identification (RFID) 159,
     166, 168, 228
ramps 35, 117, 162, 204, 209
rare books facilities 94, 233
Raymond Burton Library for Humanities
     Research 229
readers
     see users
reader's adviser desk 178
Reading Agency 11
reading rooms
     academic libraries 94, 109, 222, 224
     casual reading areas 225
     linked 226
     national libraries 69, 75, 232-3
     public libraries 117, 141
     special libraries 124, 128, 130, 233
     state libraries 232
Reading University, Main Library 228, 254
reception desks 71, 75, 106, 135, 222, 226,
     228
record offices
     see archive services
reference services 29, 59, 150, 174
     during refurbishment 165, 230-1
refreshment facilities
     see cafés, restaurants
refurbishment 145, 159
     achievements and benefits 261-2
     as a continuous process 262-3
     by stealth 208-210
     challenges and problems during 36, 64,
          74, 86, 108, 120, 129-30, 139, 152,
          168-9
     cycle of 4, 239, 263
     key issues 187
     lessons learned 39, 86, 121
     media coverage of 30, 65, 165, 189
     numbers of 6, 15-16
     partial refurbishment 257
     priorities 42-3, 147-152
     programmes 239
     rather than new build 221
     reasons for xv, 31-3, 59-64, 67-9, 79-
          80, 92, 96, 101-104, 113, 115-116,
          124-5, 133, 145, 182-4, 195-6, 203,
          208-209, 211
     temporary arrangements 129

time invested in projects 75, 86, 115,
     130, 262
     see also extensions; impact
          assessments; library service;
          phased refubishments; post-project
          reviews
renewal 5, 15-16, 225
     scenarios for the future 262-5
     see also refurbishment
re-opening 74, 260
     events 188
     previews 65
replanning
     see refurbishment
research facilities 90, 104, 119, 120-121
     inadequacies 101-102
     funds for 103
restaurants 58, 71, 75, 232
retail principles in design 22, 204
rewiring 129
risk assessment 74
robotic sorting 139, 142
roofs 36, 84, 162, 213, 214, 234
     features of 128, 134, 149, 203
     planted with sedum 225
Room Makeover Contest, USA 238
Royal Society of Medicine Library,
     London 233

SCONUL
     see Society of College, National and
          University Libraries
St Pancras Station and Hotel xv
Scarborough Library, North Yorkshire
     Libraries 185, 190, 243
scholarship 226
school libraries refurbishment 238
Scottish Funding Council 13
Scunthorpe Central Library
     see North Lincolnshire Central Library
seating 43, 46, 90, 97, 101, 106, 115, 148,
     167
     see also types of seating, e.g. sofas
Section 106 agreements (with developers)
     174
security 35, 70, 71, 75, 150, 151, 159
Selby Library, North Yorkshire Libraries
     185

self-service (issue and return) 22, 84, 87,
    130, 139, 142, 199, 204, 226, 228,
    238
  location of terminals 215
seminar rooms 94, 106, 162
Services supporting learning in Wales
    (Cymal) 14
shared buildings 22, 24, 190
Sheffield Hallam University Library 250,
    251
shelving 135, 139, 209, 216
  colour 44, 137, 167, 175, 200
  end panels 45, 83, 84
  height 35, 51, 105, 139, 151, 170, 205
  layouts 36, 187, 216
  mobile 108
  reuse of existing 46, 49, 233
  used as walls 136, 140-1
  wooden 48-9
Sherburn Library, North Yorkshire
    Libraries 193
shopping centre libraries 178-9
shops 71, 75, 222, 232
short loan collections 84, 87, 228
signs (and guiding) 45, 65, 124, 150, 167,
    185, 200, 204, 239
  bilingual 75
  external 185, 199, 209
  for disabled people 140, 162, 234
  readability 37, 108, 139-40
Single Capital Pot (funding) 33, 196, 209
site management 64, 96, 127, 259-60
sites 59-60, 92, 127, 130, 146, 147, 160,
    232
  access to 36, 72, 96
  acquisition 125
  concerns of residents 117, 127, 130
  constraints of 202
  controversy over siting 59
  'land-locked' 117, 148
  location criteria 247-8
  split 59
skylights 34
snag lists 65, 152, 169
social inclusion 150
Society of College, National and
    University Libraries (SCONUL)
    13-14

sofas 45, 46, 90, 148, 200
solar gain 95, 96, 197, 198, 203
South Lanarkshire
  see Hamilton Town House Library
Southampton University
  see Hartley Library
Southern California, University of
  see Doheny Memorial Library
space 84, 86, 98, 103, 104, 148, 149, 150
  constraints 33
  for guided tours 230
  increase in 179, 210, 217
  informal space 104, 108, 229, 234
  lack of 36, 124, 145
  multi-functional 35, 63, 149, 150, 153
  open and flexible 216
  planning assumptions 105
  rationalization of 203
  relationships 63
  reuse of 108
  sequencing of 154
  see *also* circulation space; interior
      design; layouts; zones
Spaces for Learning (SFC) 13
special collections
  academic libraries 101-2, 103, 108-9,
      225, 229
  public libraries 61, 114, 115
  special libraries 129, 233
  see also local studies provision
special libraries 15, 123-31
  heritage buildings 233
sprinkler systems 64
staff
  commitment to change 188-9, 201, 213
  deployment 140, 159, 238
  living through refurbishment 87, 109,
      207, 217
  reaction to new building 135
  reception of readers 106, 141, 215, 226
  redeployment during refurbishment
      200
  response to negative comments 261
  restructuring 30, 200
  role 5, 185
  temporary accommodation for 163-4
  uniforms for 185
  see also librarians

staff restrooms 129, 204
staff training
    customer care 185
Staffordshire Library and Information
        Services 247, 252
    see also Leek Library
stairs 25, 84, 92, 117, 213, 228
    fire protection 198
    new installations 129, 134, 224, 233
standard plans
    see design templates
State Library of Victoria, Melbourne 232,
        243, 262
stock
    audit 98
    improved arrangement of 105, 108
    inaccessible during refurbishment 107
        move logistics 86, 107
    public libraries
        better stock needed 41
        display of 28, 137-8
        face-on display 35, 46
        fiction categorization 50-1
        increases to 37, 124
        integration by subject 136
        kept to one floor 162, 212
        move logistics 165-6, 200, 210
        open access problems 135
        satisfaction with 51
        see also collections; fiction; non-
            fiction
stock presentation 22
    the 'spine' 25
stools 46, 90
storage libraries 94
storage space 36, 49, 94, 115, 222, 229
    during refurbishment 165-6
story telling facilities 141, 153
Stowmarket Library, Suffolk 202-07, **205**,
        244, 245, 248, 252, 254, 255
strategic planning 21, 41, 69, 104, 125,
        159, 173, 185, 223, 224, 239, 247
structural changes and problems 117, 179,
        255-6
    case study of Li Fing Medical Library,
        Hong Kong 256-7
students
    consultation rooms for 106
    information skills for 104
    library environment for 80, 81, 228,
        229
    services centered on 103
    subject support 106
study areas 82, 97, 104, 149, 223
    different types provided 83, 90, 104,
        228
Suffolk Libraries, Archives and
        Information
    see Felixstowe, Lakenheath, Lowestoft
        and Stowmarket libraries
Sunderland University Library 254
Sutton Library 160
Swansea Libraries
    see Oystermouth Library
Sweden
    library buildings 133-46
Swiss Cottage Library, London Borough of
        Camden xv, 7, 10, 236, 262

tables 90, 136, 139, 148-9, 200
talking books 138, 174
task lighting 139, 149, 222
teaching
    changing patterns of 92, 95, 101
teaching spaces 58, 60, 61
teenagers
    zones for 216, 237
    see also young people
televisions 46, 214
temperature control 95, 96, 230
tenders 33, 64, 96, 120, 127, 186, 215
    evaluation of 81
Thatcham Library, Berkshire 254
tiling 31, 34
toilets 33, 61, 71, 75, 90, 115, 118, 150,
        303, 213, 228, 234
    for disabled people 97, 162, 187, 234,
        235
Torbay Libraries
    see Torquay Library
Torquay Library, Torbay 41-53, **42, 45, 48,
        52,** 245, 247, 251, 261, 262
Tourist Information Centres 58, 185, 190
Trading Spaces project 264
traffic flow 22, 43, 61, 69, 75, 82, 96, 135
    see also circulation space

training suites 86, 204, 207
  for ICT 101, 104, 129, 179, 234
Trinity College, Dublin Long Room 12
turnstiles 98, 106
21ˢᵗ Century Libraries (Worpole) 174, 245

undergraduate collections 94
University College London
  see Wilkins Library
university libraries
  see academic libraries
usage
  see impact assessments
user groups 21, 24, 70, 206, 234
users
  attitudes to change 29-30, 47, 50-1,
    123, 170
  attracting non-users 176
  behaviour studies 136
  buying stock by 187
  decline in numbers and issues 29, 36,
    160, 179, 183, 200
  diversity of 154
  facilities for 124, 128-9, 130
  increase in numbers of 51, 75, 170,
    176, 179, 189, 210, 217, 226
  living through refurbishment 107, 109,
    207
  reception by staff 139
  satisfaction with refurbishment 29, 37,
    38, 48, 141-2, 170-1
  surveys 125, 183
  see also consultation; disabled people;
    impact assessments; Public Library
    User Surveys; students

Vale of Glamorgan
  see Barry County Library
value engineering exercises 82, 84
vending machines 46
ventilation 95, 97, 127, 160, 198, 203-4
  natural 34, 148, 222
Victoria Centre Campus Library,
    Westminster Kingsway College
    224-5
village libraries 173, 180
Visitor Experience project 67-75
visitors
  see users
visits
  to other libraries 63, 82, 160, 174, 212
  from architects and librarians 171

walls 116, 215
  partitions 34, 86, 162, 225
  shelving as 140-1
Walsall Library and Museum 235-6, **235**,
    254
Waterford Central Library 145-55, **146**,
    149, **153**, 248, 250, 252, 256, 259,
    260, 262
Wellcome Library 15
Westminster Kingsway College
  see Victoria Centre Campus Library
wheelchair access 94, 105, 117, 129, 140,
    204, 208, 210
Whitby Library, North Yorkshire Libraries
    194
White Plains Public Library, New York,
    USA 257
Who's in charge? (Coates) 5
Widener Memorial Library, Harvard
    University 224, 252
Wilkins Library, University College
    London 12, 223-4, 247, 258
Winchester Discovery Centre, Hampshire
    frontispiece, 59-66, **62**, **63**, **65**,
    247, 248, 249, 250, 254, 255
windows 130, 134, 148, 149, 203, 209,
    213, 237
  automatic 222
  in listed buildings 27, 116-117
  stained glass 31, 32, 34, 223
wireless networks 90, 94, 97, 228, 229, 234
Wolfson Foundation 13, 98, 101
workrooms 33, 115, 134, 140-1, 213, 225
workstations for IT
  see benching; computers; desking
'wow' factor 37, 81, 84, 116, 174

Xbox 360 47

York University
  see Raymond Burton Library for
    Humanities Research; J.B. Morrell
    Library